TAKE THIS TEST

TAKE THIS TEST

EDITED BY BARRY J. PAVELEC AND STEPHEN M. KIRSCHNER

CHILTON BOOK COMPANY   RADNOR, PENNSYLVANIA

Published in Radnor, Pennsylvania, by Chilton Book Company
and simultaneously in Don Mills, Ontario, Canada,
by Nelson Canada Limited
Library of Congress Catalog Card No. 80–972
ISBN 0-8019-6924-7

Designed by Jean Callan King/Visuality
Manufactured in the United States of America

1 2 3 4 5 6 7 8 9 0   9 8 7 6 5 4 3 2 1 0

☛ CONTENTS

ACKNOWLEDGMENTS

When editors compile a book such as *Take This Test,* it is easy to decide whom to thank. There are obvious contributors who worked to achieve the end result, and they rightly must get much of the credit. First on that list is Leslie Spraker May, who spent untold hours in libraries finding some of the best tests in this book. Were that her only contribution, it would be hard to repay her adequately, but her further support, by remaining enthusiastic throughout the project and by constantly reassuring the editors they were not insane, makes repayment impossible.

Next, there are the important people who shape the manuscript into a real book, not just an idea. For accomplishing that critical task we thank Gayle S. Hobson, Nadine Campeas, and Agnes Alexander, a good friend who always seems to come to our aid when time grows short.

In addition, we would like to give credit to individuals whose input might not be as obvious to our readers, but without whom we could not have completed the task. First, thanks go to the rather sizeable group of wives and children who gave us the freedom and help to get the job done. Then there are our co-workers (we both "earn a living" in the advertising business) who have had to spend the 9-to-5 hours with two men who were "writing a book." That isn't an easy assignment.

Finally, we want to offer sincere appreciation to employees of the many publications and organizations that gave us permission to use the material in this volume. One of the most time-consuming and worrisome tasks in creating a book such as this is securing the rights to reprint material that has appeared elsewhere. To the men and women all over the world who made this part of our work easier, we offer our heartfelt gratitude.

TAKE THIS TEST

☛ INTRODUCTION

That human beings are different one from the other has never been in question. Adam knew it just as surely as we. Throughout history certain individuals have always displayed subtle or obvious characteristics that made them better able to survive or lead in their societies. The masses, meanwhile, had to be content to keep their peculiarities hidden, because for thousands of years, being different wasn't a very wise posture for a member of the masses to assume: You could get burned at the stake, stoned or, at the very least, be labeled an eccentric. As long as you were a member of the masses, it was best to act like everyone else and keep your differences to yourself.

At the end of the eighteenth century, however, something happened to remove the stigma of being "different." It was called "America." Suddenly, being different was no longer a shortcoming; in this new land it became the key to success. How different you were in your approach to life, in your mental abilities, or in your physical assets could easily determine how quickly you might rise to the top of the American social or economic ladder. The need to remain part of the faceless crowd no longer existed.

Americans watched their country become the envy of the world largely through the exploits and leadership of men whose uniqueness was evident to everyone. Men from the backwoods became presidents; immigrants who arrived with scarcely a penny toiled to become the richest citizens; men strong enough to face the threats of thousands of miles of hard travel, wild Indians, sickness, and months of toil and boredom became millionaires overnight in far-off California.

By the end of the nineteenth century, Americans were able to follow the advancement of their unique compatriots in the pages of a blossoming popular press. Dozens of weekly and monthly magazines had been founded that took editorial delight in exposing both the risks and rewards of unusual life styles. Among the publications' vast audiences were parents from emigrant traditions where the fear of non-conformity was still strong. Despite this, an urge for success caused them to wonder, "Will my child have what it takes to make it in this land? Is he really unique?"

At about the same time this question was also being asked on the continent that many of America's parents had left behind. The social revolutions that swept most of Europe during the last half of the nineteenth century created practical examples of the concepts *liberty* and *equality*. In France, one of those examples was universal education for all children, regardless of economic or social background. In a relatively short time, a flood of students of all mental and intellectual qualifications overwhelmed their classrooms. When educators tried to apply similar teaching methods and programs to all students, they were constantly unsettled by the failures of those who should be most successful, and by the successes of those whose backgrounds "predestined" them to utter failure.

Finally, the country's minister of public instruction threw up his hands. He pleaded for someone to develop a method of predicting individual successes in the classroom, regardless of social or economic background. The result was the first practical test of intelligence, created in 1905 by Simon and Binet and based upon a child's ability to understand and reason with objects in his cultural environment. After numerous revisions, the test established a standard for measuring a child's ability to perform, which was called his mental age. This standard, divided by the child's chronological age, became his intelligence quotient, or the famous IQ.

Intelligence testing came rapidly to the United States, but it came through professional educational channels and was not broadly noticed by the general public for more than a decade. During these years, only an occasional reference to IQ testing found its way into the popular magazines. Finally, in 1918, a publishing event took place: The February 16, 1918, edition of *Literary Digest* (an extremely popular magazine of the day founded by the original team of Funk & Wagnalls) published, in its "Science and Invention" section, an article entitled "A Test of Your Intelligence."

The feature, adapted from a technical review of the new intelligence test developed by Professor Terman of Stanford, was the first to offer readers an opportunity to test *their own* intelligence. Unwittingly, the editors of the *Literary Digest* had tapped the vast combined reservoir of self-doubt and faith in success based upon one's desire to stand out as a unique American. The *Digest* even posited it in a uniquely American way: "Of course you are a superior adult. . . ." Then, for the first time, the magazine suggested its readers take the simple test to prove their superiority.

Popular magazines very quickly learned that the *Digest* had struck gold. In short order, such articles as "Are You Fit to Be a Freshman?," "How High Do You Stand on the Rating Scale?" and "How Much Do You Know?" began to appear in other publications. "Take this test" became a common editorial admonition.

Editors discovered that they could enliven any issue of their periodicals with self-scoring, easy-to-create and extremely well-received test features. In a few minutes, in the privacy of their own homes, readers could obtain the real (or apparent) equivalent of a professional analysis of their intelligence, achievement, or talents and compare their scores with the rest of the world. Here was instant gratification (or disappointment) within the pages of a magazine—a powerful attraction to readers, and one which sold copies.

By the 1920s, serious test makers had moved from intelligence to other areas of human ability. The necessity of finding qualified men for the Armed Forces during World War I had created a need for tests to discover physical abilities, emotional stability, and aptitudes for various job-related functions. Magazine publishers followed closely, with editorial features that linked tests with current reader interest: "Are You Another Babe Ruth?" "Do You Know How to Get Along with People?" "What Are You Fit For?" and the unliberated classic, "How Intelligent Is the Girl Who Elects Home Economics?"

Open discussions of "personal" psychological subjects (engendered by the need for emotional escapism during the turbulent thirties and forties) was evident in magazine editorials and programming for the newer medium, radio. This opened the way for "intimate" tests which are now commonly seen in large circulation publications. Whereas a magazine in the twenties or early thirties might have run a test called "Are You a Potential Genius?" a mass-circulation publication of the late forties and fifties would have used quizzes entitled, "Do You Have a Good Marriage?" or "What's Your Love Quotient?"

The trend toward open discussions of intimacy continued and burgeoned in the last decades, to the point where fully 90 percent of the editorial, self-scoring tests published in 1978 were of the personal social/psychological variety. Clearly, "Take this test . . ." will continue to be the advice of editors of America's magazines for decades to come, just as it has been for the last sixty years. How much more intimate the subject matter of these examinations can become is impossible to predict, but it is apparent that Americans want to know how they stand in relation to the "norm" and to others' scores. Witness the popularity of "desirable weight" tables, or the anxiety over the score when a son or daughter takes a national reading or math test. Similarly, the statistics in the first Masters and Johnson study were not fascinating merely because of what they said about society as a whole, but because they enabled each of us, as individuals, to rate our own sexual experience.

The idea for a single volume of self-scoring tests dealing with all aspects of living first came about through one of the author's wives. She asked her husband to spend a short romantic interlude in front of a roaring fire and, under guidelines put forth by one of her favorite magazines, to share, in total honesty, how he rated their marriage. That experience and the subsequent reverberations demonstrated the power and danger of following the urge to "take this test."

In compiling *Take This Test,* we have gone beyond the framework of selecting tests from magazines. We have taken the same approach as the publications themselves and gone, in many cases, to original sources of tests to share these with our readers. Here you will find tests of your ability ("Could You Qualify for Mensa?", page 86) and that of your favorite pet ("Find Your Cat's IQ," page 123). You will be able to determine how your physical condition compares with applicants to West Point ("The West Point Physical Aptitude Examination," page 56). You will be able to estimate how long you have left to to live (page 49) or whether your daughter will marry a man who is just like her mother (page 230).

In this book you will be able to test your spelling and typing skills (pages 208 and 206), find out what you really know about driving and smoking ("What's Your Driving IQ?" page 92, "The National Smoking Test," page 65), and discover if you might need psychotherapy (page 251), or if your level of depression might mean serious problems for you in the future ("The Self-rating Depression Scale," page 256). You can compare your attitudes on sex and love with famous stars ("Test Your Man's Love Rating vs. Leading Celebrities," page 171) and find out what a name reveals (page 131).

We suggest taking some of the tests alone, some with others. Give your children some of the tests ("How Fit Are Your Kids: Tests I and II" pages 224 and 226). There's a test to find out how qualified your doctor is ("How to Rate Your Doctor," page 156), and even a test for your dog to rate himself as a pet ("The Dog Ownee's Aptitude Test," page 128).

We have gathered here the best of the popular tests. Some are quite serious and can offer important indications of your physical or emotional state. Others are off-beat and may tell you nothing more than how well you know trivial facts. Many are designed to do nothing more than entertain you. Each test contains answers and scoring information immediately following the questions.

Enjoy yourself. Don't take the results too seriously or, if you do, seek out proper solutions to the shortcomings they reveal. Changing your diet or exercise habits, working at being more communicative, or driving more carefully, can help you enjoy life more and live longer, and that, perhaps, is the biggest test of all.

CHARACTER, CREATIVITY, AND CLASS

☛ HOW POPULAR ARE YOU?

People differ in their definition of, and need for, popularity. Often those who think they need it most simply do not know how to get it. On the other hand, those who really prefer their own company find themselves very much in social demand. How satisfactory it would be if you could lay down a set of rules to tell everyone how to achieve popularity to the precise extent that is wanted. Unfortunately, no single type of behavior guarantees popularity.

What this psychologist-designed quiz does, provided you answer it as accurately and honestly as you can, is help you work out the kind of popularity you want. It may also help you find out how far you have gone toward achieving your goal.

1. Last time you had friends over, was it
   a. because you find them entertaining and interesting
   b. because they like you
   c. because you thought you had to

2. When you are on vacation, do you
   a. usually make friends easily
   b. prefer to spend time alone
   c. wish to make friends, but find it difficult

3. You have arranged to meet a friend but are very tired. When you are unable to reach him/her, would you
   a. not turn up, hoping that he/she will understand
   b. turn up and try to enjoy yourself
   c. turn up to ask if he/she minds if you go home early

4. How long do you keep your friends?
   a. years mostly
   b. it varies; with something in common, it can be for years
   c. not long as a rule; you keep moving on

5. A friend confides a highly interesting personal problem. Would you
   a. try to resist telling someone else
   b. not even consider passing it on
   c. call up someone else to discuss the problem as soon as the first friend had left

6. When you have a problem, do you
   a. usually feel able to cope by yourself
   b. turn to friends you can rely on
   c. turn to your friends only if it is really bad

7. When your friends have problems, do you find that
   a. they come to you for help
   b. only those close to you come for help
   c. they tend not to bother you for help

8. Do you usually make friends
   a. through people you already know
   b. from all kinds of encounters
   c. only after a long time and with some difficulty

9. Which of these qualities is the most important attribute in a friend?
   a. the ability to make you feel happy
   b. reliability
   c. interest in you

10. Which statement most nearly applies to you?
   a. I usually make people laugh
   b. I usually make people think
   c. people feel comfortable with me

11. If you are asked to join in a game or sing at a party, would you
   a. make an excuse to get out of it
   b. join in with relish
   c. refuse outright

12. Which statement is true for you?
   a. I like to praise my friends
   b. I believe in honesty, so I sometimes have to make negative comments
   c. I do not flatter or criticize my friends

13. Do you find that
   a. you can only get on well with people who share your interests
   b. generally you can get on with almost anyone
   c. sometimes you would like to get on with someone who is unresponsive to you

14. If friends play a practical joke on you, do you
   a. join in the laughter
   b. feel angry and show it
   c. depending on your mood and the circumstances, possibly *a* or *b*

15. How do you feel about others depending on you?
   a. Up to a point I do not mind, but I like a certain amount of independence in my friends.
   b. Fine. I like to be depended on.
   c. A bit wary—I would prefer to keep clear of some responsibilities

HOW TO SCORE

Total your score from the points given for each answer.

1. a—3 b—3 c—1	**6.** a—1 b—2 c—3	**11.** a—2 b—3 c—1
2. a—3 b—2 c—1	**7.** a—3 b—2 c—1	**12.** a—3 b—1 c—2
3. a—1 b—3 c—2	**8.** a—2 b—3 c—1	**13.** a—1 b—3 c—2
4. a—3 b—2 c—1	**9.** a—3 b—2 c—1	**14.** a—3 b—1 c—2
5. a—2 b—3 c—1	**10.** a—2 b—1 c—3	**15.** a—2 b—3 c—1

WHAT YOUR SCORE MEANS

36–45: You enjoy having people around you and get a good deal of fun out of life. You are probably popular with a wide circle of friends, though you may avoid more intimate relationships.

26–35: Your popularity may fluctuate. It could be that, while you want to be liked, you try too hard, and others are not always relaxed in your company.

15–25: You may be a rather solitary person. This does not necessarily mean that you are not popular. Popularity as such may not interest you. If it does, you need to revise your relationships with those outside your usual circle.

☞ ARE YOU TOO SERIOUS OR TOO EASYGOING?

Do you take life too seriously or not seriously enough? People who take life too seriously waste a lot of time worrying about disasters that may never happen to them. And those who are too happy-go-lucky are never prepared to deal with life's difficulties. They are poor planners who fail to see problems building up and are unable to cope with them when they occur.

This fun test may help you know yourself just a little better. Take it and find out the real you.

1. You know you are going to be late for an important date. Do you
   a. dream up a brilliant excuse
   b. start rehearsing your apologies
   c. tell yourself you're worth waiting for

2. You are going on vacation. Do you
   a. start packing weeks beforehand
   b. throw a few things into a case at the last minute
   c. make a list of what to take with you

3. Would you date
   a. only someone you know
   b. anyone you found attractive
   c. or does the question embarrass you

4. Do you usually spend
   a. as much as you feel you can afford
   b. so much you end up borrowing
   c. as little as possible

5. Suppose a friend wanted to borrow some money. Would you
   a. lend it without a second thought
   b. lend it only if you could really afford to do so
   c. make any excuse not to lend it

6. Do you buy things on impulse?
   a. yes, all the time
   b. sometimes you're tempted
   c. no—or hardly ever

7. If you feel people are staring at you or talking about you, does it
   a. make you feel self-conscious
   b. amuse you
   c. bring out the devil in you

8. Check which of the following you would do without a second thought if the opportunity came your way.
   a. make a parachute drop
   b. take part in a television quiz game
   c. try to make a fortune smuggling diamonds

By Graham Fisher. Reprinted with permission of the author and *The Star*, News Group Publications, Inc., New York, NY.

9. How good are you at remembering other people's birthdays and anniversaries?
   a. not bad
   b. not good, but you keep a list
   c. you don't bother

10. Do you worry about the future?
    a. no—let the future take care of itself
    b. not really, but you do think about it at times
    c. of course

11. Check which of the following situations would cause you to tell a lie.
    a. to protect a friend
    b. to get out of an embarrassing situation
    c. to avoid losing your job
    d. to win an argument
    e. to get back at someone

12. You are on vacation with a mixed group. Someone suggests a swim in the nude. Would the idea
    a. appeal to you
    b. embarrass you
    c. probably have been your own idea

13. You say or do something stupid and your friends laugh. Would you
    a. join in
    b. get angry
    c. acutely feel embarrassed

14. Check which of the following situations you would first find amusing?
    a. an angry wife hitting her drunken husband with an umbrella
    b. a dog with a can tied to its tail
    c. a girl's skirt falling off in the street
    d. an old lady slipping on a banana skin
    e. A small girl trying to walk in her mother's high-heeled shoes

15. Which of the following do you enjoy most on television?
    a. serious plays
    b. old movies
    c. quiz games

16. Which of the following would you rather have?
    a. lots of money
    b. principles—and stick to them
    c. lots of friends

HOW TO SCORE

Score the following points for each of your answers, then total your score.

1. a—3, b—1, c—5
2. a—1, b—5, c—3
3. a—3, b—5, c—1
4. a—3, b—5, c—1
5. a—5, b—3, c—1
6. a—5, b—3, c—1
7. a—1, b—3, c—5

8. score 1 point for each check
9. a—1, b—3, c—5
10. a—5, b—3, c—1
11. score 1 point for each check
12. a—3, b—1, c—5

13. a—3, b—5, c—1
14. score 1 point for each check
15. a—1, b—3, c—5
16. a—5, b—1, c—3

WHAT YOUR SCORE MEANS

30 or under: You are a very reliable person, trustworthy and conscientious, but you take life far too seriously. Try not to worry so much—especially about things that may never happen.

31–37: You are one of the in-betweens. You are not a worrier, but you're not really lighthearted either, though you would very much like to be. You could be lighthearted if you would relax some and take things a little more in stride.

38–55: Lucky you! You are easygoing, but serious enough when you need to be. In other words, you take life as it comes, but not stupidly so. Your friends enjoy your company. They find you bright and amusing, but also know you as very sincere and genuine.

56–62: You are another of the in-betweens. Only this time you are a shade too casual, too flippant, too frivolous. Remember that there are occasionally things in life which can't be simply shrugged off.

63 or more: Oh, dear! You doubtless consider yourself lighthearted. Your friends are more likely to think of you as lightheaded. You don't have to be a bore or a worrier, but you shouldn't go to the other extreme either.

☞WHAT'S YOUR COMMUNICATING STYLE?

For a clue to your own communicating style, complete this survey. Write the number 4 beside the word or phrase that best describes you, 3 beside the one next most like you, 2 beside the next most, and 1 beside the phrase least descriptive of you.

1. I am likely to impress others as
   a. practical and to the point
   b. emotional and somewhat stimulating
   c. astute and logical
   d. intellectually oriented and somewhat complex

2. When I am involved with a problem, I tend to
   a. concentrate on reality—on things as they are right now
   b. remain open and responsive to my feelings about the matter
   c. analyze past situations and what to plan next
   d. think about concepts and relationships between day-to-day events

3. My time is important, so I want to make sure that
   a. what I do today counts
   b. my actions will become a meaningful memory

   c. I plan well and follow my plan
   d. I am getting ready for the future

4. I am most convincing when I am
   a. practical and down-to-earth
   b. in touch with my own feelings and those of others
   c. organized and logical
   d. creative and broad-gauged

5. I enjoy it when others see me as
   a. a person who gets things done
   b. warm and expressive
   c. well organized and systematic
   d. bright, with a vision

6. When others pressure me, I am
   a. likely to react immediately
   b. apt to get carried away by my feelings
   c. inclined to be highly analytical and serious
   d. prone to step back into my own world of thought

ANSWERS

Add all the numbers in front of the *a* questions (Sensor style); in front of the *b* questions (Feeler); in front of the *c* questions (Thinker); in front of the *d* questions (Intuitor). The highest score indicates your primary communicating style, and the second highest score indicates your secondary style.

WHAT YOUR SCORE MEANS

a. Sensors are easy to spot. Sensors are spirited, moving, and goal-minded. They tend to be very practical, down-to-earth people who prefer to deal with others in an open, frank, and straightforward manner. Sensors are competitive and enjoy the thrill of the chase plus a fast payoff. Their answer to feelings of doubt or anxiety is to do something. At their best, Sensors are dynamos. At their worst, they react blindly and tend to gloss over some necessary details. Sensors tend to give and demand total loyalty, and if and when they fail, they blame others for not being as aggressive or devoted as they are.

b. Feelers are emotional, spontaneous, and introspective. They are known for their love of people, adventure, and involvement. They like to read between the lines and are concerned with the people aspect of any undertaking. Feelers tend to base their decisions on feelings—whether choosing a friend or a car. They tend to be somewhat self-indulgent and are warm in their speech and letter writing. In their choices of styles and colors, they favor the bright, sunny, outrageous. For persons of other styles, the Feeler can be a real nuisance—somewhat impulsive, erratic, and cavalier. At times they can become too wrapped up in their feelings and can be seen as moody. They turn up in such fields as acting, sales, writing, social work, and nursing.

c. Thinkers are organized, structured, and detail-oriented people who seldom leap to conclusions. They prefer to gather all relevant data, weight their alternatives, and then systematically implement their solution. Thinkers usually have a conservative, well-tailored look, an orderly living and working environment, and an accurate checkbook. They give our world a badly needed sense of direction and unity. At times Thinkers can get bogged down in details and might be seen by others as somewhat indecisive or impersonal. At their worst, they can be rigid, dogmatic, and boring. Thinkers tend to be engineers, data processing specialists, lawyers, accountants, and teachers.

d. Intuitors are imaginative, futuristic, and idea-oriented. The technical details of everyday life often elude or bore them since they are looking at the big, overall picture. They prefer to think of the potentials and possibilities involved in any situation. Intuitors tend to be somewhat unconcerned or impatient with the details of implementing their ideas. Due to their futuristic, theoretical outlook, others may at times perceive Intuitors to be impractical, unrealistic, or out of touch with reality. There aren't many Intuitors in our culture—only about one person in ten. They include inventors, scientists, researchers, architects, artists, writers, and planners of one type or another.

    By knowing our communicating style, we get to know ourselves better, and we get along with others better as we develop the ability to recognize and respond to their styles.

☞ TEST YOUR PSYCHOLOGICAL FITNESS

Answer the following questions Yes or No.

Work Fitness

1. In general, do you enjoy working?
2. Are you financially successful in your work, according to your own standards?
3. Are you successfully pursuing your chosen career?
4. Are your work skills improving?
5. Do you work well alone?
6. Do you work well with others?
7. Do you have a positive opinion of the way you work?
8. Do you have a positive opinion of your potential to work?
9. Have your attitudes about work improved, compared to earlier times in your life?
10. Do you have the skills you need to work as successfully as you want to work?

Relationship Fitness

1. Do you enjoy your friendships?
2. Do you trust and depend on your friends when you need someone to lean on?
3. Do your friends trust and depend on you when they need someone to lean on?
4. Do you see friends regularly (at least three times a week)?
5. Do you have close friends of both sexes?
6. Do you have long term friendships (three years or more)?
7. Do you have a positive opinion of your ability to make and keep friends?
8. Do other people have a positive opinion of your ability to make and keep friends?
9. Are you satisfied with your friendships?
10. Do you have the skills you need to make and keep as many friends as you want?

Love Fitness

1. Do you enjoy making physical contact with your lover?
2. Are you good friends with your lover?
3. Do you share your secret thoughts with your lover?

Abridged and adapted excerpts from *Psychological Fitness: 21 Days to Feeling Good*, copyright © 1979, 1978 by Joseph Hart and Richard Corriere, reprinted by permission of Harcourt Brace Jovanovich, Inc.

4. Do you share your intimate feelings with your lover?

5. Have you ever had a long term love relationship (at least three years)?

6. Do you have a positive opinion of your present ability to love?

7. Do other people have a positive opinion of your ability to love?

8. Are you satisfied with your love relationship?

9. Do you have the interpersonal skills you need to have a love relationship?

10. Do you have a positive opinion of your potential to love?

HOW TO SCORE

Give yourself one point for each Yes and total your score for each section.

WHAT YOUR SCORE MEANS

Work Fitness

8–10: You are a worker athlete. You have a strength in work.

4–7: You are an amateur worker. This means you have the potential to be a worker athlete, but either you're working in a way that doesn't feel good to your inner self or you're not working up to the potential of your inner self.

1–3: You are a worker spectator. It's time to do something about your work patterns and behavior.

Relationship Fitness

8–10: You are a relationship athlete. That means you have the strengths necessary to build, keep, and use your relationships.

4–7: You are a weekend athlete in relationships. This often means your relationships are fine only if everything is going right.

1–3: You are a relationship spectator. You have the potential to develop a new area in your life.

Love Fitness

8–10: You are an expert in love.

4–7: You are a weekend lover. You exercise your ability to love but not often enough to establish a one-to-one relationship that changes both of you.

1–3: You are a love spectator. You could have someone in your life whom you might only fantasize about.

☛ HOW SHY ARE YOU?

Eighty-four million Americans feel that they are shy, according to psychologist Philip Zimbardo, who has studied this problem for seven years and has established a shyness clinic at Stanford University. Below is a version of the questionnaire he has given to over 4,000 people around the world (the results of which appear in his book *Shyness: What It Is, What to Do about It*). Fill out the questionnaire to see exactly how shyness affects your life.

There are no right or wrong answers to this quiz. Its purpose is to help you evaluate and understand your shyness.

1. How shy are you when you feel shy?
   a. extremely shy **b.** very shy **c.** quite shy **d.** moderately shy **e.** somewhat shy **f.** only slightly shy

2. How often do you feel shy?
   a. every day **b.** almost every day **c.** often, nearly every other day **d.** one or two times a week **e.** occasionally, less than once a week **f.** rarely, once a month or less

3. When you are feeling shy, can you conceal it and have others believe you are not feeling shy?
   a. yes, always **b.** sometimes I can, sometimes not **c.** no, I usually can't hide it

4. What do you think causes your shyness? (Check all that are applicable.)
   ____concern about negative evaluation; ____ fear of being rejected; ____ lack of self-confidence; ____ lack of specific social skills (specify): _____
   _____; ____ fear of being intimate with others; ____ preference for being alone; ____ personal inadequacy, handicap (specify): _____
   _____
   ____; other (specify): _____

5. How shy do you think the following people judge you to be? Use this scale:
   1 = extremely shy, 2 = quite shy, 3 = moderately shy, 4 = only slightly shy, 5 = not shy, 6 = don't know

Reprinted from *Shyness: What It Is and What to Do about It* by Philip G. Zimbardo, copyright © 1977, by permission of Addison-Wesley Publishing Co., Reading, MA.

____ parents; ____ your brothers and/or sisters; ____ close friends; ____ your spouse or steady boyfriend/girlfriend; ____ your children; ____ the people you work with

6. What situations or activities make you feel shy? (Check all appropriate choices.) ____ social situations in general; ____ large groups; ____ small, task-oriented groups (like seminars at school, work groups on the job, church groups, fund-raising groups); ____ small, social groups (like parties, dances); ____ one-to-one interactions with a person of the same sex; ____ one-to-one interactions with a person of the opposite sex; ____ when you are vulnerable (for example, when asking for help); ____ when you are of lower status than others (like when speaking to superiors, authorities); ____ when assertiveness is required (for example, when complaining about faulty service in a restaurant or the poor quality of a product); ____ when you are the focus of attention before a large group (for example, when giving a speech); ____ when you are the focus of attention before a small group (for example, when being introduced or being asked directly for your opinion); ____ when you are being evaluated or compared with others (for example, when being interviewed or being criticized);____new interpersonal situations in general; ____ when sexual intimacy is possible

7. What types of people make you feel shy? (Check all appropriate choices.) ____ friends; ____ strangers; ____ foreigners; ____ authorities (by virtue of their role—police, teacher, superior at work); ____ authorities (by virtue of their knowledge—intellectual superiors, experts); ____ people much older than you; ____ people much younger than you; ____persons of the opposite sex, in a group; ____ persons of the same sex, in a group; ____a person of the opposite sex, one-to-one; ____ a person of the same sex, one-to-one

8. What are the negative consequences of your being shy? ____ none; ____ creates social problems and makes it difficult to meet new people, enjoy potentially good experiences; ____ has negative emotional consequences; creates feelings of loneliness, isolation, depression; ____ prevents positive evaluations by others (your personal assets never become apparent); ____ makes it difficult to be appropriately assertive, to express opinions, to take advantage of opportunities; ____ allows incorrect negative evaluations by others (you may unjustly be seen as un-friendly or snobbish or weak); ____makes it hard to think and communicate clearly; ____ encourages excessive self-consciousness, preoccupations with yourself

9. What are the positive consequences of your being shy? ____ none; ____ creates a modest, appealing impression, makes you appear discreet, introspective; ____ helps avoid interpersonal conflicts; ____ provides a convenient form of anonymity and protection; ____ provides an opportunity to stand back, observe others, act carefully and intelligently; ____ avoids negative evaluations by others (a shy person is not considered obnoxious, over-aggressive, pretentious); ____ provides a way to be selective about the people with whom one interacts; ____ enhances personal privacy and the pleasure that solitude offers; ____ creates positive interpersonal consequences, by not putting others off, intimidating them or hurting them

10. Are you willing to seriously work at overcoming your shyness? ____ yes, definitely; ____ yes, perhaps; ____ not sure yet; ____no

Following are the techniques developed in the shyness clinic to help you build a stronger, more confident self. Each one will help you build a more positive self-image and help eradicate your shyness.

You might find the following eight steps useful in providing a structure for your efforts:

1. Don't allow yourself to indulge in guilt and shame.
2. Look for the causes of your behavior in aspects of your current situation and not in personality defects in yourself.
3. Remind yourself that there are alternative views of every event. "Reality" is no more than a shared agreement among people to call something by the same name. This attitude will enable you to be more tolerant in your interpretation of others' intentions and more generous in dismissing what might appear to be their rejection of you.
4. Never say bad things about yourself; especially don't attribute to yourself irreversible negative traits like "stupid . . . ugly . . . uncreative . . . a failure . . . incorrigible."
5. Don't allow others to criticize you as a person; it is your specific actions that are open for evaluation and improvement. Accept constructive feedback graciously if it will help you.
6. Remember that failures and disappointments are sometimes blessings in disguise that tell you your goals were not right for you, or that your effort wasn't worth it.
7. Do not tolerate people, jobs and situations that make you feel inadequate. If you can't change them or yourself enough to make you feel more worthwhile, walk on out or pass them by. Life is too short to fill it with downers.
8. Practice being a social animal. Enjoy feeling the energy that other people transmit, the unique qualities and range of variability of our fellow human beings. Imagine what their fears and insecurities might be and how you could help them. Decide what you need from them and what you have to give. Then let them know that you are open to sharing.

☞ HOW GOOD A FRIEND ARE YOU?

Our society tells us what husbands and wives are supposed to be and to do for each other. We know what traditional obligations bind parents and children. But there is still one vast and important area of human living that remains undefined—friendship.

Most of us want and need good friends. We search for an extension of, or even a replacement for, family support. We crave the bond of absolute trust. We yearn for someone we can call in the middle of the night when we're in trouble. But it isn't always easy to achieve and sustain those relationships; there are no strict rules for how to make, and keep, a friend. The paradoxes of friendship are profound. We spill our most intimate secrets to a stranger in the next airplane seat, but we ignore the death of a college roommate's child, because we don't know how to reestablish the old intimacy. For months we dread seeing a friend, then, when we're reunited, we can't understand why we waited so long. An old friend calls because she's in trouble, and we find we no longer have the strength or desire to help her. A new friend calls, and we offer to do anything she asks.

It's been said that "the only way to have a friend is to be one." Does that mean we tell our friend that her new man is unworthy of her, that her clothes are all wrong, that her prejudices constantly annoy us? Do good friends check in every day, every week, or once a month? Do friends lend each other money, or cars, or clothes? Does being a good friend mean that we can expect constant, unqualified understanding and honesty?

There are no friendship clinics to help us explore and resolve the dilemmas of friendship. In fact, only a handful of human-relations professionals have even studied the phenomenon of friendship, though it is as old as humankind's decision to live in groups. For the most part, then, we have to puzzle out our own solutions.

The following dilemmas are based on actual situations involving real people. You might want to read these vignettes together with a close friend and then discuss the possible courses of action for each one. There are no right or wrong answers. Every relationship and every situation is unique. A person faced with a troubling quandary must first consider: her own private feelings and those of her friend; the implications of her actions on all the people involved, and the depth of the attachment. Then she can act accordingly.

To find out how the real-life person involved in each dilemma actually resolved it, look in the answers.

But what about you? What would you have done?

Dilemma 1. Your closest friend, Anne, went through a bitter divorce a year ago. You haven't seen her ex-husband, Ben, since he and Anne split up. Because Ben and your husband are still friends, you are invited to Ben's wedding. (He's marrying a woman he met after his divorce.) Your husband wants you to go. Do you

   a. go and hope Anne doesn't find out
   b. ask your husband to attend the wedding alone while you spend the day with Anne
   c. ask Anne what she wants you to do and abide by her wishes
   d. tell Anne ahead of time that you plan to go even though you think she will feel betrayed
   e. tell your husband you won't go and ask him not to as well

Dilemma 2. Your fourteen-year-old daughter has told you, in confidence, about a rumor that a classmate, Heidi, is selling small amounts of marijuana to other teenagers. Heidi is the daughter of your closest friend, Gwen. Do you

   a. not say anything so as not to violate your daughter's confidence
   b. not say anything because you feel that Heidi's activities are not your concern—and besides, it's just a rumor
   c. explain to your daughter that you must tell Gwen, but you won't reveal where you heard the rumor; then tell Gwen
   d. speak to Heidi herself and warn her about the risks she is taking, legal and otherwise

Dilemma 3. Your friend, Diana, has been securely married for ten years to Ed, a decent but unexciting man. She has just become involved with someone else. He fascinates her, but she's sure she would never leave Ed for him. She has asked you to say, if asked, that she was with you when, in fact, she was with her lover. Do you

   a. agree to cover up for her simply because she is your friend
   b. explain that you aren't judging her, but you are uncomfortable with the idea of adultery and you don't want to become involved at all
   c. tell her that you could never look Ed in the face again if you lied for her
   d. tell her you think she is imposing on your friendship by asking you to lie for her, when you don't even lie about things in your own life
   e. explain that because you love her, you won't lie for her; that you feel what she is doing is risky, and advise her to seek counseling

Dilemma 4. Last year, your good friend, Nina, a serious sculptor, suggested that you enroll in the class she had been taking for several years with a renowned local artist. You enjoyed the class enormously. This year both you and Nina were late in signing up and the two of you were told that the class was filled. You call the teacher to ask whether he can possibly make room for you and Nina, but he tells you he can take only one of you. Do you

   a. take the opening yourself since you took the initiative in making the phone call
   b. tell him to enroll Nina since she is more serious about her art than you are and she got you into the class in the first place

c. call Nina and offer her the place

d. explain the situation to Nina and resolve the dilemma together

Dilemma 5. Your closest friend's only daughter, Robin, has just been swept up in a whirlwind romance and has set her wedding for a month away. When her mother, Suzanne, invites you to the wedding—an intimate celebration limited to family and a few close friends—you tell her with regret that you have already accepted a dinner invitation for that evening from the Millers. Dan Miller is a business associate as well as a friend of you husband's. Suzanne asks you to change the dinner date. Do you

    a. call Victoria Miller, explain the situation to her, and ask whether you can have a raincheck

    b. go to Robin's wedding ceremony, but instead of staying for the reception, arrive a little late at the Millers' party

    c. tell Suzanne that while you're thrilled for Robin and would love to be at her wedding, you don't feel you can gracefully get out of your other obligation without offending the Millers

Dilemma 6. You have just learned that Ken, the husband of your closest friend, Julie, definitely has been seeing other women. Ken has recently become so blatant that his activities are a subject of gossip, yet you are convinced that Julie knows nothing about it. Do you

    a. tell Julie so she can deal with the problem

    b. tell Ken that he owes it to Julie to admit his infidelities to her and urge him to seek marriage counseling

    c. send an anonymous note to Julie so she'll know what is happening but won't be embarrassed by hearing it from you

    d. say nothing to either one because it's none of your business

Dilemma 7. You owe your job to Ursula. She suggested that you apply for an open position in the department next to hers, and personally recommended you to the department head. Now, two years later, you are at a higher level than Ursula, partly because she has been leading a militant committee to upgrade the status of women employees. You learn of a good job in your department that is opening up, and you feel obligated to return Ursula's favor. Major efforts on her behalf may jeopardize your own position, however. Do you

    a. tell Ursula confidentially about the upcoming job opening and encourage her to apply for it directly, without getting more involved yourself

    b. say nothing

    c. point out Ursula's qualifications to your department head in a low-key way

    d. extend yourself as far on Ursula's behalf as she did on yours, even though your own job might be at stake

Dilemma 8. Wendy's father, to whom she was extremely close, has just died suddenly. Even though Wendy is your best friend, she has asked her husband to call you and tell you that she'd rather you didn't come to the funeral, because she is afraid that seeing you will make her lose her composure. Do you

    a. go anyway, feeling that Wendy is too distraught now to be thinking straight and that later on she might regret that you weren't with her at a time of crisis

b. stay away from the funeral but go to Wendy's house to prepare for the family's return after the service

c. stay away until you feel Wendy can deal with seeing you, but keep in touch with her or her husband by phone

Dilemma 9. Three months ago Barbara's husband left her. You rallied to her side and listened to her talk for hours at a time about her anger, fear, and sadness. Now, three months later, she is still calling you every day. Afterwards you feel so depressed and drained that your own family relationships are suffering. You'd rather talk to her less often, but you don't want to let down a friend in need. Do you

a. continue to listen to her as often and as long as she needs you to, realizing that this crisis period won't go on forever

b. tell her "I love you very much but you have to pull yourself together or you'll drag me down, too"

c. tell her that as much as you love her, you are not equipped to give her the kind of help she needs at a time like this and urge her to get professional counseling

Dilemma 10. You have made a date with your friend, Debbie, to see a movie. The afternoon of your date, you receive a call from Greg, and appealing man you recently met at a party. He has just been given two tickets for this evening's performance of a hit play and he invites you to go with him to the play and to dinner afterwards. Do you

a. accept Greg's invitation, since you and Debbie have an understanding that any dates between you will automatically be canceled if either of you is asked out by a man

b. ask Greg whether he could get a ticket for Debbie, too

c. refuse Greg's invitation with regret, piqueing his interest by letting him think you are going out with another man

d. explain to Greg that you have a prior commitment but that you would really like to see him, and pin him down to another date

ANSWERS

Here are the solutions chosen by the real-life women who were involved in the preceding dilemmas.

1. Carol chose solution *d.* She went to Ben's wedding. "I felt secure enough in my friendship with Anne to know that it wouldn't fall apart over this issue. The one thing that could have come between us though, would have been dishonesty. I never considered going to the wedding without telling Anne. She probably would have found out anyway, and I don't believe in going behind a friend's back," says Carol. Carol went to Anne and told her she was planning to go to the wedding. At first Anne was angry, feeling that Carol was betraying her, but then she realized that Carol didn't have to prove her loyalty by choosing sides.

2. Eileen chose solution *c.* She explains why she told Gwen the rumor about Heidi: "I thought about the possible consequences of fourteen-year-old Heidi getting involved in an illegal activity with unsavory characters, and I decided I would never be able to forgive myself if Heidi got into really serious trouble later, and I had never said anything that could have alerted her

parents. I explained my feelings to my daughter." Eileen set up a lunch date with Gwen, during which she asked her, "If somebody heard a rumor about your daughter doing something that might get her into trouble, would you want to know?" When Gwen said she would, Eileen told her what she had heard, emphasizing that it had been only a rumor but that she felt duty-bound to alert Gwen to the possibility that Heidi might need some help.

3. Fern chose *e*. She told Diana she would not cover up for her: "I knew that by refusing what Diana asked, and by coming on strong to get her to talk to a professional counselor, I was running the risk of alienating her. But I cared enough about my friend to chance losing our friendship," says Fern. "Which, in fact, did happen. For months Diana hasn't spoken to me. She did go on seeing this man and she and Ed almost broke up over it. I'm hoping that someday we'll be friends again."

4. Marilyn chose *d*. She telephoned Nina so they could meet to resolve the problem together. "I was dying to sign up for that class on the spot, but I didn't feel right doing that to Nina. On the other hand, I felt I deserved credit for taking the initiative and making the call," says Marilyn. "Besides, I knew we had been equally guilty because we were late in making the application. "I called Nina, we talked it over, and we finally decided to toss a coin. She won. I took a class with somebody else who isn't as good a teacher or as exciting, and both of us are making sure to send our money in early for next year. And I feel good because I'm sure I did the right thing."

5. Pat chose *c*. She kept her dinner date with the Millers. "I really hated to miss Robin's wedding," she says, "but I felt I had an obligation not only to Victoria Miller but also to my husband. And trying to get to both places wouldn't please anybody. So I went to the Millers. I went a little overboard on Robin's wedding present, and I invited both Robin and Suzanne to come to dinner with their husbands as soon as Robin got back from her honeymoon. I know there's still a lingering feeling on Suzanne's part that I should have come to Robin's wedding no matter what, but I'm sure that our friendship will weather this crisis, just as it has weathered a few others through the years."

6. Lois chose *a*. She told Julie that Ken had been unfaithful. "If I could do it all over again, though, I would keep my mouth shut," says Lois now. "The minute I saw Julie's face, I knew I had made a mistake. I could tell that she already knew about Ken's affairs and was trying to deal with the situation as well as she could. I embarrassed my friend, and things haven't been the same between us since. Now that Julie knows that I know about her problems with Ken, there's an awkwardness between us—a barrier. We don't talk about it, but we both know it is there."

7. Tina chose *a* and *c*. She told Ursula about the job opening and briefly mentioned Ursula's qualifications to her department head. "I felt cowardly not going gung-ho all the way, as Ursula did for me," says Tina, somewhat abashedly. "But the climate was different then, and Ursula had been in a stronger position than I am now. I figured it wouldn't help either of us if I were in as much disfavor as she is these days. Then I couldn't do anything to help her. If need be, I would lay down my life for Ursula, but I couldn't see giving up a perfectly good job when that wouldn't help either one of us."

8. Alison chose *a*. She went to the funeral. "I was sure that no matter how hard it would be for Wendy to see me at the funeral, she would be glad I had come," says Alison, adding, "and that's how it turned out." Wendy did break down when Alison came in, but instead of being angry, she put her arms around her friend and sobbed. "I would have felt terrible afterwards if I hadn't been with Wendy then," says Alison. "Sometimes you just have to trust your intuition—how well you know your friend and how well you know yourself."

9. Cheryl chose *b*. She told Barbara that she had cried and fumed long enough and it was time for her to deal with her life as it was, not as she wanted it to be. "I was tough," says Cheryl, "but for both our sakes I had to be. I couldn't take any more. It was either speak up or forget the friendship. And I didn't want to beat around the bush and avoid talking to Barbara the way

some of her other friends had done. I came right out and told her that if she kept this up she wouldn't find anyone to listen to her. Whatever I said, it worked, because she stopped bemoaning her fate all the time, and she was able to go back to talking about other things in life besides the break-up of her marriage and all the problems connected with it."

10. Ellen chose *d*. She kept her date with Debbie and countered Greg's invitation with one of her own for supper at her place the following week. "I used to have agreements with my women friends that our plans with each other didn't count if a man called," says Ellen, "until I realized that men usually come into my life and go out again, while my women friends are there to pick up the pieces after the man is long gone. Besides, I just don't like the whole idea that being with a woman friend is only worthwhile until something better comes along. I have my own interest at heart, really. I wouldn't want a friend to drop me every time a man calls—and I wouldn't want Greg or any man to think that I'm the kind of person who can't be counted on."

☛ HOW CREATIVE ARE YOU?

The test reflects the characteristics possessed by men and women—business leaders among them—whom psychologists have determined have the creative impulse.

After each statement indicate with a letter the degree or extent to which you *agree* or *disagree* with it: A=strongly agree; B=agree; C=in-between or don't know; D=disagree; E=strongly disagree. Answer as accurately and frankly as possible. Try not to second guess how a creative person might respond to each statement—be honest and give your *own* answer.

1. I always work with a great deal of certainty that I'm following the correct procedures for solving a particular problem. _____
2. It would be a waste of time for me to ask questions if I had no hope of obtaining answers. _____
3. I concentrate harder on whatever interests me than do most people. _____
4. I feel that a logical step-by-step method is best for solving problems. _____
5. I occasionally voice opinions that seem to turn some people off. _____
6. I spend a great deal of time thinking about what others think of me. _____
7. It is more important for me to do what I believe to be right than to try to win the approval of others. _____
8. People who seem unsure and uncertain about things lose my respect.

9. More than other people, I need to have things interesting and exciting. _____
10. I know how to keep my inner impulses in check. _____
11. I am able to stick with difficult problems over extended periods of time. _____
12. On occasion I get overly enthusiastic about things. _____
13. I often get my best ideas when doing nothing in particular. _____
14. I rely on intuitive hunches and the feeling of "rightness" or "wrongness" when moving toward the solution of a problem. _____
15. In problem solving, I work faster when analyzing the problem, and slower when synthesizing the information I've gathered. _____
16. I sometimes get a kick out of breaking the rules and doing things I'm not supposed to do. _____

17. I like hobbies that involve collecting things. _____
18. Daydreaming has provided the impetus for many of my more important projects. _____
19. I like people who are objective and rational. _____
20. If I had to choose from two occupations other than the one I now have, I would rather be a physician than an explorer. _____
21. I can get along more easily with people if they belong to about the same social and business class as myself. _____
22. I have a high degree of aesthetic sensitivity. _____
23. I am driven to achieve high status and power in life. _____
24. I like people who are most sure of their conclusions. _____
25. Inspiration has nothing to do with the successful solution of problems. _____
26. When I'm engaged in an argument, the greatest pleasure for me would be for the person who disagrees with me to become a friend, even at the price of sacrificing my point of view. _____
27. I am much more interested in coming up with new ideas than I am in trying to sell them to others. _____
28. I would enjoy spending an entire day alone, just "chewing the mental cud." _____
29. I tend to avoid situations in which I might feel inferior. _____
30. In evaluating information, the source of it is more important to me than the content. _____
31. I resent things being uncertain and unpredictable. _____
32. I like people who follow the rule "business before pleasure." _____
33. One's own self-respect is much more important than the respect of others. _____
34. I feel that people who strive for perfection are unwise. _____

35. I prefer to work with others in a team effort rather than solo. _____
36. I like work in which I must influence others. _____
37. Many problems that I encounter in life cannot be resolved in terms of right or wrong solutions. _____
38. It is important for me to have a place for everything and everything in its place. _____
39. Writers who use strange and unusual words merely want to show off. _____
40. The trouble with many people is that they take things too seriously. _____
41. I can maintain my motivation and enthusiasm for my projects, even in the face of discouragement, obstacles, or opposition. _____
42. People who are willing to entertain crackpot ideas are impractical. _____
43. I am more impressed with what I don't know than with what I do know. _____
44. I am more interested in what could be rather than what is. _____
45. I often brood about the thoughtless things I have said that may have hurt other people's feelings. _____
46. I rather enjoy fooling around with new ideas, even if there is no practical payoff. _____
47. I think the statement "ideas are a dime a dozen" hits the nail on the head. _____
48. I don't like to ask questions that show ignorance. _____
49. Once I undertake a project, I'm determined to finish it, even under conditions of frustration. _____
50. I sometimes feel that ideas come to me as if from some external source and that I am not directly responsible for them. _____
51. I sometimes get into trouble because I'm too curious or inquisitive. _____
52. People often say that I'm somewhat absent-minded. _____
53. I am more open to my feelings and emotions than are most other people. _____

54. I can more easily change my interests to pursue a job or a career than I can change a job to pursue my interests. _____

55. People who are theoretically oriented are less important than are those who are practical. _____

56. When brainstorming in a group, I am able to think up more ideas more rapidly than most of the others in the group can. _____

57. I am not ashamed to express "feminine" interests (if man), or "masculine" interests (if woman), if so inclined. _____

58. I can easily give up immediate gain or comfort to reach the goals I have set. _____

59. People who express their feelings and emotions are either unstable or immature. _____

60. In dealing with people, it is more important to be diplomatic than open and direct. _____

61. It is a waste of time to analyze one's failures. _____

62. There's nothing wrong with showing off a little now and then. _____

63. At times I have so enjoyed the ingenuity of a crook that I hoped he would go scot-free. _____

64. When someone tries to get ahead of me in a line of people, I usually point it out to him. _____

65. Problems that do not have clear-cut and unambiguous answers have very little interest for me. _____

66. I like to ponder the mystery of life. _____

67. I trust my feelings to guide me through experience. _____

68. I frequently begin work on a problem that I can only dimly sense and not yet express. _____

69. Things that I've accepted as old and familiar sometimes appear to me strange and distant. _____

70. I frequently tend to forget things such as names of people, streets, highways, small towns, etc. _____

71. During my adolescence I frequently had a desire to be alone and to pursue my own interests and thoughts. _____

72. I feel that hard work is the basic factor for success. _____

73. Many creative breakthroughs are the result of chance factors. _____

74. To be regarded as a good team member is important to me. _____

75. I was very happy in my childhood. _____

76. Below is a list of adjectives and terms that describe people. Indicate with a check mark ten (10) words that best characterize you.

energetic	perceptive	habit-bound	dynamic
persuasive	courageous	resourceful	self-demanding
observant	stern	egotistical	polished
fashionable	thorough	independent	realistic
self-confident	impulsive	good-natured	modest
persevering	determined	predictable	involved
forward-looking	factual	acquisitive	absent-minded
formal	open-minded	practical	flexible
informal	tactful	alert	sociable
dedicated	inhibited	curious	well-liked
original	enthusiastic	organized	restless
quick	innovative	unemotional	retiring
efficient	poised	clear-thinking	
helpful	cautious	understanding	

HOW TO SCORE

To compute your score add up the points assigned to each item. For each question, the first value is for A (strongly agree) or B (agree), the second is for C (in-between or don't know), and the third is for D (disagree) or E (strongly disagree).

1. 0, 1, 2	**2.** 0, 1, 2	**3.** 4, 1, 0	**4.** −2, 0, 3
5. 2, 1, 0	**6.** −1, 0, 3	**7.** 3, 0, −1	**8.** 0, 1, 2
9. 3, 0, −1	**10.** 1, 0, 3	**11.** 4, 1, 0	**12.** 3, 0, −1
13. 2, 1, 0	**14.** 4, 0, −2	**15.** −1, 0, 2	**16.** 2, 1, 0
17. 0, 1, 2	**18.** 3, 0, −1	**19.** 0, 1, 2	**20.** 0, 1, 2
21. 0, 1, 2	**22.** 3, 0, −1	**23.** 0, 1, 2	**24.** −1, 0, 2
25. 0, 1, 3	**26.** −1, 0, 2	**27.** 2, 1, 0	**28.** 2, 0, −1
29. 0, 1, 2	**30.** −2, 0, 3	**31.** 0, 1, 2	**32.** 0, 1, 2
33. 3, 0, −1	**34.** −1, 0, 2	**35.** 0, 1, 2	**36.** 1, 2, 3
37. 2, 1, 0	**38.** 0, 1, 2	**39.** −1, 0, 2	**40.** 2, 1, 0
41. 3, 1, 0	**42.** −1, 0, 2	**43.** 2, 1, 0	**44.** 2, 1, 0
45. −1, 0, 2	**46.** 3, 2, 0	**47.** 0, 1, 2	**48.** 0, 1, 2
49. 3, 1, 0	**50.** 2, 1, 0	**51.** 2, 1, 0	**52.** 3, 1, −1
53. 3, 0, −1	**54.** 0, 1, 2	**55.** −1, 0, 3	**56.** 2, 1, 0
57. 3, 0, −1	**58.** 2, 0, −1	**59.** 0, 1, 2	**60.** 1, 0, 2
61. 0, 1, 2	**62.** 2, 0, −1	**63.** 2, 0, −1	**64.** 2, 1, 0
65. −1, 0, 3	**66.** 3, 1, 0	**67.** 3, 1, 0	**68.** 2, 0, −1
69. 2, 1, 0	**70.** 3, 0, −1	**71.** 3, 1, 0	**72.** 2, 1, 0
73. 2, 1, 0	**74.** 1, 0, 2	**75.** 0, 1, 2	

76. The following have values of 2: energetic, observant, persevering, resourceful, independent, dedicated, original, perceptive, courageous, enthusiastic, innovative, curious, dynamic, self-demanding, involved, flexible.
The following have values of 1: self-confident, forward-looking, informal, thorough, open-minded, alert, restless, determined.
The rest have values of 0.

WHAT YOUR SCORE MEANS

180–200: Exceptionally creative

150–179: Very creative

110–149: Above average

60–109: Average

40–59: Below average

−30–39: Noncreative

☞TEST YOUR CREATIVE PROBLEM-SOLVING ABILITY

Creativity is alive and well. Creative thought is very useful in daily problem solving, and life's real success stories are made by men and women who aren't afraid to try new things or share different viewpoints. Through exercises like those that follow, you can not only test your creative ability but also revitalize it.

Approach these problems as stimulation and reinforcement for your creative thinking. Most importantly, have fun doing it.

1. Think of a fifth word that is related to each of the following sets of four words. (You can form compounds, hyphenate words, or use common expressions.)

   Examples:
   a. elephant, bleed, lie, wash _____
   answer: white (white elephant, bleed white, white lies, whitewash)
   b. sleeping, contest, spot, shop _____
   answer: beauty (sleeping beauty, beauty contest, beauty spot, beauty shop)
   c. style, love, jacket, span _____
   answer: life (life style, love life, life jacket, life span)

Now train your own associative powers with the following sets:

1. bug	rest	fellow	cover	_____
2. cross	baby	blood	ribbon	_____
3. see	carpet	hot	cent	_____

Reprinted from *Creative Growth Games* by Eugene Raudsepp, copyright © 1979, with permission of Creative Research, Inc., P.O. Box 122, Princeton, NJ 08540.

4. touch	palate	soap	sell	_____
5. easy	hush	belt	order	_____
6. tree	cup	cake	forbidden	_____
7. wagon	stand	aid	dance	_____
8. dust	movie	gaze	sapphire	_____
9. tooth	talk	potato	bitter	_____
10. alley	date	snow	spot	_____
11. call	nap	burgler	hep	_____
12. rest	post	linen	fellow	_____
13. bulldog	cuff	toast	windows	_____
14. opera	no	box	stone	_____
15. brain	watching	bath	house	_____
16. wire	out	feed	play	_____
17. studies	work	science	welfare	_____
18. storage	shoulder	comfort	cream	_____
19. walk	new	scape	beam	_____
20. business	suit	wrench	shine	_____
21. fire	hole	bent	catch	_____
22. days	biscuit	collar	ear	_____
23. clay	breast	english	hearted	_____
24. play	breast	pox	wire	_____
25. belt	magic	market	head	_____
26. guy	crack	up	man	_____
27. mouth	shot	stick	time	_____
28. dirty	cycle	office	school	_____
29. beater	head	roll	rotten	_____
30. dress	musical	star	prayer	_____
31. hunter	light	wind	stand	_____
32. actor	witness	sketch	odd	_____
33. shave	quarters	call	down	_____
34. belly	fever	journalism	pages	_____
35. A	B	C	E	_____
36. away	post	board	language	_____
37. star	glory	after	sickness	_____

38. seat	suit	broad	bail	_____
39. boy	bell	hand	hide	_____
40. sure	crow	eyed	fight	_____
41. age	class	brow	ear	_____
42. French	taking	alone	on	_____

2. *Medical Emergency.* Stereotyped thinking is one of the major barriers to creative problem solving. The impulse to overgeneralize about human beings is one most of us never fully conquer. But it is worth struggling with, because it can grossly mislead us—as this little puzzle illustrates.

A young man, badly injured in an auto accident, is brought into the emergency room of a hospital. The attending physician determines that immediate brain surgery is required. Accordingly, the brain surgeon is summoned. Upon seeing the patient, the surgeon exclaims, "My God, I can't operate on that boy! He's my son!"
That is so, but the surgeon is not the boy's father. How do you explain the apparent contradiction?

3. *Half of Thirteen.* This is an exercise in ingenuity and persistence. It increases your ability to look at a problem from as many different angles or viewpoints as possible. How many different answers can you think of to the question: "What is half of thirteen?"
Of course, the obvious answer is 6.5. See if you can find other acceptable answers. This exercise is not easy, but don't be discouraged. Chances are you can stump your friends with it.

4. *It's In the Bag.* This exercise shows that with some problems requiring a creative solution you need to reverse the problem, or "stand it on its head," so to speak. How would you solve the following problem?

It was the sixteenth hole in the annual Bob Hope tournament play. The tall, handsome newcomer, who looked very much like Bing Crosby, had an excellent chance of winning. His iron shot had fallen short of the green, and he had a good chance of making a birdie. Smiling broadly and singing "Thanks for the Memories," he bounded down the fairway, then stopped short in utter dismay. His ball had rolled into a small paper bag carelessly tossed there by someone in the gallery—although it was whispered that Bob Hope had placed it there. If he removed the ball from the bag, it would cost him a penalty stroke. If he tried to hit the ball and the bag, he would lose control over the shot. For a moment, he stood there pondering over the problem. Then, to Bob's chagrin, he solved it. How did he solve it?

5. *Nature's Inventions.* For many modern inventions, there already exists a counterpart in nature. Here is a list of animals and of the inventions they utilize. Try matching the animal with the invention.

1. bat		**a.** snowshoes
2. armadillo		**b.** swaddling clothes
3. chameleon		**c.** sonar
4. deep-sea fishes		**d.** gun blasts and chemical attack
5. echidna		**e.** tank
6. squid		**f.** camouflage
7. flying squirrel		**g.** suction cup
8. hummingbird		**h.** anesthesia
9. birds		**i.** electricity
10. scorpion		**j.** helicopter
11. snake		**k.** spurs
12. antelope		**l.** parachute
13. abalone		**m.** jet propulsion
14. beetle		**n.** hypodermic
15. caribou		**o.** signal code
16. silkworm		**p.** plane flaps (for braking)

ANSWERS

1. 1. bed. 2. blue. 3. red. 4. soft. 5. money. 6. fruit. 7. band. 8. star. 9. sweet. 10. blind. 11. cat. 12. bed. 13. French. 14. soap. 15. bird. 16. chicken. 17. social. 18. cold. 19. moon. 20. monkey. 21. hell. 22. dog. 23. pigeon. 24. chicken. 25. black. 26. wise. 27. big. 28. business. 29. egg. 30. evening. 31. head. 32. character. 33. close. 34. yellow. 35. vitamin. 36. sign. 37. morning. 38. jump. 39. cow. 40. cock. 41. middle. 42. leave

2. The answer, of course, is that the surgeon is the boy's mother. Although there are many women doctors—and many of them prominent specialists—our cultural stereotyping tells us that doctors are men and nurses are women. It is worth noting that the story might just as easily have been about a nurse attending the patient, because most large hospitals now have a substantial number of male nurses. The identification of a profession with a particular sex is diminishing gradually, to the great benefit of coming generations.

In a similar but much earlier story, two Indians—a tall one and a short one—arrive at a military post to negotiate with United States marshals about the land that the Indians are occupying. They look very much alike, and in fact, they are closely related. The short Indian is the son of the tall Indian, but the tall Indian is not the father of the short Indian. What is their relationship? Beware of sexual stereotyping.

3. There are seven answers: 1, 2, 3, 4, 6.5, 8, and 11. Half of thirteen is 6.5; ⅓ gives you 1 and 3; thirteen gives you 4, and X̶I̶I̶I̶ produces 8. XI/II gives you 11 and 2.

In creative problem solving, it is frequently more important to look at a problem from different vantage points rather than run with the first solution that pops into mind.

4. He reached into his pocket, extracted a book of matches, lit one and set fire to the bag. When the bag had burned to ashes, he selected an iron, swung, and watched the ball roll to the rim of the hole. Unable to get the ball away from the paper bag without a penalty, this golfer was imaginative enough to recognize that the problem could be solved by getting the paper bag away from the ball. The reversal of problems, the purging of habitual, accepted, or established ways of thinking about things has brought many important advances.

5.   1–c. The bat used sonar long before it was discovered. As it flies, it emits a series of sharp cries unheard to the human ear but audible to itself. As the cries bounce off various objects, they warn the bat of the approach of obstructions. In experiments, blindfolded bats could still fly perfectly, but bats with their ears plugged up flew into something at once.

2–e. Both armadillo and turtle antedate the tank.

3–f. Before modern warfare invented camouflage the chameleon was a master at it, rapidly changing its color from green to yellow and gray.

4–i. Some deep-sea fish have their own electrical power plants. They are equipped with electric stingers, lighted "portholes" along their bodies, and lanterns in their jaws or on their tails. Many—the electric eel particularly—have electric "batteries" strong enough to deliver a lethal shock.

5–k. The Australian spiny anteater, known as the echidna, popularized spurs before the cowboy and caballero glorified them, except that the echidna's spurs had the utilitarian purpose of defense against enemies.

6–m. Jet propulsion is used by the squid, which sucks and expels water to move along.

7–l. The flying squirrel spreads its forelegs and hind legs outward so that the skin along its sides forms a parachute as it flies from tree to tree.

8–j. The hummingbird is nature's tiny helicopter. It can hover and even fly backward.

9–p. Birds can brake with their tailfeathers exactly as planes do with flaps.

10–n. The scorpion's tail is a perfect hypodermic needle. Like a surgeon, he uses it for injections, except that he does not much care whether the patient lives.

11–h. In biting, the snake paralyzes and desensitizes its prey before eating it, applying a merciful function known in medicine only since the 1800s—anesthesia.

12–o. The army signal corps would be amazed if it watched the pronghorn antelope: it signals with its tail to tell of danger.

13–g. Suction cups, so useful today, were known in nature millions of years ago. They are especially prevalent among marine creatures like the sea snails. California abalones—the giant sea snails—have them. Their suction to rocks is so great that professional abalone divers have to pry them off with tire irons.

14–d. Even before the blunderbuss was invented, the bombardier beetle would turn its rear on the enemy and go to town with blasts for which it has been named. It combines a gun blast with chemical attack.

15–a. The caribou and the snowshoe rabbit have nature's patent on snowshoes. Both have feet designed to skim over the snow.

16–b. The Egyptians are among some of the most ancient nations to use swaddling clothes, but the silkworm made a cocoon long before man appeared on earth.

Biology and zoology are considered by many to contain the richest mine of analogies upon which significant inventions have been, and can be, built. One of the most celebrated cases is the invention of the telephone. As Alexander Graham Bell wrote: "It struck me that the bones of the human ear were very massive, indeed, as compared with the delicate thin membrane that operated them, and the thought occurred that if a membrane so delicate could move bones so relatively massive, why should not a thicker and stouter piece of membrane move my piece of steel." And the telephone was conceived.

☞AMY VANDERBILT'S ETIQUETTE QUIZ

The interpretation of etiquette rules today is sometimes a matter of one's life style. Although there is usually a right and wrong, how you behave in a given situation can often reveal your age, background, and general philosophy of life. Here's a quick quiz to find out how you fit into the etiquette picture. If you're a Traditionalist, you believe in using the established rules. If you're a Contemporary-Modern, you have good manners, but in a current idiom. If you're a non-etiquette person, you either need some know-how or you just don't care—which may lead to uncomfortable situations. In any case, take this quiz and find out your etiquette quotient, and see if you would resolve these problems the same way Amy Vanderbilt would.

Scene 1. You are going to meet a woman friend for lunch. You are wearing white gloves and a hat. Your friend turns up in pants, a body shirt, barefoot sandals, no hat. You see her, but she does not see you.
  a. You hide your gloves and remove your hat.
  b. You keep your gloves on (until the food comes) and enjoy your hat.
  c. You rush out the side entrance and phone the headwaiter, asking him to tell your friend you can't make lunch.

Scene 2. You are at home in lounging pajamas and bare feet. A neighbor drops by unannounced.
  a. You tell someone to say you are out, or you don't answer the door.
  b. You stay dressed as you are and are friendly.
  c. You insist that your neighbor remove his or her shoes, too.

Scene 3. A friend asks, "Will I see you at Anne's party?"—one to which you have not been invited.

a. You say, "I'm busy that night,"—implying that you were asked but didn't care to accept.

b. You say, "I wasn't invited."

c. You say, "I haven't decided." Then you call the hostess and imply that she forgot to ask you.

Scene 4. You know your best friend's husband is having an affair.

a. You pretend to his wife, who is suspicious, that you know nothing of it.

b. You tell his wife.

c. You confront the husband with your knowledge.

Scene 5. A friend invites you and your husband for a weekend. She later calls to ask if you mind if she also asks another couple, people you can't stand.

a. You say, "Please don't. We don't enjoy them and probably they don't enjoy us."

b. You acquiesce, feeling that the hostess has the right to invite any guests she wishes to.

c. You say, "Count us out. We'll come some other time."

Scene 6. You are going to a dinner at a house where the husband is an alcoholic and no liquor is offered.

a. You have several cocktails before you leave home.

b. You abstain graciously.

c. You bring your own bottle.

Scene 7. You are going to a wedding. Your dress, you find, is from the same designer as the one chosen by the mother of the bride—and in the same color.

a. You exchange it for something you don't like as well.

b. You wear it anyhow.

c. You wear it and call everyone's attention to the fact that the bride's mother has on the same dress, implying it is a cheap copy of yours.

Scene 8. You have a blind date. He turns out to be short, fat, bald, and much older than you had expected.

a. You go out with him anyway.

b. You slam the door in his face.

c. You go out with him and tell the friend who arranged the date that he or she was out of line, so that it won't happen again.

Scene 9. You receive flowers from a man—five purple orchids—before going to a dance with him.

a. You say, "Thank you, but I never wear corsages," then use them in an arrangement in your home.

b. You wear them, top-heavy as they are, with your scarlet dress.

c. You throw them in the wastebasket after he removes them from the box.

Scene 10. You burn a hole in your hostess's tablecloth with your cigarette.

a. You move the ashtray to cover the hole, and say nothing

b. You offer to have the hole invisibly mended.

c. You admit that you did it but suggest that the hostess's fire-insurance coverage will take care of the problem.

Scene 11. You are going to a dinner party.

a. You tell the hostess in advance what you can't eat.

b. You go, eat what you can eat, and say nothing.

c. You take all your own food and make a big production of your problem.

Scene 12. You are having dinner in a restaurant with friends. You pick up the wrong fork.

    a. You clean it with your napkin and pick up the right fork.

    b. You go on eating with the fork in your hand.

    c. You tell the hostess that the table setting is wrong, which is why you made the mistake.

ANSWERS

Scene 1. You are a Contemporary-Modern if you check *a*; a Traditionalist-Conformist if you checked *b*; lacking in savvy if you checked *c*. (In this case, I prefer *b*.)

Scene 2. You are a Traditionalist if you checked *a*; a Contemporary-Modern if you checked *b* (which I prefer); if you checked *c*, you're impossible.

Scene 3. You are a Traditionalist if you checked *a*; a Contemporary-Modern if you checked *b* (my choice); impossible if you checked *c*. (The question, of course, should not have been asked.)

Scene 4. You are a Traditionalist if you checked *a*. Contemporary-Modern if you checked *b*; foolish if you checked *c*.

Scene 5. You are Contemporary-Modern if you checked *a*, Traditionalist if you checked *b*; very rude if you checked *c*. I believe in being honest; therefore, I prefer the first answer.

Scene 6. You are Contemporary-Modern (but lacking in sensitivity) if you checked *a*; a Traditionalist if you checked *b* (my choice); rude if you checked *c*.

Scene 7. You are Contemporary-Modern if you checked *a*; a Traditionalist if you checked *b*; unkind if you checked *c* (I prefer *b*).

Scene 8. You are a Traditionalist if you checked *a*; impossible if you checked *b*; Contemporary-Modern if you checked *c* (I prefer *a*).

Scene 9. You are Contemporary-Modern if you check *a* (my preference); a Traditionalist if you checked *b*; rude if you checked *c*.

Scene 10. You are unkind if you checked *a*; a Traditionalist if you checked *b* (my choice); Contemporary-Modern if you checked *c*.

Scene 11. You are a Contemporary-Modern if you checked *a*; a Traditionalist if you checked *b*; unkind if you checked *c* (*b* is my answer).

Scene 12. You are Contemporary-Modern if you checked *a*; a Traditionalist if you checked *b* (my choice); unwise if you checked *c*.

☞ ARE YOU A RADICAL OR A CONSERVATIVE?

On any particular issue it is possible to discern those who favor the new as opposed to those who would conserve the old. As successive issues are confronted, the alignment changes somewhat, but not completely. The extent to which one conserves the old values determines one's conservatism; the extent to which one strives for new values determines one's radicalism. Radicalism abides in one's desire for changes of a deep-rooted or fundamental nature.

This simple exercise presents issues that require you to take a side. Each response will force you to take a stand with either the conservative or radical viewpoint. Your total score will determine whether you are a radical or conservative.

Instructions

Read the statements below. They are all opinions and you will agree with some and disagree with others.

If you *agree* more than you disagree with a statement, mark a plus (+). If you *disagree* more than you agree with a statement, mark a minus (−). *Be sure* to place either a *plus* or a *minus mark* to the right of each number. Try to answer all questions. If you have absolutely no opinion on a statement, leave it blank.

1. Three meals a day will always be the best general rule. (   )
2. The metric system of weights and measures should be adopted instead of our present system. (   )
3. Cleanliness is a more valuable human trait than curiosity. (   )
4. We should celebrate Pasteur's birthday rather than Washington's, as he has done the world a greater service. (   )
5. The proposal to change the present calendar to one having thirteen months of twenty-eight days is unsound. (   )
6. Even in an ideal world there should be protective tariffs. (   )
7. Our courts should be in the hands of sociologists rather than lawyers. (   )
8. Not the young men, but the old men, should fight our wars. (   )

Adapted from the "Conservatism-Radicalism Questionnaire." The C-R Opinionaire (Forms J and K) and the Manual are the result of work done by members of the Character Research Association and its Director, Theo. F. Lentz, copyright © 1935.

9. In Sunday School, only the Bible should be taught. (   )
10. Social-minded experts, rather than voters, should decide the policies of government. (   )
11. Cat meat is out of the question for the human diet. (   )
12. Conscience is an infallible guide. (   )
13. The English and the Americans have the highest standards of morality. (   )
14. Our universities should have as many research workers as teachers. (   )
15. Ministers should preach more about immortality than about social justice. (   )
16. A commission form of government would not be desirable for the nation. (   )
17. Negroes should be permitted to attend educational institutions with whites. (   )
18. People who are religious will be happier in the future life than will others. (   )
19. Married women should not be allowed to teach in public schools. (   )
20. Any science which conflicts with religious beliefs should be taught cautiously, if at all, in our schools. (   )
21. It is more important to believe in God than to be unselfish. (   )
22. Since the theory of evolution has been accepted by most scientists, it should be taught in our schools. (   )
23. Skirts which do not come to the knee should not be worn by women. (   )
24. Criminals should be treated like sick persons. (   )
25. It is to be hoped that men will improve the comfort of their dress by abandoning or replacing the present necktie and collar. (   )
26. Cremation is the best method of burial. (   )
27. Conservative people are usually more intelligent than radical people. (   )
28. Trial by jury has been, and always will be, the most effective way of securing justice. (   )
29. Our spelling should be revised and simplified. (   )
30. Capital punishment will some day be done away with. (   )
31. The average person needs greater caution more than greater daring. (   )
32. One is never justified in taking another's life, even when it would be a merciful act. (   )
33. Of all national anthems, the "Star-Spangled Banner" is the most stirring in theme and noble in sentiment. (   )
34. At the age of 21, people should have the privilege of changing their given names. (   )
35. The Bible is valuable primarily because it contains some of the world's best literature, and not because it is the word of God. (   )
36. Race prejudice is, on the whole, beneficial as it keeps many undesirable foreigners from the country. (   )
37. Democracy as practiced in the United States is the best of all modern governments because it is most suited to the needs of modern times. (   )
38. Freedom of teaching, that is, allowing teachers to teach what they think is the truth, is necessary for real education. (   )
39. American civilization may some day be wiped out, as was Roman civilization. (   )
40. It is improbable that wood ever will be converted into humanly edible food. (   )
41. The Japanese race is, on the whole, crafty and treacherous. (   )
42. Children should be brought up to have higher respect for their ancestors. (   )
43. Radical agitators and propagandists should be allowed to speak publicly in parks and streets. (   )
44. Telling a lie is worse than taking the name of God in vain. (   )

45. National boundaries may some day become as truly obliterated as state lines have become in America during the past 150 years. ( )
46. In college, students should be allowed to attend class as much or as little as they like. ( )
47. Our present system of athletics in America is at fault in that it does not provide for mass participation. ( )
48. The A.B. degree should continue to require four and only four years of work above the high school level. ( )
49. We should Europeanize our native Americans, as well as Americanize Europeans among ourselves. ( )
50. We cannot say whether Christianity is sound or not because we have never practiced it systematically. ( )
51. Preaching is one of the most effective ways of teaching people to lead better lives. ( )
52. Our present system of law, based upon outdated conditions, should be replaced by a progressive system based upon the conditions of our present order. ( )
53. We owe our progress to radically minded people rather than to the "middle of the road" folk. ( )
54. Generally speaking, Americans are more intelligent and enterprising than people of most any other country. ( )
55. The naval custom for a captain to stay with his ship until she sinks is outmoded, sentimental, and unnecessary. ( )
56. It would not be possible to invent an ice cream that could be made merely by opening a tin can and exposing the contents to the air. ( )
57. Deformed babies whom we can be sure will be permanently helpless should be put to death at the outset. ( )
58. Something more effective than our present brooms and mops and vacuum cleaners should be devised for cleaning our homes. ( )
59. All children should have some sectarian religious training either on Sunday or week days. ( )
60. Most members of the D.A.R. would repudiate as dangerous characters modern personalities equivalent to the progenitors through whom they claim membership in the organization. ( )

HOW TO SCORE

To arrive at your score, take the total number of answers agreeing with this key and add one-half of those you have omitted.

1. +	16. +	31. +	46. −
2. −	17. −	32. +	47. −
3. +	18. +	33. +	48. +
4. −	19. +	34. −	49. −
5. +	20. +	35. −	50. −
6. +	21. +	36. +	51. +
7. −	22. −	37. +	52. −
8. −	23. +	38. −	53. −
9. +	24. −	39. −	54. +
10. −	25. −	40. +	55. −
11. +	26. −	41. +	56. +
12. +	27. +	42. +	57. −
13. +	28. +	43. −	58. −
14. −	29. −	44. −	59. +
15. +	30. −	45. −	60. −

WHAT YOUR SCORE MEANS

The scoring of this test is done from the point of view of conservatism. Consequently, a high score is a conservative score and a low one, a radical score.

Of 580 college students of all ages and both sexes taking this test a percentile ranking standard was established. Locate your score below to determine your general position. Remember, the highest scores are ultra-conservative, the lowest super-radical.

Total Score	Percentile Ranking
50 and above	99
40–49	78–98
35–39	61–74
30–34	47–58
25–29	36–45
20–24	24–34
15–19	14–22
10–14	10–12
9 and under	5

HEALTH AND FITNESS

☞ WHAT DO YOU REALLY KNOW ABOUT EXERCISE?

There is so much contradictory, and sometimes erroneous advice about exercising that one can easily be confused. To help take some of the confusion out of the burgeoning world of exercise advice, take the following quiz. It is basic and informative and will confirm what you really do know about exercise.

1. The best way to reduce the midsection is to do abdominal exercise.
True   False

2. To maintain an adequate level of physical fitness one needs to exercise at least___days a week.

3. You should perspire freely during an exercise period.
True   False

4. You burn more calories jogging one mile than walking the same distance.
True   False

5. If your breath doesn't return to normal within ten minutes after you finish exercising, you've exerted yourself too much.
True   False

6. Walking is one of the best exercises.
True   False

7. Vigorous stretching exercises keep muscles flexible.
True   False

8. It is possible to get enough exercise from one's ordinary daily activities.
True   False

9. The minimum amount of time you should spend exercising is 1, 3, 4, 10, 20, 30, 60 minutes. (Choose one answer.)

10. It takes 7, 14, 21, 30, 60, 120 days to become physically fit. (Choose one answer.)

ANSWERS

1. False. Many people believe that when certain muscles are exercised, the fatty tissues in the immediate area are burned up. In other words, if you bend at the waist often enough, you'll trim down your midsection. Despite claims to the contrary, however, "spot reducing" just doesn't work. It is impossible to reduce the amount of fat in a particular area without affecting the amount in other parts of the body.

2. Three. After extensive testing, NASA scientists concluded that, while daily exercise is desirable, three nonconsecutive days of programmed activity each week will maintain an adequate level of physical fitness. Just as the body cannot store certain vitamins but must have them regularly, it likewise cannot store certain of the conditioning effects of exercise. After forty-eight to seventy-two hours one must use the muscles again to reestablish the desirable physical effects. Therefore, you should exercise at least three days a week, with at least one day in between. Of course, you can use a daily schedule.

3. False. Sweating doesn't do anything other than lower body temperature. It does not help you reduce. You may weigh less immediately after a workout, but this is due to a loss of water. Replace the lost liquid and you'll make it all up. Sweating does not clean the pores, either; there is no evidence that it is of any value in removing toxic materials from the body. Nor does perspiration promote fitness. Fitness is developed by exercising the muscles of the body, not the sweat glands.

4. False. Work is defined as the energy required to move a given weight through a given distance. A 120-pound woman expends equal amounts of energy (i.e., does the same amount of work) traveling one mile, whether she walks or jogs. The speed at which one covers a particular distance is not related to the number of calories used. In fact, you can easily calculate how many calories you will burn jogging (or walking) one mile by multiplying your body weight by 0.73. Remember, of course, that you can jog a mile faster than you can walk it. Therefore, if you jog rather than walk for thirty minutes, you'll cover more distance and, consequently, burn more calories.

5. True. Exercise does not have to be strenuous to be beneficial. In fact, if it is too difficult, it can prove harmful. A good rule of thumb is that your breathing should return to normal within ten minutes after you've finished your routine.

Here are some other guidelines to help you determine if you are working too hard: Ten minutes after exercising you shouldn't feel your heart pounding in your chest nor should you be "all pooped out." In fact, you should begin to experience a come-back sensation. Too much exercise may make sleeping difficult and can produce fatigue into the next day. Exercise should not be strenuous, unpleasant, and exhausting; it should be moderate, enjoyable, and refreshing.

6. True. Physical anthropologists say human bone structure makes us the perfect walkers—ever notice how long your legs are in proportion to the rest of your body? Walking gets the blood circulating again. As the muscles in the legs move they squeeze the nearby veins. This action forces the blood back to the heart and makes you feel good all over.

7. False. Flexibility comes from stretching the muscles and tendons that move the joints. Most people choose the right activities; the problem is that they don't practice them properly. For example, if you want to stretch the hamstrings—the muscles that run up the back of your thighs—you should sit on the floor, legs flat in front of you, and bend forward. Most people, anxious to get on with it, will start bouncing and bobbing in an attempt to stretch out those tight hamstrings. But what they are actually doing is defeating the purpose. The muscles will become tighter, not more flexible.

Stretching exercises should be done slowly, deliberately, and carefully, allowing the muscles to relax and let go. Vigorous straining encourages tightness. When doing stretching exercises, move slowly. When the first sign of pain occurs, hold that position for several seconds, then relax. Repeat the exercise several times.

8. False, although the answer is debatable. Exercise used to be commonplace. Not that people went around touching their toes or doing push-ups, but before the industrial revolution most work was physical. It entailed movement and exercise. Today we use machines to do many tasks—and to do all the exercising involved. Unless your job involves manual labor, it's almost impossible to find an opportunity to exercise in the course of an ordinary day.

9. Twenty. There are more than 400 skeletal muscles in the body. A good exercise routine should contract and stretch all the major muscle groups, and this simply can't be done with four or five exercises in five minutes. From experience, it has been found that about twenty minutes is the minimum amount of time needed for an adequate workout.

10. How long it takes you to become physically fit depends on how fit or unfit you are when you start. If you are out of condition, you certainly can't shape up in twenty-one days, as one book claims. You can, however, make significant progress in three weeks and be well on the way to becoming physically fit in time. But the question is really moot, because shaping up doesn't do any good unless you plan to stay in shape, and that means consistent exercising. Don't think in terms of how long it will take you to get in shape, but rather, in terms of a life plan to keep that way. There is no such thing as a maintenance program in exercise. It takes as much exercise to stay in shape as it does to get there. But the work won't seem as hard after a while, because your body will be conditioned, and all the moves will seem easier. Then you'll be glad you started when you did.

☞ HOW FIT ARE YOU?

Here's a simple five-minute test designed for men and women to measure physical fitness and to predict their ability to sustain arduous work. The test predicts the maximal ability to take in, transport, and utilize oxygen—maximal oxygen intake or aerobic capacity being the best measure of physical fitness. Persons with known heart ailments or serious respiratory problems should not take the test without a physician's approval.

Equipment Needed

1. sturdy bench: 15¾ inches high for men; 13 inches high for women
2. stopwatch
3. metronome or other audible signaling device such as a tape recording, set for 90 beats per minute.
4. chairs
5. scale accurate to ±2 pounds
6. thermometer
7. quiet room at 65-75°F

Directions

1. Have subject rest a few minutes before the test (do not take test after exercise, meals, coffee, cigarettes).
2. Start the metronome (90 beats per minute).
3. Have subject step up onto bench, and back to floor, keeping time with the metronome beat. If subject can't keep up with the beat because of poor condition, stop and retake after several weeks of conditioning. Change the lead leg if it becomes tired. Stop the test if the subject shows obvious physical distress or cannot keep pace with the timer.
4. After *five minutes* of exercise, stop metronome and have subject sit down.
5. Count subject's pulse (at wrist or throat) for *exactly fifteen seconds,* starting *exactly fifteen seconds* after the step test exercise.
6. Use post-exercise pulse count and body weight on tables below to determine fitness score.

HOW TO DETERMINE YOUR FITNESS RATING

1. Find body weight.
2. Locate the post-exercise pulse count in column.
3. Opposite pulse count, find fitness score on table.

Derived from the Fitness Test published by the U.S. Department of the Interior.

MEN'S FITNESS SCORE

Body Weight	120	130	140	150	160	170	180	190	200	210	220	230	240
45	33	33	33	33	33	32	32	32	32	32	32	32	32
44	34	34	34	34	33	33	33	33	33	33	33	33	33
43	35	35	35	34	34	34	34	34	34	34	34	34	34
42	36	35	35	35	35	35	35	35	35	35	35	34	34
41	36	36	36	36	36	36	36	36	36	36	36	35	35
40	37	37	37	37	37	37	37	37	36	36	36	36	36
39	38	38	38	38	38	38	38	38	38	38	38	37	37
38	39	39	39	39	39	39	39	39	39	39	39	38	38
37	41	40	40	40	40	40	40	40	40	40	40	39	39
36	42	42	41	41	41	41	41	41	41	41	41	40	40
35	43	43	42	42	42	42	42	42	42	42	42	42	41
34	44	44	43	43	43	43	43	43	43	43	43	43	43
33	46	45	45	45	45	45	44	44	44	44	44	44	44
32	47	47	46	46	46	46	46	46	46	46	46	46	46
31	48	48	48	47	47	47	47	47	47	47	47	47	47
30	50	49	49	49	48	48	48	48	48	48	48	48	48
29	52	51	51	51	50	50	50	50	50	50	50	50	50
28	53	53	53	53	52	52	52	52	52	52	51	51	51
27	55	55	55	54	54	54	54	54	54	53	53	53	52
26	57	57	56	56	56	56	56	56	56	55	55	54	54
25	59	59	58	58	58	58	58	58	58	56	56	55	55
24	60	60	60	60	60	60	60	59	59	58	58	57	—
23	62	62	61	61	61	61	61	60	60	60	59	—	—
22	64	64	63	63	63	63	62	62	61	61	—	—	—
21	66	66	65	65	65	64	64	64	62	—	—	—	—
20	68	68	67	67	67	66	66	65	—	—	—	—	—

POST-EXERCISE PULSE COUNT

WOMEN'S FITNESS SCORE

Body Weight	80	90	100	110	120	130	140	150	160	170	180	190
45	—	—	—	—	—	—	—	—	—	29	29	29
44	—	—	—	—	—	—	—	30	30	30	30	30
43	—	—	—	—	—	—	31	31	31	31	31	31
42	—	—	32	32	32	32	32	32	32	32	32	32
41	—	—	33	33	33	33	33	33	33	33	33	33
40	—	—	34	34	34	34	34	34	34	34	34	34
39	—	—	35	35	35	35	35	35	35	35	35	35
38	—	—	36	36	36	36	36	36	36	36	36	36
37	—	—	37	37	37	37	37	37	37	37	37	37
36	—	37	38	38	38	38	38	38	38	38	38	38
35	38	38	39	39	39	39	39	39	39	39	39	39
34	39	39	40	40	40	40	40	40	40	40	40	40
33	40	40	41	41	41	41	41	41	41	41	41	41
32	41	41	42	42	42	42	42	42	42	42	42	42
31	42	42	43	43	43	43	43	43	43	43	43	43
30	43	43	44	44	44	44	44	44	44	44	44	44
29	44	44	45	45	45	45	45	45	45	45	45	45
28	45	45	46	46	46	47	47	47	47	47	47	47
27	46	46	47	48	48	49	49	49	49	49	—	—
26	47	48	49	50	50	51	51	51	51	—	—	—
25	49	50	51	52	52	53	53	—	—	—	—	—
24	51	52	53	54	54	55	—	—	—	—	—	—
23	53	54	55	56	56	57	—	—	—	—	—	—

POST-EXERCISE PULSE COUNT

4. Find age-adjusted score opposite nearest age.

AGE-ADJUSTED SCORE

Nearest Age / Fitness Score	30	31	32	33	34	35	36	37	38	39	40	41	42	43	44	45	46	47	48	49	50
15	32	33	34	35	36	37	38	39	40	41	42	43	44	45	46	47	48	49	50	51	53
20	31	32	33	34	35	36	37	38	39	40	41	42	43	44	45	46	47	48	49	50	51
25	30	31	32	33	34	35	36	37	38	39	40	41	42	43	44	45	46	47	48	49	50
30	29	30	31	32	33	34	35	36	37	38	39	40	41	42	43	44	45	46	47	48	49
35	27	28	29	31	32	33	34	35	36	37	38	39	40	41	42	43	44	45	46	47	48
40	26	27	28	30	31	32	33	34	35	36	37	38	39	40	41	42	43	44	45	46	47
45	25	26	27	29	30	31	32	33	34	35	36	37	38	39	40	41	42	43	44	45	46
50	24	25	26	28	29	30	31	32	33	34	35	36	37	38	39	40	41	42	43	44	45
55	23	24	25	27	28	29	30	31	32	33	34	35	36	37	38	39	40	40	41	42	43
60	22	23	24	25	26	27	28	30	31	32	33	34	35	36	37	37	38	39	40	41	42
65	21	22	23	24	25	26	27	28	29	30	31	32	33	34	35	36	37	38	38	39	40

Nearest Age / Fitness Score	51	52	53	54	55	56	57	58	59	60	61	62	63	64	65	66	67	68	69	70	71	72
15	54	55	56	57	58	59	60	61	62	63	64	65	66	67	68	69	70	71	72	74	75	76
20	52	53	54	55	56	57	58	59	60	61	62	63	64	65	66	67	68	69	70	71	72	73
25	51	52	53	54	55	56	57	58	59	60	61	62	63	64	65	66	67	68	69	70	71	72
30	50	51	52	53	54	55	56	57	58	59	60	61	62	63	64	65	66	67	68	69	70	71
35	49	50	51	52	53	54	55	56	57	58	59	60	60	61	62	63	64	65	66	67	68	69
40	48	49	50	51	52	53	54	55	55	56	57	58	59	60	61	62	63	64	65	66	67	68
45	47	48	49	50	51	52	52	53	54	55	56	57	58	59	60	61	62	63	64	65	65	66
50	45	46	47	48	49	50	51	52	53	53	54	55	56	57	58	58	59	61	61	62	63	64
55	44	45	46	46	47	48	49	50	51	52	53	53	54	55	56	57	58	59	59	60	61	62
60	42	43	44	45	46	46	47	48	49	50	51	51	52	53	54	55	56	57	57	58	59	60
65	41	42	42	43	44	45	46	46	47	48	49	50	50	51	52	53	54	54	55	56	57	58

5. With adjusted fitness score, find your physical fitness rating on the following table.

PHYSICAL FITNESS RATING—MEN

Nearest Age	Superior	Excellent	Very Good	Good	Fair	Poor	Very Poor
15	57+	56–52	51–47	46–42	41–37	36–32	31–
20	56+	55–51	50–46	45–41	40–36	35–31	30–
25	55+	54–50	49–45	44–40	39–35	34–30	29–
30	54+	53–49	48–44	43–39	38–34	33–29	28–
35	53+	52–48	47–43	42–38	37–33	32–28	27–
40	52+	51–47	46–42	41–37	36–32	31–27	26–
45	51+	50–46	45–41	40–36	35–31	30–26	25–
50	50+	49–45	44–40	39–35	34–30	29–25	24–
55	49+	48–44	43–39	38–34	33–29	28–24	23–
60	48+	47–43	42–38	37–33	32–28	27–23	22–
65	47+	46–42	41–37	36–32	31–27	26–22	21–

PHYSICAL FITNESS RATING—WOMEN

Nearest Age	Superior	Excellent	Very Good	Good	Fair	Poor	Very Poor
15	54+	53–49	48–44	43–39	38–34	33–29	28–
20	53+	52–48	47–43	42–38	37–33	32–28	27–
25	52+	51–47	46–42	41–37	36–32	31–27	26–
30	51+	50–46	45–41	40–36	35–31	30–26	25–
35	50+	49–45	44–40	39–35	34–30	29–25	24–
40	49+	48–44	43–39	38–34	33–29	28–24	23–
45	48+	47–43	42–38	37–33	32–28	27–23	22–
50	47+	46–42	41–37	36–32	31–27	26–22	21–
55	46+	45–41	40–36	35–31	30–26	25–21	20–
60	45+	44–40	39–35	34–30	29–25	24–20	19–
65	44+	43–39	38–34	33–29	28–24	23–20	19–

☞ HOW LONG WILL YOU LIVE?

Your chances for a long life have never been better, according to the lastest government statistics. But whether you will be among those who enjoy a generally longer lifespan still depends on how well you take care of yourself now.

Doctors say you need to take more responsibility for your own health, protecting yourself from life-shortening factors. Dr. Donald M. Vickery, president of the Center for Consumer Health Education, Inc., explains how you can do this in his book, *Life Plan for Your Health*. He also presents the LifeScore quiz, excerpted below.

Using the LifeScore quiz, you can analyze your own health history and predict how long and how well you will live. The questionnaire deals only with facts known to have an impact on health, not with every piece of information that might be of interest to a doctor at some point in the future. By taking it today, studying the results, and making plans to change your minus signs to plus signs wherever possible, you may put yourself on the road to a longer, healthier life.

How Much You Should Weigh
MEN OF AGES TWENTY-FIVE AND OVER
(In indoor clothing, including shoes)

Height (with one-inch heels)		Small frame	Medium frame	Large frame
FEET	INCHES	POUNDS	POUNDS	POUNDS
5	2	112–120	118–129	126–141
5	3	115–123	121–133	129–144
5	4	118–126	124–136	132–148
5	5	121–129	127–139	135–152
5	6	124–133	130–143	138–156
5	7	128–137	134–147	142–161
5	8	132–141	138–152	147–166
5	9	136–145	142–156	151–170
5	10	140–150	146–160	155–174
5	11	144–154	150–165	159–179
6	0	148–158	154–170	164–184
6	1	152–162	158–175	168–189
6	2	156–167	162–180	173–194
6	3	160–171	167–185	178–199
6	4	164–175	172–190	182–204

Reprinted from *Lifeplan for Your Health* by Donald M. Vickery, MD, copyright © 1978, by permission of Addison-Wesley Publishing Co., Reading, MA.

WOMEN OF AGES TWENTY-FIVE AND OVER
(In indoor clothing, including shoes)

Height (with two-inch heels		Small frame	Medium frame	Large frame
FEET	INCHES	POUNDS	POUNDS	POUNDS
4	10	91- 98	96-107	104-119
4	11	94-101	98-110	106-122
5	0	96-104	101-113	109-125
5	1	99-107	104-116	112-128
5	2	102-110	107-119	115-131
5	3	105-113	110-122	118-134
5	4	108-116	113-126	121-138
5	5	111-119	116-130	125-142
5	6	114-123	120-135	129-146
5	7	118-127	124-139	133-150
5	8	122-131	128-143	137-154
5	9	126-135	132-147	141-158
5	10	130-140	136-151	145-163
5	11	134-144	140-155	149-168
6	0	138-148	144-159	153-173

I. Habits

1. Exercise

To qualify as a minute of conditioning, it must be a minute with the heart rate at 120 beats per minute or more. Beware of overestimating activities in which there may be a lot of standing around, e.g., tennis. As a rule, golf, bowling, baseball and volleyball do not result in conditioning. If you have 15–29 minutes of conditioning per week, or less, score   0

30–44 minutes	+2
45–74 minutes	+6
75–119 minutes	+12
120–179 minutes	+16
180–more minutes	+24

2. Weight

Look at the weight table to determine how many pounds overweight you are. If you are 0–5 pounds overweight, score   0

6–15 pounds	−2
16–25 pounds	−6
26–35 pounds	−10
36–45 pounds	−12
46 or more	−15

3. Diet

If you eat a well-balanced diet, score   +4

If you avoid saturated fats and cholesterol, score   +2

4. Smoking

One cigar is considered to be the equivalent of one cigarette. If you smoke only a pipe, score− 4. If you smoke

0 cigarettes per day, score	0
1–9 cigarettes	−10
10–19 cigarettes	−13
20–29 cigarettes	−15
30–39 cigarettes	−17
40–49 cigarettes	−20
50 or more cigarettes	−24

5. Drinking

Cocktails are assumed to contain one-and-a-half-ounces of hard liquor. If you are pouring doubles, multiply accordingly. One pint equals sixteen ounces or about ten cocktails. One eight-ounce beer is the equivalent of one cocktail. Six ounces of wine also is the equivalent of one cocktail. If you drink: 0–1 cocktails per day, score   0

2–3 cocktails	−4
4–5 cocktails	−12
6–8 cocktails	−20
9 or more cocktails	−30

6. Seat Belts

The actual time you wear a seat belt while driving is probably one-half your first guess (unless the guess was zero). Take a minute to come up with a more accurate estimate. If you wear a seat belt less than 25 percent of time,

score	0
about 25 percent	+2
about 50 percent	+4
about 75 percent	+6
about 100 percent	+8

7. Contraception (for women only)

If you have had a hysterectomy, tubal ligation, or have reached menopause, skip this section. If you use

nothing and would not have an abortion, score	−10
mechanical method and would not have an abortion	0
birth control pills and would not have an abortion	+4
nothing, but would have an abortion	+4
birth control pills and would have an abortion	+5
mechanical method and would have an abortion	+10
bad bonus: if you smoke or use birth control pills	−10
Habits total	_____

II. Stress

Calculate your stress level from the Holmes Stress Scale on page 264, then record your score in the appropriate space. If your Holmes score is

less than 150, score	0
150–250	−4
250–300	−7
more than 300	−10
Stress total	_____

III. Immunity (age thirteen and up)

If you are not current on tetanus (booster every ten years), score	−4
diphtheria (booster every ten years for those with high risk of exposure only)	−2
Immunity total	_____

IV. Personal History

Tuberculosis: If you have been in close contact for a year or more with someone with tuberculosis, score	−4
Radiation: If you have had radiation (x-ray) treatment of tonsils, adenoids, acne or ringworm of the scalp	−6

Asbestos:

If you work with asbestos regularly and do not smoke	−2
If you work with asbestos regularly and do smoke	−10

Vinyl chloride:

If you work regularly with vinyl chloride	−4
Urban environment: If you live in a city	−6

Risk of venereal disease (men and women):

If sexual activity has been frequent and with many different partners	−1

Risk of uterine cancer (women only):

If you began regular sexual activity before age eighteen	−1
If sexual activity has been frequent and with many different partners	−1
If you are Jewish	−1
Personal History total	_____

V. Family History

Heart Attacks (myocardial infarction): For each parent, brother or sister who had a heart attack before age forty, score	−4

For each grandparent, uncle, or aunt who had a heart attack before age forty   − 1

High blood pressure (hypertension):

For each parent, brother, or sister with high blood pressure requiring treatment, score   − 2

For each grandparent, uncle, or aunt with high blood pressure requiring treatment   − 1

Diabetes:

For each parent, brother, or sister with juvenile-onset diabetes, score   − 6

For each grandparent, uncle or aunt with juvenile-onset diabetes   − 2

For each parent, brother, or sister with adult-onset diabetes who required treatment with insulin, score   − 2

For each grandparent, uncle, or aunt with adult-onset diabetes who required treatment with insulin   − 1

Cancer of the Breast (women only):

If your mother or a sister has had cancer of the breast, score   − 4

Glaucoma:

If you have a parent, grandparent, brother, sister, uncle, or aunt with glaucoma, score   − 2

Gout:

If you have a parent, grandparent, brother, sister, uncle or aunt with gout   − 1

Ankylosing spondylitis (a type of arthritis):

If you have a parent, grandparent, brother, sister, uncle, or aunt with ankylosing spondylitis, score   − 1

Family History total _____

HOW TO SCORE

I. Habits   _____

II. Stress   _____

III. Immunity   _____

IV. Personal History   _____

V. Family History   _____

Total

Now add   200

to obtain your life score   _____

Be sure to get the plus and minus signs right so that you add or subtract correctly.

A LifeScore of 200 is about average. A LifeScore above 210 indicates a positive lifestyle, which gives you an excellent chance of enjoying health beyond the average life expectancy of 69 years for men and 77 years for women. A LifeScore below 185 means your chance of a healthy future is clearly decreased. If your LifeScore is below 170, consider your life to be in danger. Below 150, make out a will and get your affairs in order.

To determine how long you're going to live, make these simple calculations.
For men, the formula is:

$$\frac{\text{_____}}{\text{LifeScore}} \div 200 \times 70 \text{ years} = \underset{\text{Life Expectancy}}{\text{_____}}$$

For women:

$$\frac{\text{_____}}{\text{Lifescore}} \div 200 \times 75 \text{ years} = \underset{\text{Life Expectancy}}{\text{_____}}$$

☞MEASURE YOUR OWN PHYSICAL QUOTIENT, OR PQ

These five tests are designed to measure the three basic qualities essential for fitness: strength, flexibility and endurance. They can be taken alone, or with a companion. The only equipment you'll need is a piece of chalk, a watch with a second hand, a yardstick, and paper and pencil.

Of the test's five parts, three can be taken indoors on the floor of any room with enough space to lie down. A fourth requires jumping and reaching high on a wall. The fifth involves running some distance and can best be done at a marked high-school track or on a quiet, flat stretch of road.

It is important to remember the PQ is not a competition but simply a measure. You should not overexert yourself; the aim of the test is to encourage people to find their physical-fitness level, not to cause injuries.

Test 1. *Abdominal curl.* This modified sit-up tests the strength of the abdominal muscles, without causing back strain. Lie flat on back, with hands on thighs and feet slipped under a bed, couch or heavy chair. Raise the head, then the shoulders and upper trunk, in an upward curl, sliding hands forward until fingertips just touch the kneecaps. Return to flat position. Do as many as you can without stopping to rest.

Test 2. *Chalk jump.* This test measures your ability to summon up a burst of muscular power. (It is important to warm up with partial knee bends and squats, to avoid pulling a muscle or a tendon.) Make a chalk mark as high as you can reach on a wall, keeping your heels on the ground. Then, holding the chalk, jump as high as you can, crouching down first and swinging your arms up to carry you higher, and make another mark as far up on the wall as possible. Best of three tries counts. The number of inches between the two marks is your jump height.

Test 3. *Forward bend.* This test measures flexibility (first warm up by stretching). Sit on the floor legs extended. Heels should be about five inches apart, touching a strip of tape, edge of carpet or other marker line. Place a yardstick on the floor between and parallel to the legs so the fifteen-inch mark is on the line between your heels, and the thirty-six-inch end is farthest from you. With fingers extended, slowly reach with both

Appeared as "Measure Your Own Physical Quotient" by Judson Gooding. Reprinted with permission from the October 1976 *Reader's Digest.* Copyright © 1976 by The Reader's Digest Association, Inc.

hands as far forward as possible without straining or jerking, and note the farthest point you can touch on the yardstick. Best of three tries counts. Your score is determined from the table by the distance reading in inches.

Test 4. *Push-ups.* This measures strength in the upper arms, back, and shoulders, and provides some measurements of endurance. Lie prone, hands outside shoulders, fingers pointing forward.

Men: With feet on floor, keeping back straight, raise body by straightening arms, then lower yourself slowly so body again touches floor. Repeat as many times as possible without strain and without stopping to rest.

Women: Begin in a similar prone position. Keeping back straight, do push-ups so that the weight rests on your knees when the body is raised.

Test 5. *Twelve-minute distance test.* Designed to measure endurance, this test consists of determining the distance you can cover—running, walking, even stopping to rest if necessary—in exactly twelve minutes. It should be taken only if you have had a recent physical examination and have obtained a doctor's approval; for those over thirty-five, a stress electrocardiogram should be taken first. In doing this test, stop if discomfort is felt, and try again only after a period of conditioning and a physical examination.

Use the second hand on your watch to time your start. To calculate the actual distance covered, use track markings (most high-school tracks are ¼ mile around).

How to Arrive at Your Scores

1. ABDOMINAL CURL (MEN)

Score Age:	15–25	26–35	36–45	46–over
		SIT-UPS		
100	104	56	42	37
90	100	55	40	35
80	90–95	50	35–37	32
70	75–85	45	30	25–30
60	55–70	35	25	20
50	40–50	25–30	20	15
40	30–35	20	15	10
30	20–25	10–15	10	7
20	10–15	5	3–5	3–5
10	5	3	1	1
0	1	1	0	0

ABDOMINAL CURL (WOMEN)

Score Age:	15–25	26–35	36–45	46–over
		SIT-UPS		
100	45	41	32	27
90	43	38–40	30	22–25
80	40	35	24–27	19
70	35	25–30	21	14–16
60	25–30	20	15–18	10–12
50	20	15	12	8
40	15	10	8–10	6
30	10	7	6	3–4
20	5	3–5	4	2
10	2–3	1	2	1
0	0–1	0	0–1	0

2. CHALK JUMP (MEN)

Score Age:	15–25	26–35	36–45	46–over
	INCHES	INCHES	INCHES	INCHES
100	26.5	25.2	24	19
90	26	25	23.5	18
80	25	24	23	16–17
70	23–24	22–23	21–22	14–15
60	21–22	19–21	18–20	13
50	18–20	16–18	14–16	9–11
40	14–17	14	10–12	6–7
30	10–12	8–12	6–8	4–5
20	6–8	6	3–4	3
10	3–5	2–4	2	2
0	0–2	1	1	1

CHALK JUMP (WOMEN)

Score Age:	15–25	26–35	36–45	45–over
	INCHES	INCHES	INCHES	INCHES
100	18	16	14	11.8
90	17.5	15.5	13.5	11
80	17	15	13	10
70	15–16	13–14	12	9
60	14	12	10–11	7–8
50	12–13	9–11	8–9	5–6
40	8–10	6–8	5–7	4
30	6	4–5	4	2–3
20	3–4	2–3	2–3	1–2
10	1–2	1	1	1
00	0	0	0	0

3. FORWARD BEND:

SCORE	MEN INCHES	WOMEN INCHES
100	22–23	24–27
75	20–21	21–23
50	14–19	16–20
25	12–13	13–15
0	0–11	0–12

4. PUSH-UPS (MEN)

Score Age:	17–19	30–39	40–49	50–over
100	27	17	15	13
75	20	15	12	8
50	15	10	8	4
25	7	5	3	2
0	0	0	0	0

PUSH-UPS (WOMEN)

Score Age:	17–29	30–39	40–49	50–over
100	50	30	15	10
75	20	15	10	7
50	13	10	8	5
25	8	6	4	3
0	0	0	0	0

5. TWELVE-MINUTE DISTANCE   **MEN**

Score Age:	Under 30	30–39	40–49	50–over
	DISTANCE IN MILES COVERED IN 12 MINUTES			
100	1.75	1.65+	1.55+	1.50+
75	1.50–1.75	1.40–1.64	1.30–1.54	1.25–1.49
50	1.25–1.49	1.15–1.39	1.05–1.29	1.0 –1.24
25	1.0 –1.24	.95–1.14	.85–1.04	.80– .99
0	under 1.0	under .95	under .85	under .80

WOMEN

Score Age:	Under 30	30–39	40–49	50–over
	DISTANCE IN MILES COVERED IN 12 MINUTES			
100	1.65+	1.55+	1.45+	1.35+
75	1.35–1.64	1.25–1.54	1.15–1.44	1.05–1.34
50	1.15–1 34	1.05–1.24	.95–1.14	.85–1.04
25	.95–1.14	.85–1.04	.75– .94	.65– .84
0	under .95	under .85	under .75	under .65

SCORING AND WHAT YOUR SCORE MEANS

To calculate your composite score, or PQ, add the point scores from each test, and then divide by 2.5. A completely average person would get 50 on each test, for a total of 250, which when divided by 2.5 would give a PQ of 100. Thus a score of 100 is the norm for any given age group, just as an IQ of 100 is normal, at every age. A person who scored 75 on each test, totaling 375 for the five, would have a PQ of 150.

Anyone who is in fairly good physical condition can expect to score above 100, since there are many people who are totally out of shape; their fitness level—or unfitness—brings the general scoring level down. A score of 150 means you are in good shape. A score of 50 or less indicates that you should do something soon about getting some supervised exercise and conditioning.

It's likely that you will score higher on repeating the test because you will be more familiar with the movements required. Also, people who have learned their PQ generally want to improve it. Many do so through such simple measures as going out of their way to stretch and bend, reducing their weight, or walking, bicycling, and running more.

☛THE WEST POINT PHYSICAL APTITUDE EXAMINATION

Here's the physical aptitude test that is given to prospective male and female cadets at West Point. See how your physical aptitude compares with a recent class of plebes at the United States Military Academy.

Test 1. *Pull-ups* (men). From the arm hang position on a horizontal bar, palms away from the face, elevate the body until the chin is above the bar.

Test 2. *Flexed-arm hang* (women). With arms fully flexed, grasp the bar with the palms of the hands away from the face, the thumbs under the bar, and chin over the bar. Hold this position for time.

Test 3. *Standing long jump.* Jump for distance.

Test 4. *Basketball throw.* Throw a basketball overhand from a kneeling position for distance.

Test 5. *Shuttle run.* Run back and forth between two lines, 25 yards apart, to cover a distance of 300 yards.

SCORING AND WHAT YOUR SCORE MEANS

The final score of the Physical Aptitude Examination is an accumulated total for all items in a given examination series. A low or high score on any one test item does not determine success or failure on the entire examination.

Reprinted from the 1979 West Point admissions catalogue.

WEST POINT PHYSICAL APTITUDE EXAMINATION
Candidate Population for a Recent Class

	Pullups (MEN) / Flexed Arm Hang (WOMEN)	Standing Long Jump (MEN)(WOMEN)	Basketball Throw (MEN)(WOMEN)	300 Yard Shuttle (MEN)(WOMEN)	PERCENTILE
	19—59 sec	8'8"—7'11"	90'—62'	55 sec—60 sec	100%
	15—51 sec				
TOP QUINTILE					
	13—45 sec		80'—54'	56 sec—63 sec	
	12—40 sec	8'0"—6'11"	75'—50'		80%
	11—36 sec		70'—47'	57 sec—	
	9—34 sec				
		7'8"—6'8"	67'—46'		
		7'6"—6'7"		58 sec—66 sec	
	—30 sec				60%
MIDDLE QUINTILE	8—		65'—44'		
	7—28 sec		61'—42'	59 sec—67 sec	
		7'4"—6'4"			40%
		7'2"—6'2"			
	6—26 sec			61 sec—68 sec	
	5—22 sec			62 sec—69 sec	
			60'—39'		
	4—18 sec	7'0"—6'0"			
			55'—36'		
				64 sec—72 sec	20%
	3—16 sec	6'8"—5'9"			
			50'—33'	65 sec—75 sec	
BOTTOM QUINTILE				68 sec—78 sec	
		6'4"—5'5"	40'—25'		
	1—11 sec	5'8"—4'10"			

☞ HOW'S YOUR VISION?

The eye is a delicate and vital organ. Doctors recommend eye examinations on a yearly basis after age five. This is important for early detection of eye disease and can prevent blindness in fifty percent of all cases.

As you get older, the eye muscles, like others in our body, weaken and change. This can cause both nearsightedness and farsightedness. While it is recommended that you regularly see a professional eye doctor, you can find out your present visual acuity by using this simple eye test.

Instructions

1. Place this chart twenty feet away at eye level.

2. Cover your left eye with a card or your hand and begin reading across the chart (from left to right) with your right eye. Read down as far as possible without straining. Note the number beside the last line you were able to read. This number represents your visual acuity.

3. The 20/20 line indicates the average healthy eye. If you can go beyond this line to the 20/15 or 20/10 line your visual acuity is exceptional—better than average.

4. Now reverse this procedure and test your left eye.

5. If you wear glasses or contact lenses you might try reading the chart with and without them. This way you can determine the effectiveness of your corrective lenses.

WHAT YOUR SCORE MEANS

While standards vary, a visual acuity rating of 20/40 or better is required to drive in most states. If you require glasses, your vision must be corrected to this level or better when wearing them.

You are categorized as legally blind with a visual rating of 20/200 or less.

$\dfrac{20}{200}$

$\dfrac{20}{100}$

Z	E	D	C
	L	F	Z
O		C	P
	D		E
T	X	E	D
		P	F
$\frac{20}{70}$	$\frac{20}{50}$	$\frac{20}{40}$	$\frac{20}{30}$

T A D O Z E C P
20/25

D E F A P O T C
20/20

L N F O D P C T
20/15

D A Z T C E O P
20/13

D E F A P O T C Z
20/10

☞ WHAT'S YOUR NUTRITION IQ?

How much do you know about obtaining good nutrition for yourself or your family? If your knowledge is similar to that of a majority of American food shoppers, you probably share some widespread misconceptions about nutrition.

If you would like to compare your own nutritional knowledge with that of the Food and Drug Administration's respondents, answer the twelve questions below. Each deals with a common misconception. Ten of the questions are adapted directly from the FDA surveys; two others involve similar misconceptions about weight reduction.

1. You'll get proper nourishment if you just eat a variety of foods.
   True   False

2. People who don't eat meat, poultry, or fish can still stay healthy.
   True   False

3. The proper food eaten between meals can be just as healthy for you as food eaten at regular meals.
   True   False

4. Fresh vegetables cooked at home are always more nutritious than canned or frozen vegetables.
   True   False

5. A high-protein, low-carbohydrate diet is ideal for losing weight.
   True   False

6. When dieting, avoid starchy foods, such as bread and potatoes.
   True   False

7. If you weigh what you should, you're getting proper nourishment.
   True   False

8. Taking extra vitamins beyond the RDA's won't give you more pep and energy.
   True   False

9. Supplements of natural vitamins are better than supplements of synthetic vitamins.
   True   False

10. Older people need the same amount of vitamins as younger people.
    True   False

11. Food grown in poor, worn-out soil is lower in vitamins than food grown in rich soil.
    True   False

12. Food produced with chemical fertilizers is just as nutritious as food grown with natural, organic fertilizers.
    True   False

ANSWERS

1. False. Variety may be the spice of life, but it's not a guarantee of good nutrition. "Eating a variety of foods is not the same as selecting appropriate foods for a nutritionally balanced diet," says the FDA. A useful guide to selection is to include some choices daily from each of the four main food groups: the milk group (milk, cheese, yogurt, and other dairy foods); the meat group (meat, poultry, fish, eggs, and meat alternates such as dried beans, lentils, and nuts); the bread group (bread, cereal, noodles, and other grain products); and the vegetable group (vegetables and fruit).

2. True. People don't need meat, poultry, or fish to stay healthy. So long as they eat enough dairy foods (milk group) and eggs (meat group), they can readily obtain the essential high-quality protein that meat provides. Meat alternates, such as peanut butter, dried beans, and lentil soup, can also fill part of a person's protein needs. However, strict vegetarians who eat no eggs or dairy foods may have difficulty achieving a diet that's adequate in proteins, and some may require supplements of vitamin B_{12} tablets.

3. True. Nutritional value depends on what types of food you eat, not when you eat them. Snacking on a toasted-cheese sandwich, a hard-boiled egg, or an orange can contribute to a well-balanced diet. On the other hand, excessive consumption of relatively high-calorie, low-nutrient snacks, such as candy, potato chips, and soft drinks, may be detrimental to health if they take the place of nutritious foods eaten at regular meal times.

4. False. "The fact is," says the FDA, "that food can lose nutrients in processing, cooking, and storage whether in the home or in the factory." Overcooking destroys many nutrients. Vegetables cooked in an excess of water that's later discarded can lose a significant amount of water-soluble vitamins, such as vitamin C and some of the B vitamins. Storing fresh vegetables too long, at improper temperatures, or in open containers can also reduce nutrients, and the same applies to canned or frozen vegetables. Thus, the difference lies more in how vegetables are handled or prepared than whether they are bought fresh or packaged.

5. False. Despite the promotion of numerous fad diets based on high-protein, low-carbohydrate intake, there's nothing magical about protein. The simple truth is that you either have to eat fewer calories or use up more in order to lose weight.

   There are many promotional claims for high-protein, low-carbohydrate diets partly because they seem to work—at least initially. One reason for this is that such a diet can cause minor degrees of nausea and resultant loss of appetite, leading to lower caloric intake. Another reason is that high-protein diets tend to be high in fat (as much as seventy percent or more of the calories on such regimens may come from fat). Such diets seem to keep our appetites satisfied for longer periods. Conversely, a meal low in fat may rouse hunger pangs sooner. The common joke about Chinese food has a basis in fact: some Chinese dishes contain mainly vegetables of high moisture content and lean meat with little fat, which may cause you to feel hungry an hour after eating a meal.

6. False. While protein foods are high in some vitamins, carbohydrate foods are also important sources of many nutrients. Cut out starchy vegetables, such as peas and potatoes, or starchy grain products, such as bread and cereals, and you cut out very good sources of several B vitamins, vitamin C, and other nutrients. Moreover, the common notion that bread and potatoes are particularly fattening is inaccurate. Ounce for ounce, bread and potatoes— baked, boiled, or mashed—have fewer calories than sirloin steak, roast beef, and some other staples of the high-protein diet. A reasonable amount of bread and potatoes is desirable in a weight-reducing diet.

7. False. Proper weight is one sign that a person may be getting adequate nutrition. But weight alone doesn't reveal whether a diet is deficient in vitamins and minerals. A person whose diet includes a significant amount of sweets, alcoholic beverages, or other high-calorie, low-nutrition foods may maintain an appropriate weight (or even be over-weight) but still be missing important nutrients.

8. True. Vitamins enter into a wide variety of chemical reactions in the body that are essential to good health and survival. If your diet is seriously deficient in vitamins, those body processes can be impaired. But taking more vitamins than the body needs doesn't make it function better than it should, any more than over-filling your gas tank makes your car run better.

9. False. A vitamin has the same properties and specific chemical structure whether synthesized in a laboratory or extracted from plant or animal parts. "There are no known nutrition advantages that justify a preference for 'natural' vitamins," says the FDA. "This is especially significant because of the higher prices the 'natural' vitamins often command."

10. True. Except for calories, the RDA's for people over fifty are the same as those for people of twenty-five—and that includes the RDA's for vitamins and minerals as well as that for protein. In short, nutrient needs don't change much throughout adult life, so long as a person remains in good health. Certain illnesses do raise the requirements for some vitamins, but that is true for the young as well as for the elderly.

11. False. Poor soil is largely the farmer's headache, not the eater's. The fact is that the vitamin content of plants is determined primarily by their heredity, just as the color of our eyes is. If the nutrients a plant needs are missing from the soil, it simply won't grow. The vitamins in our foods are manufactured by the plants themselves through genetically controlled processes. They don't come from the soil.

12. True. The preference for natural over chemical fertilizers may be perceived by health-food marketers, but it's not a distinction recognized by the plant world. Organic fertilizers cannot be used directly by plants, they must first be broken down by soil bacteria into inorganic compounds. The inorganic compounds actually absorbed by the plant are identical to those supplied directly by man-made, chemical fertilizers.

HOW TO SCORE

If you answered at least eight of the questions correctly, bon appetit. Your knowledge of nutrition is probably similar to those shoppers judged "well-informed" by the FDA. If you answered only a few questions correctly, additional nutrition information may help you to improve your diet or save money on food purchases.

☞ THE NATIONAL SMOKING TEST

This test is compiled from the CBS "National Smoking Test" and concerns tobacco and what you get out of it. The first section determines how you feel about smoking, the second asks what you know about smoking, and the third helps you draw your own personal smoking profile. Each section will be scored independently.

I. How You Feel about Smoking

The questions take the form of statements. Decide whether you generally agree or generally disagree with each.

1. It has not been proved that smoking causes disease because the evidence is based only on statistics.
Agree   Disagree

2. Breathing the polluted air in our major cities is more dangerous than smoking a pack of cigarettes a day.
Agree   Disagree

3. Being fifty pounds overweight is usually more harmful to health than smoking a pack of cigarettes a day.
Agree   Disagree

4. You run a greater risk crossing busy streets every day than smoking a pack of cigarettes every day.
Agree   Disagree

II. What You Know about Smoking

5. More than half of all Americans over twenty-one are cigarette smokers.
True   False

6. At least one half of all high school seniors smoke cigarettes.
True   False

7. Most children who smoke cigarettes have a parent who smokes.
True   False

8. Approximately what percentage of people who try to give up cigarette smoking actually succeed?
a. 20%   b. 40%   c. 60%

9. Statistics indicate that people who smoke cigarettes for a long time and then stop have lower death rates than people who continue to smoke.
True   False

10. The percentage of cigarette smokers among doctors is lower than among the general adult population.
True   False

11. Cigarette manufacturers have had to pay court-awarded damages to people

who claimed that cigarette smoking led to illness or death.
True   False

12. In 1967, the number of cigarettes sold was higher than in 1964 (the year before the Surgeon General of the United States issued a Report on Smoking and Health).
True   False

13. Of all the money spent for cigarettes, about how much goes for taxes?
a. 25%   b. 50%   c. 75%

14. The average man smoker smokes more cigarettes per day than the average woman smoker.
True   False

15. Heart and lung diseases occur as often among pipe and cigar smokers as among cigarette smokers.
True   False

16. The cigarette smoker gets the greatest concentration of tars and nicotines from the first few puffs.
True   False

III. Your Smoking Profile

1. I smoke cigarettes to keep myself from slowing down.
   a. seldom or never
   b. occasionally
   c. frequently or always

2. Handling a cigarette is part of the enjoyment of smoking it.
   a. seldom or never
   b. occasionally
   c. frequently or always

3. Smoking cigarettes is relaxing.
   a. seldom or never
   b. occasionally
   c. frequently or always

4. I light a cigarette when I feel angry about something.
   a. seldom or never

   b. occasionally
   c. frequently or always

5. When I run out of cigarettes, I find it almost unbearable until I can get them.
   a. seldom or never
   b. occasionally
   c. frequently or always

6. I smoke cigarettes automatically, without even being aware of it.
   a. seldom or never
   b. occasionally
   c. frequently or always

7. I smoke cigarettes to stimulate myself, to perk myself up.
   a. seldom or never
   b. occasionally
   c. frequently or always

8. Part of the enjoyment of smoking a cigarette comes from the steps I take to light it.
   a. seldom or never
   b. occasionally
   c. frequently or always

9. I find cigarettes pleasurable.
   a. seldom or never
   b. occasionally
   c. frequently or always

10. When I feel uncomfortable or upset about something, I light a cigarette.
   a. seldom or never
   b. occasionally
   c. frequently or always

11. When I am not smoking a cigarette I am very much aware of it.
   a. seldom or never
   b. occasionally
   c. frequently or always

12. I light a cigarette without realizing I still have one in the ashtray.
   a. seldom or never
   b. occasionally
   c. frequently or always

13. I smoke a cigarette to give me a lift.
   a. seldom or never

b. occasionally
c. frequently or always

14. When I smoke a cigarette, part of the enjoyment is watching the smoke as I exhale it.
    a. seldom or never
    b. occasionally
    c. frequently or always

15. I want a cigarette most when I am comfortable and relaxed.
    a. seldom or never
    b. occasionally
    c. frequently or always

16. When I feel blue or want to take my mind off cares and worries I smoke a cigarette.

a. seldom or never
b. occasionally
c. frequently or always

17. I get a real gnawing hunger for a cigarette when I haven't smoked for a while.
    a. seldom or never
    b. occasionally
    c. frequently or always

18. I have found a cigarette in my mouth and could not remember putting it there.
    a. seldom or never
    b. occasionally
    c. frequently or always

ANSWERS AND WHAT YOUR SCORE MEANS

I. How You Feel about Smoking
A national survey taken by CBS in 1968 showed that the single factor that determined how these four questions were answered was whether or not the person taking the test was a smoker.

1. Non-smokers tended to say that the case against smoking has been proved. They supported the statement from the United States Public Health Service which says, "the overwhelming conclusion from these studies is that certain diseases occur more often among smokers, and that smokers die at an earlier age than non-smokers," and that no one has found any reason for this except that these people smoke cigarettes.
   Smokers tended to believe statements which say the cause is not proved. The Tobacco Institute, an industry association, says, "There is no biological proof either experimental or clinical that smoking is the cause of diseases with which it has been statistically associated."

2. Non-smokers tended to believe the American Cancer Society, whose studies show that lung cancer occurs most frequently among cigarette smokers whether they live in air-polluted cities or not.
   Smokers tended to go along with the Tobacco Institute, which says that certain chemicals which may be harmful are more prevalent in some polluted air than in cigarette smoke.

3. Non-smokers echo the Public Health Service, which says that cigarette smoking is as dangerous or more dangerous than gross obesity. They put it this way: One study shows that healthy men between five-feet-seven and five-feet-ten average 165 pounds. If these men were fifty pounds overweight they would have a fifty percent higher death rate than normal. Compare this, says the Public Health Service, with smokers of a half pack to a full pack a day whose death rate is seventy-five percent greater than non-smokers.
   The Tobacco Institute believes that obesity, not cigarettes, is a major factor in heart disease. It says, "Several studies have not shown any association between smoking and heart disease."

4. Again, non-smokers went along with the Public Health Service, which says pedestrian accidents took about nine thousand lives last year, according to the National Safety Council. The Public Health Service says, there are 250,000 "excess deaths"—people who die before

their time—among cigarette smokers in this country every year. At least half of these, Public Health says, would not have died early had they not been cigarette smokers.

The Tobacco Institute says, "there just isn't any documentation available," and they add, "Until we know of any way in which cigarette smoking is in fact harmful to health there is no way for us to say whether this statement is anything more than just speculation."

II. What You Know about Smoking

Each correct answer is worth 5 points.

5. False. Fewer than half the adults in this country are cigarette smokers. Forty-two percent is the current figure, and it has held about the same for the last twelve years. But smoking patterns for men and for women are moving in opposite directions. Ten years ago, six out of ten men were cigarette smokers. Now it's down to five out of ten. Ten years ago about twenty-five percent of the adult women were cigarette smokers. Now it's about thirty-three percent.

About one million people take up cigarette smoking every year. Surveys show they are mostly from the younger population. Regular smoking of some cigarettes almost every day is on the increase even in the elementary grades.

6. False. About one-third of all high school seniors are cigarette smokers.

Among sophomores, age fifteen, thirty percent are smokers. Among high-school freshmen, fourteen years old, twenty-four percent are regular cigarette smokers. And a recent survey suggests that girls are joining the smoking ranks at an increasing rate and at an earlier age than girls did several years ago.

7. True. Only about one in five junior and senior high-school smokers comes from a home where neither parent smokes cigarettes. Four out of five young people who smoke have at least one parent who smokes.

8. a. The figure twenty percent includes all people, including those who decide quite casually to try and quit smoking.

9. True. Statistics show that smokers who quit do have lower death rates than those who continue.

10. True. Doctors are smoking less than the general adult population; far less than all adult men.

11. False. There is no report that any cigarette manufacturer has been ordered to pay damages. In one case the jury did find that the victim's death was related to smoking, but the jury decided, in effect, that damages should not be granted because the manufacturer had not breached his implied warranty to the victim.

12. True. Cigarette sales were higher in 1967 than they were in 1963, the year before the Report on Smoking and Health was issued.

13. b. About fifty percent of the total amount paid for cigarettes goes for taxes. The total tax earned from cigarettes through all levels of government is over three billion, six hundred million dollars a year.

14. True. More than half of all men smokers smoke a pack or more a day. Among women smokers less than half smoke a pack or more, but figures for recent years suggest that among women the trend is upward. New York's working women are a particularly heavy smoking group.

15. False. People who smoke pipes and cigars suffer from heart and lung diseases at far lower rates than cigarette smokers, almost at the same low rate as non-smokers.

16. False. The smoke from the first few puffs works its way through the cigarette, and the tobacco acts as a kind of filter. The tars and nicotine pile up farther back in the cigarette and the smoker gets the strongest dose of them in the last few puffs if he smokes all the way down. That's why many experts suggest you should not smoke your cigarettes to the end.

Total your score.

Above **60**:	Excellent
50–60:	Good
40–45:	Fair
Less than **35**:	Poor

(Editor's Note: Only 7 percent of the CBS national sample was in the excellent category; 26 percent was in the good category; 37 percent rated fair, and 30 percent rated poor.)

III. Your Smoking Profile

The National Clearinghouse for Smoking and Health recognizes six basic reasons why people smoke. The results of questions in this section will help you understand why you smoke. Certain groups of questions indicate how much you count on cigarettes for one particular reason.

To score this section, assign 1 point for each *a* answer, 2 points for each *b*, and 3 points for each *c*. Each group of questions has its own total score and meaning.

Questions 1, 7, and 13: This group shows how much you use cigarettes to stimulate yourself. If your total score is 8 or 9, this aspect of smoking is important to you.

A typical example of the person who smokes for stimulation is the smoker who doesn't begin to live in the morning until he has had at least one cigarette at breakfast. Anyone in this stimulation group who wants to give up smoking would have to find an alternative way of getting such stimulation if it is so necessary. Since other stimulating activities such as eating and drinking can create their own problems when carried to excess, one has to choose carefully.

Questions 2, 8, and 14: These ask about the enjoyment of handling the cigarette. If you scored 8 or 9, this aspect of smoking is important to you. About one smoker in ten is in this group.

Whatever other satisfactions this smoker may get from a cigarette, a high score measures the gratification of having something to hold, something to manipulate, or something to watch. For smokers who get this kind of pleasure from cigarettes, rolling a pencil between the fingers often works just as well as a cigarette. Doodling is another form of the same kind of behavior.

Questions 3, 9 and 15: These ask whether smoking cigarettes is relaxing for you. If you scored 8 or 9 this is true. About two-thirds of all smokers score high in this category.

The test of the true relaxation smoker is that he enjoys smoking most when he is relaxed and comfortable, thus increasing his enjoyment. Most people who are relaxation smokers find they can get along quite easily without cigarettes.

Questions 4, 10, and 16: Here your use of cigarettes for support as a kind of crutch in moments of pressure or strain is tested. If your score is 8 or 9, cigarettes serve this role. About one-third of all smokers use cigarettes as a support crutch.

This type of smoker may find it easy enough to quit smoking during a calm period, but it may be hard to stay off cigarettes completely, because the next personal crisis may result in lighting up again.

Questions 5, 11, and 17: These measure what is called the psychological addiction to cigarettes. If your total is 8 or 9, psychological addiction is evident. About one out of every three smokers fits in this category.

For the person who is psychologically addicted to cigarettes the craving for the next cigarette begins to build up the moment he puts out the last one. The indications for this kind of smoker are that he must quit completely, all at once. It's called "going cold turkey." Tapering off is not likely to work for this person, because each cigarette starts the cycle of craving for the next cigarette.

Questions 6, 12, and 18: These measure the extent to which smoking is a habit with you. If you total 8 or 9, much of your smoking is just habit. About one out of ten smokers is a habit smoker.

Such smokers no longer get much satisfaction from their cigarettes. They just light them frequently without even realizing they are doing so. Habit smokers, when motivated, usually find it rather easy to quit by cutting down gradually; they do not have to cut out cigarettes all at once.

The key to success in giving up smoking is in making oneself aware of each cigarette by asking, "Do I really want this cigarette?" Smokers will be surprised to find that the answer is frequently, "No."

Look back over your scores. If you are a light smoker, or have not been smoking for very many years, you may not have scored higher than 5 or 6 on any of these factors. But even scores at this level, and especially a score of 7, may indicate the direction in which your smoking is going. You may use cigarettes for a number of purposes. For most smokers, one or two of these factors will describe a large part of your smoking.

Recognizing what you get out of smoking can be a big help in guiding you in how best to give up smoking, if that is what you really want to do. Knowing how you use cigarettes can help direct you to the most appropriate substitute for them.

☞DR. JOYCE BROTHERS ASKS: DO YOU KNOW HOW MARIJUANA AFFECTS YOU?

According to a survey published in *Public Health Reports,* the Public Health Service's magazine, the use of marijuana is on the rise. How much do you know about this drug?

1. Marijuana improves sex and tends to make males more virile.
   True   False

2. Smoking a joint before a test may help a person to perform somewhat better because it relaxes him or her.
   True   False

3. Because marijuana is non-addictive, there's no way to become dependent upon this drug.
   True   False

4. Whether or not a person smokes marijuana and how much he smokes often depends upon how he feels about himself.
   True   False

5. Teen-agers who have a close relationship with their parents are less apt to use marijuana.
   True   False

6. The psychological implications of the young marijuana abuser may be more dangerous than the physiological effects.
   True   False

7. Most pot users look down on alcohol.
   True   False

8. A person who smokes grass is no more apt to hallucinate than someone who gets drunk on alcohol.
   True   False

ANSWERS

1. False. Many males think it improves their sex but their female companions don't agree. Several different research teams have found that marijuana may cause temporary sterility—and possibly even impotence in males. In one test, the level of testosterone, the male sex hormone, was an average of forty-four percent lower among marijuana users than in the control group of non-users.
2. False. It does relax you, but unfortunately, it also impairs the memory and this obviously won't help in any test. Marijuana affects both the short-term and long-term memories, according to Dr. Hardin Jones, a University of California professor. Alcohol also affects the memory, but the long-range impairment isn't as serious as for an average marijuana smoker.
3. False. Marijuana is physiologically non-addictive, although one's tolerance does build up. Some people become psychologically addicted or dependent on the drug. Of course, it's possible to become psychologically addicted to coffee, sugar, peanuts, or eggs, but the chances of becoming dependent are greater with mood-altering drugs. Most people don't get "highs" from eggs or peanuts.
4. True. According to psychotherapist Dr. David Izenzon, who has started a program called Potsmokers Anonymous, the one reason that most people smoke comes down to a feeling of inadequacy. Potsmoking, he says, like alcohol, overeating, and tobacco smoking, provides a way of medicating the anxiety of not feeling good enough, or of dulling some kind of pain.
5. False. Youngsters who have a close relationship with their parents are, however, less apt to abuse marijuana or any other drug. Drug use is often an attempt at adaptation by a young person, prompted by inner emotional, social, and family pressures. The teen-ager who has a warm, friendly relationship with his family is more able to talk out his problems and his feelings of inadequacy.
6. True. Many experts feel the use of marijuana, alcohol and any drug is especially dangerous for youngsters because such drugs hinder and endanger the maturation process. Young people may use drugs as a way of escape, to avoid personal conflict. The emotional turmoil associated with adolescence makes adolescents particularly vulnerable to drug abuse.
7. False. Marijuana is commonly used with alcohol, rather than as an alternative to it.
8. False. Hallucinations from alcohol usually occur only with far advanced disease, whereas marijuana's effect on the brain can cause hallucinogenic effects of distorted time, space, and sound at any time. It may even occur when the drug is used in small doses.

☞ HOW MUCH DO YOU KNOW ABOUT YOUR PET'S HEALTH?

Domestic dogs and cats can't shop, cook or know when to visit the vet. So your pet's health and happiness depend on how informed and responsible you are. To find out how much you know about your animal's health, answer the ten questions below.

1. Raw eggs are a healthful addition to a dog's diet.
True   False

2. Dogs and cats get virus colds from people.
True   False

3. Just before you take your pet on a trip—either by car, train or plane—you should give your animal something to eat and drink.
True   False

4. Fish, as an integral part of the diet, is not healthy for cats.
True   False

5. Canine heartworm can be transmitted only through mosquitoes.
True   False

6. If a dog or cat is fed a dry food diet, meat and other proteins should be added.
True   False

7. Foaming at the mouth usually means a dog or cat has rabies.
True   False

8. Dogs and cats eat grass or plants when they are not receiving enough vegetables in their diet.
True   False

9. Dogs that live indoors should wear coats when they go out in cold weather.
True   False

10. Cats need more protein than dogs.
True   False

Appeared as "Pet Journal Quiz" by Karen Larson in January 1977 *Ladies' Home Journal.* © 1977 LHJ Publishing, Inc. Reprinted with permission of *Ladies' Home Journal.*

ANSWERS

1. False. Raw egg whites actually prevent an essential nutrient called biotin from being absorbed into the animal's system. However, a dog or cat can eat moderate amounts of cooked eggs and raw egg yolks without harmful effects.
2. False. Dogs and cats have their very own kinds of colds and virus diseases, which they cannot give to, or get from, human beings. Nevertheless, your animal may come down with symptoms resembling those of the human cold, including a runny nose, red and running eyes, sore throat and fever.
3. False. Don't feed your pet for at least six hours before a trip. And don't give it water within two hours of traveling, unless the weather is very hot. (A healthy dog or cat can go for twenty-four hours without water—unless the environmental temperature is high—and longer without food.) Such precautions prevent the animal from relieving itself during the trip and lessen the chance of motion sickness.
4. True. Contrary to popular belief, fish is not a natural food for cats. A diet consisting mostly of raw fish can produce a thiamin deficiency, which can eventually lead to convulsions and paralysis. Too much canned fish—unless fortified with vitamin E—can cause a vitamin E deficiency disease called pansteatitis which, if untreated, can be fatal.
5. True. Mature heartworms reside in the animal's heart and produce larvae that circulate in the blood. When a mosquito bites a dog with heartworm, the mosquito ingests the larvae. When the insect bites another dog, it releases infectious larvae and thus transmits the disease. If untreated, heartworm can cause fatal damage. If you live in a mosquito-infected area, have a vet check your dog for heartworm every six months. Note: Heartworm is rarely found in cats and never in people.
6. False. Commercially prepared dry food is a balanced diet for a dog or cat; extras are not necessary. But remember: Dogs and cats have different nutritional needs. A food designed for dogs is not adequate for cats, and vice versa.
7. False. Hundreds of ailments and diseases besides rabies, including simple nausea, can cause frothing and foaming at the mouth.
8. False. A dog or cat usually does not eat grass because something is missing from its diet. Pets eat greenery out of boredom, because they like the taste, or to induce vomiting when they have overeaten or consumed something indigestible.
9. True. Dogs that are accustomed to living in a warm environment have trouble adjusting to sudden dips in temperature. A coat that covers your pet's chest and stomach will prevent chills. However, large, husky dogs that spend as much time outside as in will adjust to the cold; they do not need protective clothing.
10. True. Although the minimum nutritional requirements for cats have not yet been firmly established, the protein requirement from eggs, meat, fish, soybeans, etc., is estimated to be from two to four times more than that needed by dogs at equivalent growth stages.

WHAT YOUR SCORE MEANS

10: Expert
7–9: Very knowledgeable
4–6: Enlightened
1–3: Average
0: You have a lot to learn

☞ COLD WEATHER FIRST-AID SKILLS

You can save a life in a cold-weather emergency by brushing up on your first-aid skills. Test your winter crisis response by marking the action you would take if one of the following medical emergencies were to befall you or a loved one. Then check to see if your answer is the best one, and why.

1. It's been snowing outside and your elderly mother has been napping in a drafty room. Upon awakening, she complains of dizziness and unusual fatigue. You would
   a. advise her to draw a hot bath and soak in it
   b. cover her with blankets, give her a warm, non-alcoholic drink and promptly call the doctor
   c. give her an aspirin and a warm brandy

2. Your husband burns his finger while stacking logs in the fireplace. Would you advise him to
   a. spread a protective layer of butter on the burn
   b. submerge the burned finger in cold water
   c. wait until a blister forms, then pop it

3. Your young son has been playing in the snow and comes inside bearing a numb, whitened thumb. You would promptly
   a. submerge the thumb in warm water
   b. apply ice to the thumb
   c. rub the thumb vigorously

4. You're busily chopping vegetables for a beef stew when you cut your finger with a paring knife. You would do the following to the wound
   a. clean it, stop the bleeding, and allow it to "air heal"
   b. apply an ice pack
   c. clean it, medicate it, and cover it with an adhesive bandage

5. Your husband shovels snow from the driveway, then complains of pain in his lower back. You would recommend
   a. jogging five miles to exercise the sore muscles
   b. taking an aspirin and ignoring the pain
   c. applying wet heat to the sore muscles and resting

Appeared as "Cold Weather" in *The Star*, February 6, 1979. Copyright © News Group Publications, Inc., 1979.

ANSWERS

1. b. Every winter, thousands of elderly Americans suffer hypothermia—a dangerous drop in body temperature caused by overexposure to cold. Good diagnosing if you recognized the symptoms of dizziness and lethargy. Doctors warn against using methods *a* and *c:* trying to warm the body too rapidly can cause the core temperature to drop even more drastically, and alcoholic beverages can depress the system.

2. b. While most people believe butter is the best burn remedy, doctors have refuted this old wives' tale. The best method of soothing minor burns is application of cold water. It's never wise to try *c*—breaking a blister.

3. a. First-aid experts recommend promptly rewarming the frozen area by immersing it in warm (not hot) water. Swelling may rapidly develop after thawing, so discontinue warming the area as soon as the affected part becomes flushed. Responses *b* and *c*—rubbing and refreezing— are both damaging.

4. c. The majority of doctors believe wounds heal best when covered. Applying ice would be senseless, and in spite of those old wives' tales, air healing is not always best for minor cuts.

5. c. When back strain plagues your husband, a little pampering is usually in order. This is definitely not the time to jog or rely on aspirin alone. Apply hot, damp, compresses to the aching muscles, or use a heating pad if wet heat isn't convenient. Consult your doctor if the problem persists.

☞ WHAT MINERALS AND VITAMINS DOES YOUR BODY NEED?

This Muscle Response Test appears to be related to acupuncture points and the lines of energy used for centuries in Chinese medicine to direct the body's own healing powers. The test is an indicator, a simple workable gauge, that will give a reading on your body's inner functioning.

The testing procedure itself is quick and simple: in a carefully controlled test situation, an arm muscle is used to indicate which vitamins and minerals—and how much of each—you need for your well-being. MRT uses the comparative strength of the test muscle to answer these questions. If the test muscle is strong, it means that you do *not* need additional quantities of a particular vitamin or mineral. If the muscle is weak, it means you *do*.

To take the MRT all you need is a brief practice session and a friend or family member to perform the actual testing.

The Testing Procedure
- Begin by relaxing for five to ten minutes. Simply sit quietly and give yourself a chance to unwind. Both the person administering the test and the one taking it should remove all metal objects (watches, jewelry, coins) from themselves.
- Neutralize the subject. Begin with a fifteen-second massage of the points two inches to the right and left of the notch directly below the collarbone (see illustration). Using the tips of the three middle fingers of each hand and a firm circular motion, the tester presses firmly enough to move the skin and some of the underlying tissue, but not so hard as to cause the subject any discomfort.
  The second massage points are at the tip of the mastoid bone behind each ear. Repeat the circular motion again for fifteen to twenty seconds there. Finish by

Adapted by permission of Richard Marek Publishers, Inc., from *The Muscle Response Test*, copyright © 1979 by Dr. Walter Fischman and Dr. Mark Grinims.

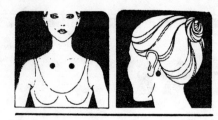

pressing and releasing the tip of the mastoids six times, applying three to five pounds of pressure. If you're not sure how much pressure this represents, test your touch on a bathroom scale first.

- Practice test for baseline strength. The person being tested should stand or sit in as relaxed a posture as possible, but he shouldn't cross his legs.

  The subject leaves one arm (it doesn't matter which) hanging loosely by his side and raises the other arm, palm down, to an angle slightly wider than 90°; that is, the wrist should be a bit higher than the shoulder. The tester places the pads of his fingers on the top of his subject's shoulder, thus stabilizing the subject's body.

  In the course of the test, the tester will press downward on the subject's wrist while the subject *resists* that force. In no way should this be a contest of wills. The idea is to determine the baseline strength of the subject, not who is the stronger of the two.

  The correct degree of pressure and resistance will be easier to maintain if the tester and subject follow these guidelines

  Subject: Keep your elbow straight. Do not clench your fist. Keep your fingers flat, with the palm facing the floor.

  Tester: Do not hang on the subject's arm; simply press down on his wrist for a second or two. The force you apply should be smooth and progressive. In other words, within that two-second period, gradually increase the amount of pressure until you can move the subject's arm downward.

  Note the moment when the arm moves. This tells you that you've applied too much force and overpowered the subject. Apply a little less pressure for the actual test. Keep the feeling of that adjusted force in your mind so you can relate to it again in the second half of the MRT procedure.

- The subject will now touch various points on his body, each corresponding to a particular vitamin or mineral, while the tester checks whether the arm muscle weakens or remains strong. The subject touches each body point with the three middle fingers of his hand. The proper position is the little finger folded to the palm, the thumb pressed down over it, the other three fingers extended. The contact is made with the fingertips, and the touch can be light, as no real pressure is necessary. If, while touching the body points, the subject is able to resist the pressure, then he doesn't need supplements of the particular vitamin or mineral being tested. If the arm gives way, however, the subject *does* have need of that particular nutritional factor.

- The tester should keep a record of those vitamins and minerals that produce a weak response. The items on that list will then be tested to determine how much of the nutrient the subject needs.

Remember that *a strong muscle feels as though it had locked into place.* It doesn't feel a bit spongy. You cannot move the arm down without applying undue force; in fact, the arm seems to spring up a bit. *A weak muscle gives way.* And it will do so quite suddenly. It isn't a matter of wearing down your subject's physical strength. Instead, when you apply force to his arm, he may resist for an instant, but then his strength will be broken. It will feel as if he had surrendered. You can move his arm downward quite easily now.

Take care not to tire the arm muscle. Five or six items at a time is enough, and you should take a five-minute break before you continue to test. Be sure to neutralize the subject again when you resume testing.

Vitamin Touch Points

Vitamin A (R.D.A.*—5,000 I.U.†): The right eyelid.

Vitamin C (R.D.A.—45 mg.): Just below the collarbone on the *left* side, 2½ inches from the center of the body.

Vitamin D (R.D.A.—400 I.U.): Midway across the stomach/thigh fold on the left side of the body.

Vitamin E (R.D.A.—15 I.U. for men; 12 I.U. for women): Just below the collarbone on the *right* side, 2½ inches from the center line of the body (the opposite of vitamin C touch point).

Note: You may be wondering why none of the B vitamins are included in this list. A contact point for the B complex as a whole—the tip of the tongue—has been isolated, but it seems to us more precise to subject *each* of the B vitamins to a dosage test (see below). This way you'll be able to tell which of the individual components of this vitamin group you need (and how much), rather than lumping them all together and possibly taking more of one than is necessary simply because another in the group is called for:

B_1 (thiamine): R.D.A.—0.5 mg. per 1,000 calories.

B_2 (riboflavin): R.D.A.—1.6 mg. for men, 1.2 mg. for women.

B_6 (pyridoxine): R.D.A.—2 mg. for each 100 grams of protein.

B_{12}: R.D.A.—3 mcg.

Folic Acid: R.D.A.—400 mcg.

Niacin: R.D.A.—8 mg. for men, slightly less for women.

Pantothenic acid: No R.D.A. established. Between 5 mg. and 50 mg. often recommended.

Mineral Touch Points

Calcium (R.D.A.—800–1,400 mg.): Locate the sterno muscle on the left side and slide your fingers down till you find the point at which muscle meets collarbone. The touch point is one-half inch above this.

Iron (R.D.A.—10 mg. for men; 18 mg. for women): Midway across the stomach/thigh fold on the right side of the body (see vitamin D; this is the same location but on the opposite side of the body).

Magnesium (R.D.A.—350 mg. for men, 300 mg. for women): The middle of the navel.

*R.D.A. - Recommended Daily Allowance.

†I.U. - International Units.

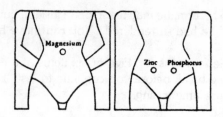

Phosphorus (R.D.A.—800 mg.): Picture a line running from the front of the left hipbone to the pubic bone. The touch point is midway between the two along the imaginary line.

Zinc (R.D.A.—15 mg.): Visualize a line running from the front of the right hip bone to the pubic bone. The touch point is midway along that imaginary line (see phosphorus; this is the same location but on the opposite side of the body).

• Testing to determine the dosage of each vitamin and mineral you need.

Once you have a list of the nutritional elements you need, it's an easy matter to find out just *how much* to take. Essentially, you use a variation on the basic MRT routine. Again, you'll need a companion to test you. In addition, you should have a bottle of tablets for each vitamin and mineral you need.

To begin, follow the preparatory steps already detailed, being sure to "neutralize" the subject. This time the subject makes contact with each substance while the tester does the arm pressure test and observes the response.

There are two ways to establish contact between the test tablets and the subject. The subject can hold them in his or her hand or place them in his or her mouth. While the subject does this, the tester tests the strength of the muscle of the other arm. If it remains strong, increase the quantity to two tablets. Keep increasing the dose until the muscle weakens. What is happening here? It is very simple: When the muscle weakens you have gone beyond the optimum dose of that material for the individual being tested.

Reduce the dosage by one or two tablets and you'll wind up with the maximum amount the subject can utilize effectively.

Run through each item on your list, keeping track of the dosages you establish. (Be sure to test the individual B vitamins in the same way to determine need and dosage of each member of the complex.)

Note: If the MRT-determined dosage is much greater than the R.D.A. given, consult your doctor about the safety of taking the larger amount.

A note of caution about mineral supplements: They do tend to have a cumulative effect. Your body will excrete amounts greater than you need, but it will do so quite slowly. If you take quantities of mineral supplements, they may build up faster than you can use or get rid of them. If the MRT test indicates a deficiency in a particular mineral, it's best to add it gradually, working up over the course of several weeks to the optimum dosage. Do retest frequently during this period. It may take as long as two or three months to reach optimum dosage. And be aware that testing for amounts is time consuming and can tire both subject and tester. You may wish to do the test over a period of several days. Once dosages have been established, it is also advisable that you retest periodically—every two months is recommended as a reasonable interval.

IQ: WHAT'S YOUR BRAIN POWER?

☞ CITIZENS' DISASTER TEST

What's your disaster IQ? Would you know what to do in case of civil emergencies? How you score on this quiz could be the difference between life and death for you and your loved ones, in an earthquake, hurricane, flood or worse.

Circle the correct answer in the multiple choice questions that follow. After completing the quiz, check your score and see how well you could perform in a crisis. Be sure to check all the answers you missed. This will help you avoid a "wrong answer" if faced by any of these disasters in a real life situation.

1. If you are in open country when a tornado strikes, the safetest thing to do is:
   a. get under a tree
   b. keep running until you find shelter
   c. lie flat in the nearest ditch or ravine
   d. head for water and immerse your body beneath it

2. If you are in your home when a tornado strikes and you do not have a basement, you should:
   a. go into a small closet or bathroom in the center of the house
   b. enter an upstairs bedroom away from the approaching tornado
   c. go outside and hide beneath the porch

   d. lie on the floor beneath an open window

3. You are in an area without manmade shelter. If an electrical storm comes, you should:
   a. try to outrun it to the nearest shelter
   b. crouch in the open far from isolated trees
   c. seek the shelter of a tall tree
   d. stand in the roadway away from trees

4. You and the family are hiking along a dry creekbed and notice a heavy storm off in the distance. You should be wary because:
   a. a storm miles away could fill the dry creek in a flash flood

b. severe winds could blow trees into your path

c. darkness could make it difficult to find your way

d. the banks of the creek could cave in

5. If you're caught in a flood at home, it is best to:

a. try to get out of the house

b. get in the car and try to drive to higher ground

c. stay indoors and keep above the water level

d. open windows to allow the current to flow through and reduce water pressure

6. When cleaning up after a flood, you should:

a. boil all water used by your family

b. throw out all food that comes in contact with flood waters

c. try to clear away mud and wreckage around your home

d. all of the above

7. You and your family are driving in a winter snow storm; you cannot go any further and become stranded. You should:

a. leave the car to get help

b. stay in the car, turn off the motor and close all of the windows to keep the heat in

c. stay in your car with the motor running intermittently with one window cracked open

d. stay in the car with the motor running and all windows closed

8. While in the car that is stranded in the snow storm, you should prevent frostbite and exposure by:

a. clapping hands and moving arms vigorously from time to time

b. huddling in a group

c. sitting perfectly still to prevent loss of body heat

d. rubbing different parts of your body from time to time

9. If you're indoors during an earthquake, you should:

a. stay there and get under a heavy table

b. go outside and get protection from a solid building

c. go outside and seek shelter beneath a bridge or overpass

d. any of the above

10. If you are driving your car when an earthquake strikes, you should:

a. keep driving to try and outrun it

b. pull off the road, stop, and remain inside

c. drive beneath an overpass to avoid falling debris

d. find the nearest garage and pull the car inside

11. During a family outing in the woods, you notice a forest fire sweeping across in the distance. You can avoid danger by running across its path and out of its way because you know that forest fires spread:

a. downhill and upwind

b. uphill and downwind

c. downhill and downwind

d. uphill and upwind

12. If a hurricane warning is issued in your area, you should remain inside. To prevent explosion within your home and injury from flying glass, windows should be:

a. boarded up and shut tight

b. left open at top and closed at bottom

c. boarded up, with storm windows left in the open position

d. boarded up, with all windows slightly ajar

ANSWERS

1. c	**4.** a	**7.** c	**10.** b
2. a	**5.** c	**8.** a	**11.** b
3. b	**6.** d	**9.** a	**12.** d

WHAT YOUR SCORE MEANS

11–12 Have no fear, travel far and near

9–10 Look to the sky

7–8 Enroll in a Civil Defense course

6 or less Be sure the Red Cross knows where you are at all times

☞ COULD YOU QUALIFY FOR MENSA?

Do you know your IQ? While valid IQ scores usually require a full battery of standardized testing, with this quiz you can see how you measure up against the super-intelligent.

Mensa, an international society of high IQ performers, has prepared this mini-test based on their test for admission. To qualify for membership in Mensa you must score higher than 98% of the general population taking a particular test. Their members represent almost every occupation: businessmen, clerks, doctors, editors, factory workers, farm laborers, housewives, policemen, prisoners, lawyers, teachers, soldiers, scientists and students.

Just how smart are you? Have some fun with this Mensa Mini-Test, then check your answers. If you answer at least six questions correctly you've done fairly well and may want to join Mensa. Good luck.

1.

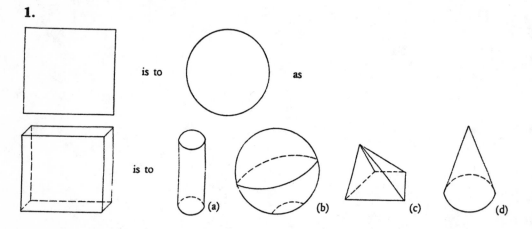

The Mensa Mini-Test is reprinted with permission from Mensa, 1701 West 3rd Street, Brooklyn, NY 11223.

2. The arrows represent a simple code. What word(s) could they spell when re-arranged?

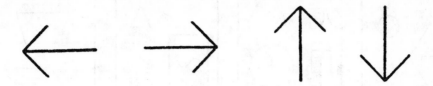

3. Given the statement, "You'd *better* solve the problem or *I'll* solve it for you!" pick out the relationship most likely to be represented.
   a. doctor to patient
   b. examiner to test taker
   c. father to son
   d. lawyer to client

4. Find a word meaning the same as the left hand word in one sense and the right hand word in another sense.
   hard _____ company

5. If M x E = 6; N x S = 20; E x S = 15; E x N = 12; S x A = 30
   then M x E x N x S x A = ?

6. Alex, Allan, Carol, Celia and Sharon took intelligence tests. Celia scored higher than Carol. Allan scored higher than Celia, and Carol outscored Alex. Sharon scored lower than Allan. Therefore
   a. Celia scored higher than Alex but lower than Carol
   b. both Alex and Allan outscored Celia
   c. Celia outscored Alex by more than she outscored Carol
   d. Sharon scored higher than Carol
   e. none of the above
   f. a–d are all true

7. Which one of these would usually not belong?
   design, equation, paragraph, poem

8. 3 is to 9 and 18, as 2 is to 8 and ?

9. All Mensans who reside in New Hope have become members by taking a supervised intelligence test. The barber in New Hope qualified for Mensa through a school achievement test score.
   a. the barber should be required to take a supervised test to qualify.
   b. the barber does not live in New Hope.
   c. the barber was unable to take the supervised test when it was given.
   d. the barber formerly lived in New Hope and then moved out.

10. Which bottom figure belongs with the top figures?

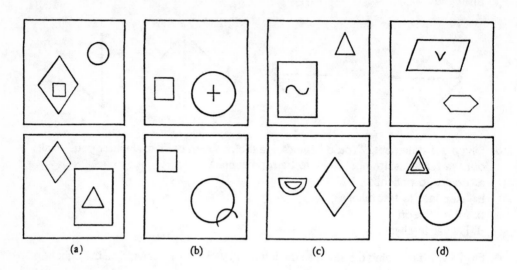

(a)   (b)   (c)   (d)

ANSWERS

1. b

2. News, Sewn, Wens

3. c

4. firm

5. 720

6. c

7. design

8. 24

9. b

10. a

WHAT YOUR SCORE MEANS

Do not get discouraged. These are real brain busters. Why even after looking at the answers you may ponder the questions to understand. Six or more correct and you are of above average intelligence. Why not contact Mensa and find out how you can qualify for admission into their society.

Write: Mensa, 1701 West 3rd Street, Brooklyn, NY 11223.

☞TEST YOUR LEGAL IQ

Do you know the law and your legal rights? Find out by reading these mini-cases. Check your answers carefully. These situations could happen to you.

1. Before Bob and Janet got married, they signed a so-called marriage contract, which carefully spelled out future privileges and responsibilities. They would take turns cooking meals and cleaning house. They would be entitled to take separate vacations. Janet would continue her career, and Bob would not take a job in another city without her approval. After two years of marriage, Bob is not keeping his part of the bargain. Janet doesn't want a divorce but feels Bob is not living up to their legal agreement. Has she grounds for a lawsuit?

   Yes   No

2. Ted and Alice signed a premarital agreement in which Alice keeps complete control of a sizeable inheritance from her grandfather's estate. Ted also promised to pay Alice's way through graduate school after he finished his own training to become an orthodontist. He is now in private practice, and Alice insists that he pay her way through law school. He wants her to use the money from her inheritance. Has she a legal case?

   Yes   No

3. Eighteen-year-old Sam runs a red light on Main Street. He is stopped by a policeman who thinks he detects a faint aroma of marijuana in the car. He asks Sam to get out so he can search it. When Sam asks to see a search warrant, the officer tells him none is needed. Is the officer right?

   Yes   No

4. Fourteen-year-old Susan is stopped by a store detective in a local department store as she carries a record from the music department on the second floor down to the first floor. She tearfully insists that she was only planning to buy a birthday card on the first floor to send along with the record. The store calls the police and has her arrested. Was the arrest legal?

   Yes   No

From *You and the Law* by Ellen Switzer and Wendy Susco. Reprinted by permission of the authors. Copyright © 1979, The Family Circle, Inc. First published in *Family Circle* magazine, May 15, 1979.

5. Agatha buys an expensive food-processing machine at a local discount store. When she uses the machine, it doesn't blend, chop, or mix. Since the warranty says the appliance is guaranteed for one year, she takes it back to the store to be fixed. She is told that she will have to send the machine to the factory in California for repairs (she lives in Vermont), which may take months. Is the store responsible for giving her a new appliance, or at least repairing the machine within a more reasonable length of time?
Yes   No

6. Elizabeth picked the best qualified doctor in her community for gallbladder surgery, which was completed successfully. Accidentally she found out that her doctor only stood by and supervised as a young resident actually wielded the scalpel. Can the surgeon make her pay his $1,000 fee for an operation he did not perform?
Yes   No

7. Anthony and Ellen own a laundromat. One night a defective dryer explodes and ruins the whole establishment. They retain an attorney who promises to file suit against the manufacturer. After more than a year has elapsed, Anthony and Ellen have not heard a word about the progress of their case. They call their lawyer (for the tenth time), and he confesses that he forgot to file the necessary papers. Now it's too late, he says, because in their state, the statute of limitations has run out. Can Anthony and Ellen still sue anybody?
Yes . No

8. Beverly, age fifty-three, has been working as a receptionist for a wholesale cosmetics firm for five years. One day she is called into the manager's office and told that times are bad and that the staff is being cut. She gets two weeks' severance pay. A few days later, she comes back to pick up a plant she forgot to take home and finds a very attractive woman, probably no older than twenty, sitting in her former desk. She suspects that she was fired because the management wanted a younger, better looking receptionist. Can she file a legal complaint?
Yes   No

9. Twenty-six-year old Sandy has been going steady for more than five years with Ben, who has told her he is single and promises to marry her as soon as "certain financial matters" have been straightened out. One day, she meets an old friend who has known Ben for years and who tells Sandy that he has a wife and three children in Oklahoma. Can she sue Ben?
Yes   No

10. Althea has signed a two-year lease on an apartment, which specifically prohibits subletting. When she is transferred to another city, Althea decides to "lend" her sister Dorothy the apartment. Althea then sends a rent check to the landlord every month, and Dorothy reimburses her. One day, the landlord discovers who is really living in the apartment and evicts Dorothy. Can he do this?
Yes   No

ANSWERS

1. No. Such contracts governing personal behavior are considered by the courts to be private agreements and therefore of no concern to the state. Besides, courts rarely interfere in

ongoing marriages. If Janet wishes to divorce Bob, then she may be able to use his breach of marriage contract as evidence.

2. Yes. A court's concern with financial matters dates back to times when women brought dowries into marriage and husbands-to-be settled sums of money on future brides. So-called prenuptial financial agreements are legal contracts and will usually be regarded in that light by the court.

3. Yes. The United States Supreme Court recently ruled that a police officer may search the car of a driver stopped for a traffic violation. The reason: A warrantless search of the immediate premises is legal if an offense has already been committed, and this includes traffic violations. Parents should tell children this simple legal fact.

4. No. Shoplifting charges can be brought only if the suspect has actually left the store. Susan's parents may have grounds to sue the store for falsely accusing and arresting their daughter.

5. No. Agatha's warranty stated explicitly that the manufacturer was responsible for repairing the machine during a twelve-month period, unless the store made special provisions. It's wise to read warranties before making a purchase and to ask about a store's policy for appliance breakdowns. If the store indicates that the repairs will be done locally, get this promise in writing.

6. Yes. Elizabeth had "ghost surgery," which occurs frequently, especially in teaching hospitals. Before her operation Elizabeth signed a consent form that probably said something like this: "Dr. Jones is authorized to perform a gallbladder operation, assisted by any physicians he may designate." The courts define the word "assisted" very broadly. As long as Dr. Jones was in the operating room, he has the right to charge his customary fee. If Elizabeth encounters any serious problems after her gallbladder surgery, and it turns out that the resident bungled the job, she may, of course, sue Dr. Jones for medical malpractice. To avoid a similar problem the next time she needs an operation, Elizabeth may cross out that line about "assistance by other physicians," or she may get a written promise that Dr. Jones will indeed perform the operation himself.

7. Yes. They can sue the lawyer for malpractice. Most people don't realize that all professionals are liable to malpractice suits if through failure to perform their duties in a responsible manner they damage their clients.

8. Yes. Federal law prohibits job discrimination on grounds of age, as well as on grounds of sex, race, religion, and place of national origin. If her employer felt a younger receptionist was needed, he could have transferred Beverly to another job at a comparable salary. She should file a complaint with her state's Equal Opportunity agency and/or with the nearest office of the United States Department of Labor.

9. No. Breach-of-promise suits went out with crinolines. Most states have eliminated them from their books, and even those that still have such laws refuse to enforce them. Remember one legal principle: Usually hurt feelings don't count. A plaintiff must prove real physical or financial damage or serious injury to his reputation before any award will be considered.

10. Yes. Althea is doing exactly what she had contractually agreed not to do: Subletting the apartment. That the tenant happens to be her sister has absolutely nothing to do with the case.

WHAT YOUR SCORE MEANS

Tally the number of right answers.

9–10: F. Lee Bailey, move over

7–8: Better brush-up for Law Boards

5–6: Don't sign anything

4 or less: Watch Perry Mason reruns

☞ WHAT'S YOUR DRIVING IQ?

Sure, you passed your driving test, and after all these years behind the wheel you must be an expert. But how long ago was that test? Why not test your present driving IQ and find out just how much you know about the rules of the road. The results of this little exercise may shock you.

Just choose the correct answer from those given, total your score and find out if the rest of the world is safe with you behind the wheel.

1. When you park on a hill facing upward, in which direction should your wheels be facing?
   a. keep wheels straight ahead
   b. turn wheels toward the curb
   c. turn wheels away from the curb
   d. keep wheels straight ahead with parking brake on

2. What is the main reason night driving speed should be reduced?
   a. danger from oncoming glare
   b. longer reaction time
   c. reduced visual warning signals
   d. reduced visibility

3. When should you dim your headlights?
   a. when following or meeting a vehicle within 500 feet
   b. when following or meeting a vehicle within 100 feet
   c. when passing another vehicle
   d. when following or meeting a vehicle within 250 feet

4. At a speed of 50 MPH what is the reaction distance you must allow for when applying the brakes?
   a. 25 feet   b. 35 feet   c. 55 feet   d. 75 feet

5. What is the *total* stopping distance required when applying the brakes on a dry road at 50 MPH?
   a. 200 feet   b. 243 feet   c. 297 feet   d. 325 feet

6. When you are being overtaken by another car what is the correct thing to do?
   a. do not increase speed
   b. wave him on if it looks clear
   c. signal him with your horn
   d. slow down and pull over to the left

7. What is the proper way to enter from the ramp of a high speed expressway?
   a. speed up and try to enter before the approaching cars reach you
   b. ask your passenger to check for approaching cars
   c. yield the right of way to cars on the expressway

d. slow down and enter the expressway very slowly

8. How could you best dry your brakes after traveling through water?
  a. brake gently and feed the gas at the same time
  b. get out of the car and wipe the brake linings
  c. drive fast and let them air-dry
  d. allow the car to sit at the side of the road until brakes dry

9. Diamond shaped yellow traffic signs stand for:
  a. No U Turn
  b. Do Not Pass
  c. Yield
  d. Road Condition Warning

10. The most common cause of traffic accidents is:
  a. poor roads
  b. bad weather
  c. bad drivers
  d. mechanical failure

11. If your temperature gauge shows your car overheating, where would you check if the radiator appears to be normal?
  a. oil pressure gauge
  b. heater
  c fuse
  d. power brakes

12. How should you position your hands on the steering wheel when turning?
  a. both hands at the bottom of wheel
  b. both hands at the top of wheel
  c. hand-over-hand motion with a light grip
  d. twisting motion of the arms without moving the hands

13. What are the chances of your survival in an accident when you are wearing your seat belts as opposed to not wearing them?
  a. 2 times better **b.** 3 times better **c.** 5 times better **d.** no better

14. How far away from a turn should you begin signaling?
  a. 150 feet **b.** 100 feet **c.** 75 feet **d.** 50 feet

15. What is the best way to warm up a car engine?
  a. keep car in park or neutral and gun the engine
  b. start driving immediately at moderate speed
  c. keep car in park or neutral and pump the gas pedal
  d. run it just fast enough to keep from stalling for five minutes

16. How can you best determine the general meaning of a traffic sign?
  a. color **b.** shape **c.** size **d.** height

17. On a four lane street, in which lane should you be to make a left turn?
  a. immediately to the right of the center line
  b. immediately to the left of the center line
  c. next to the parked cars or on the shoulder
  d. in the center lane

18. What is a grade separation?
  a. a road divider that separates the road from opposing traffic
  b. an intersection separating traffic on intersecting roads
  c. a banked curve
  d. a divider built on mountain roads

19. When is an icy road most dangerous?
  a. when the ice is frozen solid
  b. when the ice is melting
  c. when the temperature is near zero
  d. when you are the first to drive on it

20. At what point should you reduce your speed when driving a curve?
  a. on the sharpest part of the curve
  b. prior to entering the curve
  c. gradually, for the entire length of the curve
  d. half way through the curve

ANSWERS

Score one point for each correct answer.

1. c	**6.** a	**11.** a	**16.** b
2. d	**7.** c	**12.** c	**17.** a
3. a	**8.** a	**13.** b	**18.** b
4. c	**9.** d	**14.** b	**19.** a
5. d	**10.** c	**15.** d	**20.** b

WHAT YOUR SCORE MEANS

19–20: Drive around the world with pride.
17–18: Proceed with caution.
15–16: Let your friends drive when possible.
Less than 13: Learn to jog!

☞ BUSINESS IQ TEST

Have you always insisted you belong at the helm of a multi-national conglomerate? Now you may be able to prove it, says Largent Parks Jr., a Dallas executive-search consultant.

Parks claims a Business IQ test he began administering for laughs has proven itself surprisingly effective in sizing up executive ability.

The quiz is based on the theory that there are three types of business intelligence: concrete, the type possessed by salespeople, clerks and other workers; functional, found in successful middle-managers and supervisors, and abstract, usually associated with top executives.

The test is composed of thirteen pairs of words. The person being tested is to say what he or she thinks each pair has in common. It is important to give the first answer that comes to mind.

1. lemon–banana
   a. yellow, come from trees
   b. food
   c. fruit

2. coat–dress
   a. clothing
   b. made of cloth
   c. people wear them

3. ax–saw
   a. tools, cutting implements
   b. carpenters use them
   c. made of metal

4. dog–lion
   a. live outdoors
   b. have fur and tails
   c. animals, four-legged mammals

5. north–west
   a. compass points, direction
   b. on maps, charts
   c. tell where you're going

6. nose–ear
   a. sense organs, receptors of stimuli
   b. flesh, attached to the head
   c. parts of the body

7. air–water
   a. elements of the environment
   b. necessary for life
   c clear, invisible

8. table–chair
   a. furniture
   b. have four legs
   c. used for meals

9. egg–seed
   a. beginnings of life, points of origin
   b. they grow
   c. food

By Largent Parks, Jr. Reprinted by permission of Newspaper Enterprise Association, 200 Park Ave., New York NY 10017.

10. poem–statue
   a. artists create them
   b. found in books, museums, etc.
   c. art

11. wood–alcohol
   a. both words have two o's
   b. fuel, used in manufacturing
   c. organic substances

12. praise–punishment
   a. both words start with p
   b. motivators
   c. training tools, means of discipline

13. fly–tree
   a. found outdoors
   b. living organisms
   c. both have limbs

ANSWERS AND HOW TO SCORE

Give yourself the following points for each a, b, or c answer.

1. a–0, b–1, c–2
2. a–2, b–0, c–1
3. a–2, b–1, c–0
4. a–0, b–1, c–2
5. a–2, b–1, c–2

6. a–2, b–0, c–1
7. a–1, b–2, c–0
8. a–2, b–0, c–1
9. a–2, b–0, c–1
10. a–1, b–0, c–2

11. a–0, b–1, c–2
12. a–0, b–2, c–1
13. a–1, b–2, c–0

Award yourself points for age:

from 35–39 = 1 point
from 40–49 = 2 points
from 50–54 = 3 points
55 or older = 4 points

Total your score and convert it to the Business IQ as follows:

Score	IQ	Score	IQ
13	100	22	121
14	109	23	125
15	111	24	126
16	113	25	128
17	114	26	130
18	115	27	132
19	116	28	135
20	118	29	138
21	120	30	140

WHAT YOUR SCORE MEANS

Business IQ of 128 or above: You are an abstract thinker and would no doubt perform well in the executive suite.

116—127: You are a functional thinker and could probably succeed as a manager or supervisor.

115 or less: You are a concrete thinker and could probably become a successful salesperson, clerk, or office worker.

SO YOU THINK YOU KNOW EVERYTHING!

☞THE NATIONAL SCIENCE TEST

Here's the National Science Test developed by CBS News in 1967. The questions are about some of the things we see, do, and feel every day and major scientific developments that are changing our lives. Some of the questions involve situations encountered daily. Others deal with the world around us, outer space, and Mother Nature. Watch out, certain seemingly simple questions may have surprising answers!

1. They had some bananas on sale at the store today. A housewife bought quite a few, some green and some ripe enough to eat right away. She doesn't want to be forced to throw any of them out if they get too soft. Should she put the ripe bananas in the refrigerator?
Yes   No

2. Mashed potatoes are on tonight's menu, and the problem is to get the potatoes cooked in the shortest possible time. Should you cut them up or cook them whole? Will cutting up the potatoes make them cook faster?
Yes   No

3. Among the housewife's required reading is the frozen food wrapper: how long to thaw, how long to cook. One direction for many frozen vegetables is add a teaspoonful of salt to the water before boiling. Does the salt make the food cook faster?
Yes   No

4. By now, the kitchen has become uncomfortably warm and our cook looks for relief. She would like to cool down the kitchen. The coolest air obviously is inside the refrigerator. Will keeping the refrigerator door open cool the kitchen?
Yes   No

5. But our kitchen is still uncomfortably warm—it's cooler outside than inside. The window is the answer, but what's the best way to open it—from the top, bottom, or both top and bottom? Our housewife remembers that hot air rises. Will the room cool quickest by opening just the top window?
Yes   No

6. Two children weighing exactly the

same are placed side by side on playground swings. Child A is on a short swing, child B on a long swing. If both are pulled back and released from the same height at exactly the same time, which will swing back and forth more times in ten seconds?

a. Child A on the short swing.
b. Child B on the long swing.
c. They will swing the same number of times.

7. Do you know how your body performs and moves. Specifically, how does a muscle work in the body?
   a. Only by pushing.
   b. Only by pulling.
   c. By pushing and pulling.

8. Two children are on a see-saw. Child A is heavier than child B. To balance the see-saw the heavier A should move toward the center of the see-saw.
   True   False

9. What do you know about the birth of twins? Identical twins result from the fertilization of a single egg cell.
   True   False

10. How does a picture appear on your home TV screen, and what is the process that brings it to you? Specifically, is the picture created by a light beam projected from inside your picture tube?
    Yes   No

11. When you fly in a plane, you feel secure knowing that certain scientific principles keep it aloft. Do you know how? When a plane is in flight is the air pressure on the top of the airplane wing the same as the air pressure on the bottom?
    Yes   No

12. Airplanes breaking the speed of sound cause a sonic boom. Does a plane cause a continuous sonic boom as long as its speed is greater than the speed of sound?
    Yes   No

13. Here's a statement about the world around us. The sun is visible before its rim comes over the horizon.
    True   False

14. Benjamin Franklin knew that lightning was an electrical discharge. Lightning is seen before the resulting thunder is heard because the sound has farther to travel.
    True   False

15. Here's a statement about the elements. The oceans are the major source of rain water.
    True   False

16. It would be nice to think birds sing because we like to listen, but it isn't so. Why do they sing? Most birds sing to summon other birds.
    True   False

17. If Daniel Boone hadn't carved his name on a tree, we would never have known he shot a bear in the Kentucky hills. But what happens to those carvings? Initials carved on a tree will be higher off the ground after the tree has grown for twenty years.
    True   False

18. When a spacecraft is in orbit around the earth, gravity provides the force that keeps the capsule in orbit.
    True   False

19. When an astronaut walks in space, he floats eerily around and needs special equipment to get him where he wants to go. An astronaut in orbit has weight.
    True   False

20. The moon revolves around the earth, held in orbit by the earth's gravity. The moon, like all bodies, has a gravitational pull of its own, and a scale on the surface of the moon could measure this pull on the astronaut toward the moon's center. On the surface of the moon, an astronaut will weigh more than he does on earth.

True   False

ANSWERS

1. Yes. Put the ripe bananas in the refrigerator to slow down the chemical action which would cause over-ripening. Chiquita's current advice is to let the green bananas ripen at room temperature until they suit your taste and then put them in the refrigerator.

The same rule applies to tomatoes, pears, melons, or any other fruit which undergoes a chemical ripening process. Not just chemical action, but the growth of bacteria is also slowed by lower temperatures. That's why you put perishables like meat, dairy products and fresh vegetables in the refrigerator.

2. Yes. Cut them into small pieces so that more surface area is exposed to the boiling water. Cutting them in smaller pieces also means the heat will penetrate more quickly. The increased surface area of granulated sugar will cause it to dissolve faster than a sugar lump. This explains why you digest food better when you've chewed it well, and why you use kindling to start a fire.

3. No. The salt is for flavoring. Even if you've remembered that adding salt does lower the temperature at which water boils, that bit of scientific knowledge won't help you cook faster unless you want very salty vegetables. It would take an excessive amount of salt to lower the boiling point of that small amount of water even a few degrees. The time you'd save, as they say, is not worth the salt.

4. No. Propping the door open won't cool the kitchen, because all a refrigerator can do is draw the heat out of something and pump it somewhere else. Normally, the coils and motor draw the heat from the food inside the refrigerator and pump it into the kitchen air. With the door open, the system just pushes the same heat around and around. In fact, the refrigerator motor must work overtime and get hotter, the net effect making the kitchen warmer than it was before. This is why room air conditioners are placed in a window so that heat can be pumped outside.

5. No. The top and bottom should be opened. Warm air rises, and it collects at the top of the room. Opening the top allows it to escape. Outside air will enter more easily if the bottom window is opened. This starts a flow of air in a large circular pattern, carrying off the warm air in the fastest possible way. Radiators are placed near the floor to take advantage of this principle and start similar circular patterns.

6. a. Child A on the short swing will swing back and forth more times in ten seconds. The swings behave like the pendulum on a clock, and the length of the rope is the important factor.

7. b. Only by pulling. When the body performs any action, even what seems to be a pushing action, it happens because one set of muscles is contracting and pulling a tendon, which moves a bone.

8. True. The children can only balance and see-saw easily if the heavier one shifts toward the center.

9. True. Identical twins come from a single egg, fertilized by a single sperm. The fertilized cell then divides to produce two identical children.

10. No. It is not a light beam but a beam of electrons. A magnet affects the movement of electrons, moving back and forth, changing the path of the electrons, and aligning the picture. If the picture were created by a light beam, this magnet would have no effect.
More precisely, the beam of electrons strikes a coating on the inner face of the tube, causing different portions to glow with varying intensities and thus create a picture.

11. No. The pressures are not the same because of the way the air flows around the wing. The air passing above the wing travels farther and faster than the air passing below. Because it is traveling faster over the wing, it is not pushing as hard against the wing as the air underneath. The air underneath thus pushes the wing and the plane upward.

12. Yes. The shock wave, the sonic boom, is being made during the entire time the plane is flying faster than the speed of sound. On the ground, you will hear it as a single explosive bang, but actually it's a rumble moving behind the plane, striking point after point along its route.

13. True. You can see the image of the sun before it comes over the horizon because the light from the sun is being bent by the atmosphere of the earth. This means we can see the sun around a corner. Light bends whenever it moves from a medium of one density—the vacuum of outer space—to a medium of another density, in this case the atmosphere of the earth.

14. False. They both travel the same distance. The flash and the thunder clap both occur at the same instant, in the same place, but the flash reached you first. Light travels almost one million times faster than sound.

15. True. The oceans are the major source of rain because they are the major collecting points for water in the water cycle. The sun heats the water to vapor, which forms clouds that drift until cooler air turns the vapor back into water. This falls as rain, which runs downhill into the oceans, and then the whole cycle repeats.

16. False. Birds do not sing to summon other birds, but to chase them away. Song is their way of posting a No Trespassing sign. A bird sings from perches to stake a claim to enough territory to provide food for himself and his family. And he sings even louder when another bird moves across his boundary.

17. False. Trees grow up from the top, not from the bottom. The bottom branch remains the same distance from the ground, and the carving remains the same height off the ground, though the carving will spread out.

18. True. Without the pull of gravity the spacecraft would go straight out into space. But gravity pulls it downward. The result is the curving path of the orbit.

19. True. An astronaut does have weight in orbit, because weight is a measure of gravitational pull toward the center of earth. Like the spacecraft, the astronaut is still falling toward the earth, pulled by gravity. But his forward speed makes him fall in orbit around the earth instead of falling toward it. We can calculate his weight, but we can't measure it, because a scale in space would be falling just as he is, and there would be no pressure against the scale to indicate his weight.

20. False. The astronaut's weight will be less, because the pull of gravity will be less. The pull of gravity between two objects depends on the mass, or bulk, of each of them, and how far apart their centers are. We know the mass of the moon, and how far the surface is from the center, so we can calculate that a man on the moon will weigh one-sixth of his weight on earth.

☛ ARE YOU A KNOWLEDGEABLE CITIZEN?

This test is compiled from actual tests given to immigrants seeking United States citizenship. As a birthright American you have much to be thankful for. After taking this quiz, you may be glad that a citizenship test is not required for you to remain in America.

1. Which of these is *not* a purpose of the United States Constitution?
   a. to tell people where they must live
   b. to tell the states how to work with the federal government
   c. to tell the states how to work with each other
   d. to set out the purpose and authority of the federal government

2. What is the meaning of the word "republic"?
   a. to ask in writing
   b. the final authority of persons or things
   c. a system of representative government
   d. some part of a town or country where people live close together

3. What is the flag of our country often called?
   a. The Stars and Bars
   b. The Stars and Stripes
   c. The Union Jack
   d. The Tricolor

4. Which of these statements is true about the flag of the United States?
   a. the stripes represent the states of the United States
   b. the blue color represents the president, the white represents Congress, and the red represents the people
   c. there is no United States flag, only state flags
   d. none of the above is true

5. We say that the people of the United States govern themselves. How do they do this?
   a. by electing their own government officials
   b. by voting on every action taken by the government

Derived from *Our Constitution and Government*, U.S. Department of Justice, Immigration and Naturalization Service.

c. by attending required classes on government

d. all of the above

6. Which one of the following statements best describes the Declaration of Independence?

   a. the Declaration of Independence is the Constitution of the United States

   b. the Declaration of Independence said that the colonies were free from the control of Great Britain

   c. the Declaration of Independence declared war on Great Britain

   d. the Declaration of Independence gave slaves their freedom

7. When was the Declaration of Independence signed?

   a. 1763

   b. 1776

   c. 1781

   d. 1789

8. Which one of the following states was *not* one of the original thirteen colonies?

   a. New Hampshire

   b. Vermont

   c. New York

   d. Virginia

9. What three branches of government are provided for in the Consitution?

   a. legislative, judicial, executive

   b. congressional, judicial, presidential

   c. parliamentary, judiciary, administrative

   d. legislative, judiciary, governmental

10. What is the "Bill of Rights"?

    a. a statement of the rights for United States citizens

    b. a statement of the rights for non-citizens living in the United States

    c. the first ten amendments to the Constitution

    d. all of the above

11. A written change in the Constitution is called

    a. an amendment

    b. a bill

    c. a patent

    d. a treaty

12. Who has the final authority in state government in the United States?

    a. the governor of each state

    b. the people of each state

    c. the state representatives

    d. judges who rule on the constitutionality of state laws

13. Which one of the following groups of people is not legally allowed to vote in United States elections?

    a. criminals

    b. mentally ill people

    c. non-citizens

    d. none of the above groups are allowed to vote.

14. Which of these is *not* an objective of the United States Constitution, as stated in the Preamble?

    a. the federal government would have the power to defend all of the states

    b. the country would be a better union of states

    c. the government would work for the good of all people

    d. the country would be free from the control of England

15. The branch of the federal government that makes the laws is the

    a. executive branch

    b. judicial branch

    c. legislative branch

    d. diplomatic branch

16. The two parts of the Congress are the Senate and

    a. the House of Commons

    b. the House of Representatives

    c. the House of Legislation

    d. the House of Justice

17. How many Senators are there in Congress?
  a. 50
  b. 535
  c. 285
  d. 100

18. To be a United States Senator, a person must be thirty years of age, reside in the state from which elected, and
  a. be a citizen for nine years
  b. be a natural-born citizen
  c. be a registered voter
  d. have a college law degree

19. To be a United States Representative, a person must be twenty-five years of age, reside in the state from which elected, and
  a. be a natural-born citizen
  b. be a high school graduate
  c. be a citizen for seven years
  d. have paid at least $100 in taxes in the previous year

20. Which state has the largest number of Representatives in the Congress?
  a. Alaska
  b. Texas
  c. California
  d. New York

21. What officer presides over the United States Senate?
  a. the president pro tempore of the Senate
  b. the Speaker of the House of Representatives
  c. the president
  d. the vice-president

22. How does a bill usually become a law?
  a. It must be approved by both Houses and signed by the president.
  b. It need be approved only by the Senate and signed by the president.
  c. It need be approved only by the House of Representatives and signed by the president.

d. It only needs to be signed by the president.

23. How are the president and vice-president of the United States elected?
  a. by receiving a majority of the registered voters' votes
  b. by the Supreme Court
  c. by receiving a majority of the votes of the electoral college
  d. by a two-thirds majority in the Senate

24. The United States Supreme Court is made up of
  a. five justices
  b. six justices
  c. nine justices
  d. eleven justices

25. How many members are on the president's cabinet?
  a. six
  b. nine
  c. eleven
  d. thirteen

26. Before a treaty can become effective, who must it be approved by?
  a. majority of the states
  b. Supreme Court
  c. United States House of Representatives
  d. United States Senate

27. Which of the following is *not* a branch of the state government?
  a. executive branch
  b. judicial branch
  c. lawmaking branch
  d. mayoral branch

28. Who makes the laws for your state?
  a. the United States Congress
  b. the state legislature
  c. the city council
  d. the state supreme court

29. Who is responsible for enforcing the laws of the state?
  a. the mayor of each city and town

b. the governor and his administrative staff

c. the United States Senate

d. none of the above

30. How does the governor get into office?

    a. through appointment by the previous governor

b. through election by the members of the state legislature

c. through appointment by the United States Senate

d. through election by the voters of the states

ANSWERS

1. a	**9.** a	**17.** d	**25.** c
2. c	**10.** d	**18.** a	**26.** d
3. b	**11.** a	**19.** c	**27.** d
4. d	**12.** b	**20.** c	**28.** b
5. a	**13.** c	**21.** d	**29.** b
6. b	**14.** d	**22.** a	**30.** d
7. b	**15.** c	**23.** c	
8. b	**16.** b	**24.** c	

WHAT YOUR SCORE MEANS

27–30: Wave old glory, you're "All-American."

23–26: "This Land Is Your Land."

20–22: Triple AAA—Average American Adult.

19 or less: Discover America! It's your duty.

☞ HOW GREEN IS YOUR THUMB?

Do you have a green thumb or a very, very black one? One way to tell is by looking at your houseplants. People with green thumbs usually have green plants. People with black thumbs have dead ones. If you're like most people, you're somewhere in between—say, a brown thumb. Your house plants are probably leggy, wilting, dropping leaves or turning yellow. After you've looked over your house plants, take the following test. Not only should it confirm what your plants have already told you (the color of your thumb), but it may help you to figure out what you've been doing wrong.

1. It is usually better to overwater a plant than to underwater it.
True   False

2. The best way to water is to establish a regular watering schedule, then stick to it.
True   False

3. Since most house plants come from tropical or subtropical climates, they do best in rooms held at a fairly high temperature (say, 75°+).
True   False

4. When a plant grown in a greenhouse is first brought home it often drops leaves and flowers. This is entirely normal
True   False

5. The tinfoil usually wrapped around a potted plant at the florists should be removed as soon as possible after you get the plant home.
True   False

6. Drafts cause more house plant problems than cool room temperatures do.
True   False

7. House plants should be moved outdoors in the summer and placed in the full sun.
True   False

8. House plants generally do best in rooms where night temperature is higher than day temperature.
True   False

9. In many cases, the environmental conditions needed to *maintain* house plants differ widely from those needed to *grow* them.
True   False

10. The chlorine in treated tap water does not harm plants.
    True   False

11. Dust on house plant leaves significantly reduces the amount of light that they receive.
    True   False

12. Flowering house plants generally require much more water and stronger light than foliage plants.
    True   False

13. Plants in clay pots require less frequent watering than those in plastic pots.
    True   False

14. Houseplants should be fertilized sparingly, especially in winter, when light intensity is so low.
    True   False

15. Most house plants benefit from periodic misting.
    True   False

16. Natural light is far better for plants than artificial light from incandescent or fluorescent tubes.
    True   False

17. Which of the following plants would do best in a terrarium?

    a. selaginella
    b. dumbcane
    c. Christmas cactus
    d. African violet

18. Which of the following plants would tolerate a room with no windows, where several fluorescent lights are turned on from 8:00 A.M. to 5:00 P.M.?

    a. cattleya orchid
    b. aglaonema
    c. chrysanthemum
    d. spider plant

19. Which of the following plants would be a good candidate for a hanging basket?

    a. fuchsia
    b. rubber plant
    c. jade plant
    d. elephant's ear

20. The best place to grow African violets would be:

    a. in a southern bedroom window near a warm air duct.
    b. in an eastern bedroom window near a warm air duct.
    c. in an eastern bathroom window.
    d. in a southern bathroom window.

ANSWERS

1. False because overwatering reduces the amount of air in the soil and air is vital to a healthy root system. When you water, the soil's open spaces become filled and air is driven out. If plants are overwatered, the soil spaces never dry, and air never has a chance to reenter them.

2. False because the soil around the plant roots does not always dry out at the same rate. Drying rates vary with changes in air temperature and humidity. You should check plants daily, drenching them thoroughly when they become moderately dry, then waiting to water again until they are once more moderately dry.

3. False. Though most of our house plants do come from the tropics or semi-tropics, they actually do better at cool temperatures in the house. This is primarily because the humidity in our homes is so much lower than that of the tropics. At high temperatures and low humidity, plants lose much more water to the air than they do at low temperatures and low humidity.

4. True. Plants used to the favorable conditions of a moist greenhouse generally go through a period of adjustment to the drier air and lower temperatures in the home. They may lose a few

leaves and drop flowers. Within a few weeks, however, they should be thriving happily in their new environment. Keep them well watered during their adjustment period.

5. False. The tinfoil helps to reduce water loss from the root system to the dry air of the home. Keep the tinfoil on the plant for at least two weeks, while it adjusts to its new environment.
6. True because drafts increase the amount of water lost from the plant to the dry air of the home.
7. False. While house plants usually benefit from a move outdoors in the summer, they should be placed in slightly shaded conditions, similar to those they have been accustomed to indoors. Remember that the greater air movement of the outdoors and high summer temperatures will increase the amount of water lost by the plants to the air. You will probably need to water more frequently. Don't count on the rain to do it!
8. False. House plants do best in rooms where the night temperature is *lower* than the day temperature. Plants manufacture food in sunlight only, but they burn it up twenty-four hours a day. At high temperatures, they burn up more food, so high night temperatures cause the plant to burn more food than it would at low temperatures. And at night, plants are not making any food. High night temperatures, therefore, make it difficult for a plant to build up reserves of food.
9. True. Plants need ideal conditions for optimum growth, but at considerably less than ideal conditions, they are able to maintain themselves. To keep the perfect house plant from getting too big, in fact, you can reduce water, fertilizer, and light, without hurting it. The plant will remain in healthy condition, but cut back on active growth.
10. Chlorine is poisonous, and it does limit plant growth. If you are anxious to encourage growth, aerate the water by allowing it to stand for a day in an open container. Under most conditions, however, unaerated tap water is fine for maintaining plants.
11. True. Wash your plants' leaves every now and then to permit optimum light penetration.
12. True, partly because a plant with flowers has more surface area and loses more water to the air, and partly because the flowers produce little food themselves and must be supported by the plant's stem and leaves.
13. False. Clay pots are porous and allow more evaporation of water from the soil than do plastic pots. Plants in clay pots usually need more frequent watering than those in plastic ones.
14. True. Overfertilizing house plants when light conditions are low encourages leggy growth.
15. True. Because most of our house plants come from humid climates, they appreciate misting in the dry environment of our houses.
16. True—but not entirely. Plants derive most benefit from the red and blue portions of the light spectrum, found in all natural light. Most artificial white light is designed to provide yellow and green, which are considered best for reading. There are, however, special fluorescent lights designed to meet the needs of plants, and these are every bit as good as most natural sunlight in the house.
17. b. Christmas cactus and most African violets are too large for most terrariums, and the Christmas cactus would probably not appreciate the still air of a terrarium. There are miniature African violets which would be well-suited to these conditions, however, since African violets thrive on high humidity.
18. b. The only one of these that would tolerate so little light is the aglaonema, or Chinese evergreen.
19. a. Hanging basket plants should, by definition, hang. Fuchsia is the only one of these plants that does so.
20. c. African violets need filtered shade and high humidity. A southern window would be too bright, and a hot air duct would make it difficult to maintain high humidity. Light from an eastern window, however, is weaker, and plants in a bathroom would benefit from the steam generated by showers and from the frequent running of water.

WHAT YOUR SCORE MEANS

Give yourself one point for every correct answer.

15–20: You definitely have a green thumb! But, of course, you already knew that. People compliment you on your plants constantly.

10–15: Your thumb is showing tinges of yellow and brown. So too, I expect, are your plants. You probably tend to overwater and overfertilize.

5–10: A definite brown thumb. You forget to water often—too often. Your avocado is probably withering in a corner right now. (Some people enjoy reading about plants more than taking care of them.)

0–5: Unfortunately, you have a classical case of black thumb. Buy a plastic philodendron.

☞ DO YOU HAVE A SCIENTIFIC MIND?

It's hard to even read a newspaper without stumbling across some technological lingo or scientific explanation. Even the movies and weekly TV screens are filled with scientific adventures. Test your level of scientific knowledge.

1. The ratio of the kilometer to the mile is roughly
   a. 1 to 10
   b. 5 to 8
   c. 8 to 5
   d. 2 to 1

2. Water freezes at
   a. zero degrees Fahrenheit
   b. 32 degrees Fahrenheit
   c. 100 degrees Celsius
   d. absolute zero

3. A lunar eclipse can occur only when
   a. the earth is between the sun and the moon
   b. the moon is between the earth and the sun
   c. the sun is between the moon and the earth
   d. there is a new moon

4. The conservation-of-energy principle refers to the fact that
   a. it is essential not to waste natural gas and oil, for these are limited in supply.
   b. solar heating makes use of the sun's energy, which would otherwise be wasted

   c. energy can be neither created nor destroyed
   d. nuclear power plants recycle spent fuel

5. The splitting of an atomic nucleus into two large fragments and several smaller ones is known as
   a. fusion
   b. alpha decay
   c. fission
   d. thermonuclear energy

6. Atoms are believed to be composed of
   a. protons, neutrons and electrons
   b. protons and electrons
   c. positrons, neutrinos and electrons
   d. protons and antiprotons

7. The period of revolution of the moon about the earth is approximately
   a. one hour
   b. one day
   c. one month
   d. one year

8. Identify the nonastronomical objects:
   a. white giants and red dwarfs
   b. white dwarfs and black holes
   c. quasars and supernovae
   d. neutron stars and galaxies

Appeared as "Do You Have a Space-Age Mind?" by Grace Marmor Spruch and Larry Spruch in *The New York Times*, August 2, 1976. © 1976 by The New York Times Company. Reprinted by permission.

9. The Pythagorean theorem states that
 a. in any triangle the square of the longest side equals the sum of the squares of the other sides
 b. in any triangle the square of the longest side equals the square of the sum of the other sides
 c. in a right triangle the square of the hypotenuse equals the sum of the squares of the other sides
 d. in an isosceles triangle the third side equals the sum of the two equal sides

10. One type of radioactivity involves
 a. gamma rays
 b. sunspots
 c. pulsars
 d. magnetic fields

11. Thirteen billion years corresponds most closely to the presumed
 a. age of the universe
 b. age of the earth
 c. time since the dinosaurs were on earth
 d. time man has been on earth

12. Helium was first discovered
 a. in mines
 b. in the depths of the ocean
 c. on the moon
 d. on the sun

13. A planet that is never visible to the naked eye is
 a. Mercury
 b. Venus
 c. Mars
 d. Neptune

14. The chain reaction that forms the basis of the atomic bomb was first achieved by a group directed by
 a. Albert Einstein
 b. Neils Bohr
 c. Edward Teller
 d. Enrico Fermi

15. The gravitational force between two spherical objects is known to be inversely proportional to the square of the distance between their centers. If that distance is made three times larger, the gravitational force will be
 a. 3 times smaller
 b. 9 times smaller
 c. 2 times smaller
 d. 3 times larger

16. Who did not make fundamental contributions to the science of electricity?
 a. Charles Coulomb
 b. Michael Faraday
 c. Benjamin Franklin
 d. Isaac Newton

17. The Big Bang is related to
 a. the hydrogen bomb
 b. the maximum noise level in an amplifier
 c. a theory of the origin of the universe
 d. supersonic aircraft

18. Nuclear physics does not deal with
 a. alpha particles
 b. beta rays
 c. deuterons
 d. deoxyribonucleic acid

19. Identify the incorrect statement. Transmutation of the elements
 a. was a goal of the alchemists
 b. occurs in ordinary chemical reactions
 c. was first achieved by Ernest Rutherford
 d. occurs in some nuclear reactions

20. Radiocarbon dating is a technique by which
 a. persons who might get along well together are identified by computer
 b. the fading of carbon copies is used to tell the age of documents
 c. the age of art objects is measured

d. the length of time a patient has had cancer is determined

21. A laser is not
  a. a source of light that can be focused to a tiny area
  b. a device conceived by Jules Verne for propelling a man to the moon
  c. employed in some delicate eye operations
  d. a device that was used to measure the distance to the moon

22. Light
  a. can travel in a vacuum
  b. can travel at infinite speed
  c. always travels in perfectly straight lines
  d. cannot travel through solid objects

23. A rocket moves because
  a. its shape permits air to support it
  b. it has exceptionally powerful propellers
  c. it weighs less than the air it displaces
  d. there is a reaction to the gases it exhausts

24. The speed of sound is most nearly
  a. 10 feet per second
  b. 1,000 feet per second
  c. 10,000 feet per second
  d. 186,000 miles per second

25. Acceleration
  a. is the change in velocity
  b. is the rate of change of velocity
  c. always increases
  d. is the force on an object

26. Newton's three laws relate to
  a. electricity
  b. atomic physics
  c. heat
  d. motion

27. There is no conservation of
  a. angular momentum
  b. momentum
  c. force
  d. charge

28. A hologram is
  a. a rapid means of communication
  b. a slide that can be used to produce three-dimensioned images
  c. an atom smasher
  d. a future mode of transportation

29. The "Red Planet" is
  a. Saturn
  b. Venus
  c. Sputnik
  d. Mars

30. The ancient Greek scientist one associates with an atomic theory is
  a. Archimedes
  b. Pythagoras
  c. Eureka
  d. Democritus

31. A half life is
  a. a molecule that cannot be classed as definitely organic or definitely inorganic
  b. half the average life expectancy of a group of people
  c. the time for half a given amount of radioactive material to decay
  d. the radiation dose that will be lethal to half the subjects in an experiment

32. Choose the proper order of the names Archimedes, Copernicus, Einstein and Galileo so that they correspond to these statements:
  . . . was the first to view the moons of Jupiter through a telescope.
  . . . showed the equivalence of mass and energy.
  . . . stated that a floating body displaces a volume of water the weight of which equals the weight of the body.

. . . stated that the sun, rather than the earth, is at the center of the solar system.

a. Archimedes, Einstein, Galileo, Copernicus

b. Copernicus, Einstein, Archimedes, Galileo

c. Copernicus, Archimedes, Galileo, Einstein

d. Galileo, Einstein, Archimedes, Copernicus

33. A topic not likely to arise in SALT talks is

a. NaCl

b. ICBM

c. MIRV

d. U-235

ANSWERS

1. b	**10.** a	**19.** b	**28.** b
2. b	**11.** a	**20.** c	**29.** d
3. a	**12.** d	**21.** b	**30.** d
4. c	**13.** d	**22.** a	**31.** c
5. c	**14.** d	**23.** d	**32.** d
6. a	**15.** b	**24.** b	**33.** a
7. c	**16.** d	**25.** b	
8. a	**17.** c	**26.** d	
9. c	**18.** d	**27.** c	

WHAT YOUR SCORE MEANS

30–33: Exceptional. Ever consider science as a profession?
26–29: Excellent. Maybe you could get a job with NASA.
22–25: Fair. Time for some refresher lab courses.
21 or below: Maybe you should watch some Mr. Wizard reruns.

☞ THE METRIC QUIZ

Do you remember your school days, when you learned to convert pints into quarts, feet into miles, ounces into pounds? Now, we are being told to get ready to "metricate"—to join the rest of the world in using the metric system of measurement.

Must we learn the metric system? Probably, since most of the world already measures metrically. The United States is the only major nation that has no plan underway to convert totally to the metric system, although there are signs that we are finally inching (if you'll pardon the expression) toward this sensible system that avoids fractions and uses multiples of ten.

To see if you're ready for the metric system, take this quick quiz.

1. The height of a first-grader is closest to
   a. 1 centimeter
   b. 1 meter
   c. 1 kilometer
   d. 1 kilogram

2. A teenaged girl's waistline is usually close to
   a. 20 cm
   b. 40 cm
   c. 60 cm
   d. 80 cm

3. The maximum legal United States highway speed is closest to
   a. 44 kilometers per hour
   b. 55 kilometers per hour
   c. 77 kilometers per hour
   d. 88 kilometers per hour

4. Normal human body temperature is closest to
   a. 7° Celsius
   b. 17° Celsius
   c. 27° Celsius
   d. 37° Celsius

5. The width of a large paper clip is approximately
   a. 1 millimeter
   b. 1 centimeter
   c. 1 meter
   d. 1 kilometer

6. The volume of a large milkshake is closest to
   a. 1 meter
   b. 1 milliliter
   c. 1 cubic centimeter
   d. 1 liter

Reprinted with permission of the author, Chris Buethe, from October 1976 *Ladies' Home Journal.* © 1976 LHJ Publishing, Inc. Reprinted with permission of *Ladies' Home Journal.*

7. The weight of a quart of milk is about
   a. 1 gram
   b. 100 grams
   c. 1 kilogram
   d. 100 kilograms

8. Of these, the most metric United States industry is
   a. drugs
   b. automobiles
   c. textiles
   d. foods

ANSWERS

1.   b. A meter (m) is about 40 inches (actually 39.37 inches). To make a good guess, just add a little to the yard estimate that you now use. For example, if it is about one yard from your nose to your fingertips, add the width of your hand and you have a meter length.

2.   c. A centimeter (cm) is almost 0.4 inch, or the width of your little finger. It takes about 2.54 centimeters to make an inch. So a teenager's 24-inch waist is a bit over 60 cm.

3.   d. A kilometer (km) is 1,000 meters. That's approximately 5/8 of a mile. So 5 miles per hour is about 8 kilometers per hour. Thus, 55 miles per hour, the United States highway speed limit, is 88 kilometers per hour.

4.   d. In metric degrees Celsius, water freezes at 0°C and boils at 100°C. Twenty degrees Celsius makes a comfortable house, and 25°C is a nice temperature outdoors. A normal body temperature of 37°C is the same as one of 98.6° Fahrenheit.

5.   b. The width of a large paper clip is about one centimeter (cm), or one hundredth of a meter.

6.   d. A quart volume is almost a liter. A large milkshake is close to one liter. A milliliter is one thousandth of a liter.

7.   c. A kilogram is the weight of a liter of water. Since a liter is nearly 1.1 quarts and milk is mainly water, the weight of a quart of milk is nearly 1 kilogram (kg.).

8.   a. Pharmaceuticals have been metric for years. Recently, some foods have begun to be marked in metric units. Watch for a 454-gram package of butter or a 170-gram can of frozen juice on your next grocery shopping venture.

WHAT YOUR SCORE MEANS

If you answered more than half the questions correctly, you either use the metric system regularly, have traveled extensively abroad or are a good guesser.

☞ WHAT'S YOUR MOVIE/TV TRIVIA QUOTIENT?

1. The young sex symbol of the fifties was James Dean. His first picture was *East of Eden* in 1955. What was his last in 1956?

2. What was the famous rabbit's name in Walt Disney's cartoon classic, *Bambi*?

3. What child actor was always giving W.C. Fields all he could handle?

4. What was Clark Gable's famous last line in the movie epic *Gone With the Wind?*

5. Who played the role of The Invisible Man in the 1933 thriller by that name?

6. What glamourous actress played the role of the twelve-year-old leading lady in 1944's *National Velvet?*

7. James Cagney received an Academy Award for the leading role in the 1942 musical film *Yankee Doodle Dandy.* This film portrays the life of what famous singer/songwriter?

8. In Walt Disney's *Pinocchio,* what is the name of the friendly goldfish?

9. In what movie did Humphrey Bogart win an Academy Award playing opposite Kathryn Hepburn?

10. In what movie did Marlon Brando star as an infamous Mexican bandito?

11. Jim Backus played Judge Stevens in what early TV sitcom?

12. Who played Jackie Gleason's lovable wife Alice on the "Honeymooners"?

13. What was the regular announcer's name on Groucho Marx's quiz show "You Bet Your Life"?

14. What was the name of the dragon on "Kukla, Fran, and Ollie"?

15. In what TV western did actor James Garner have a starring role?

16. Who played Chester on the original TV "Gunsmoke" show?

17. Who played the role of Spin on the Mickey Mouse Club serial "Spin and Marty"?

18. Who played Dr. Zorba on TV's medical show "Ben Casey"?

19. Who played the wacky neighbors Fred and Ethel Mertz on "I Love Lucy"?

20. What western TV series did Will Hutchins star in during the 1950s?

ANSWERS

1. *Giant*
2. Thumper
3. Baby Le Roy
4. "Frankly, my dear,
   I don't give a damn."
5. Claude Rains
6. Elizabeth Taylor
7. George M. Cohan

8. Cleo
9. *The African Queen*
10. *Viva Zapata*
11. "I married Joan"
12. Audrey Meadows
13. George Fenneman
14. Oliver J. Dragon

15. "Maverick"
16. Dennis Weaver
17. Tim Considine
18. Sam Jaffe
19. William Frawley,
    Vivian Vance
20. "Sugarfoot"

WHAT YOUR SCORE MEANS

19–20: Genius, Move over C.B.

17–18: Excellent. You deserve an Oscar and an Emmy.

15–16: Good. Keep your ears open at cocktail parties.

13–14: Fair. Spend more time reading "TV Guide."

0–12: "Say goodnight, Gracie!" Better stay up and watch the Late Late Show.

☞SEEKING REDRESS, OR WHAT'S YOUR RAG-Q?

Are you fully exploiting your wardrobe potential? Here's a fun quiz to give you insight on your ability to dress for success as a working woman in a male chauvinist's business world. Find out your "Rag-Q."

1. I always wanted my boss to notice my
   a. unpuckered seams
   b. paisley report covers
   c. dedication
   d. shabby salary

2. I'd like my work clothes to make people in the office
   a. afraid of me
   b. genuflect
   c. recognize my expertise
   d. learn my name

3. When I am properly dressed, I usually find myself
   a. promoted
   b. having my name put on the door
   c. without a subway token
   d. making tuna-fish sandwiches

4. I feel most comfortable in
   a. medium-range gray
   b. 100 percent wool
   c. John Kloss nightgowns
   d. fetal position

5. If there's no time to change before dinner, I usually add
   a. a sequined sweater
   b. false eyelashes
   c. my credit card
   d. an apron

6. At the most important moment of my life, I was wearing
   a. a skirted suit
   b. a little hatband feather
   c. sterile draped sheets
   d. white satin and a veil

7. Constricting undergarments make me
  a. look thinner
  b. more aware of myself
  c. ooze
  d. very hostile

8. I spend most of my free time
  a. comparison shopping for quality clothing
  b. plotting corporate takeover
  c. in sexual fantasy
  d. sucking my thumb

9. Opaque fabrics best conceal my
  a. nipples
  b. competitive nature
  c. essential paranoia
  d. torn underwear

10. A babushka is not good business headgear because it
  a. lacks a brim
  b. flattens my hairdo
  c. reveals my socioeconomic background
  d. arouses a pogrom impulse in others

11. To ensure I'm not imitating men, I try to avoid
  a. wearing a three-piece, pinstripe pantsuit
  b. carrying heavy sample cases
  c. ring around the collar
  d. growing a beard

12. Complete the following sentence: Clothes make
  a. the man
  b. the woman
  c. the person
  d. more laundry

HOW TO SCORE

Award 4 points for each *a* answer, 3 for each *b*, 2 for *c*, and 1 for *d*. Then subtract one point for each garment you still have in your closet that doesn't zip anymore (be honest!).

WHAT YOUR SCORE MEANS

Above 40: The winner! But beware the cloneliness of a life devoted to the slavish suit of success.

25 to 40: Danger zone; there's not much between you and an old bathrobe and slippers.

0 to 24: Commence emergency procedures. Increase your height. Give up wearing lobster bibs. Molt.

☞FIND YOUR CAT'S IQ

Now you can find out just how smart your cat really is with an amazing IQ test exclusively for felines. The Cat-Q test was developed by Ohio psychologist Elizabeth Bard, who says cats do not have to be able to perform extraordinary feats to take it. The Cat-Q includes an observation scale and a performance scale, both of which are scored on a point system. The first section consists of twenty-five questions to be answered by the cat's owner. On the performance scale, your cat's senses are put to the test.

Nine test items are geared to how your cat reacts to such stimuli as the sound of a bell, the sight of a feather, a rolling ball, and the touch of a pencil inside its ear.

To get an idea of how well your cat would score on the Cat-Q test, sample part of the performance scale, here excerpted from the Cat-Q. You will need a shoestring, ball, bell, pencil, and feather. The number of points your cat gets are specified in the answer section. You will need approximately fifteen minutes for this part of the test. Each item may be repeated up to five times to obtain a response.

1. Touch or stroke your cat gently on the nose and around the mouth area with your finger.
   a. closes eyes
   b. shakes head
   c. licks mouth

2. Touch gently on back with finger or pencil tip.
   a. ripples (moves coat)
   b. shakes fur
   c. licks spot touched

3. Touch inside hair of either ear very lightly with finger or pencil tip.
   a. shakes entire head
   b. twitches one ear
   c. rubs or touches ear with paw

4. Ring bell quickly behind your cat.
   a. moves or twitches ears
   b. moves head partially
   c. turns head completely

5. Place string on cat's back. Do not let string hang down or touch the floor.
   a. ripples
   b. removes string (in any manner)

6. Run string in right to left motion in front of cat.
   a. watches with eyes
   b. touches with nose
   c. grabs with paw

7. Place feather on floor two to four inches in front of your cat.
   a. touches with paw(s)

b. touches with nose
c. begins to chew feather
d. picks up feather with paw
e. transfers from paw to paw

8. Move pencil on floor slowly toward the cat.
a. touches with paw(s)

b. touches with same paw two or more times

9. Roll the ball on the floor toward the cat.
a. touches ball with paw(s)
b. touches ball with nose
c. begins to play with ball

HOW TO SCORE

Tally your cat's score from the following points.

1. a–1, b–1, c–2
2. a–1, b–1, c–2
3. a–1, b–2, c–2

4. a–1, b–1, c–2
5. a–1, b–2
6. a–1, b–1, c–2

7. a–1, b–1, c–1, d–2, e–2
8. a–1, b–2
9. a–1, b–1, c–2

WHAT YOUR CAT'S SCORE MEANS

15 or above: Superior—he may, indeed, be smarter than you are!

11–14: A charmingly average feline.

10 or less: Lovable, but scarcely a Rhodes scholar.

☞ THE DOG OWNER'S APTITUDE TEST

Are you fit to own a dog? Well you may think so, but many of our four-legged friends have been abandoned or mistreated because owners were not aware of their full responsibility. Answer these questions and try to see the consequence regarding each of your responses. If you pass, why not let the prospective dog try to qualify for his place in your family with "The Dog Ownee's Aptitude Test" following this one.

Circle the correct answer to each of the following questions.

1. If a strange dog barks at you, do you
   a. make an obscene gesture
   b. chase him away
   c. run away in fright
   d. bark back until he shuts up
   e. reassure the dog in a friendly tone that you mean no harm and walk away slowly

2. If you felt like a bit of exercise, would you
   a. promise yourself to do some sit-ups tomorrow
   b. run over to the television and turn on the football game
   c. take a walk in the park and leave the dog home
   d. walk the dog down to the corner for a six-pack and walk back home to watch the football game
   e. take the dog on your daily two-mile jog

3. If your dog made a "mistake" on the living-room rug, would you
   a. throw a newspaper on top of it and walk around it
   b. erect a run in the living room, figuring if that's where he's going to go, that's where he's going to go
   c. tell him to get out and never come back
   d. rub his nose in it and hit him with a newspaper
   e. say "no" firmly, take him outside for five minutes, and keep alert the next time the dog is in the living room

Taken from *Mutt* by Nancy Dolensek and Barbara Burn. Copyright © 1978 by Nancy Dolensek and Barbara Burn. Used by permission of Clarkson N. Potter, Inc.

4. If you had to shop for dog food, would you
   a. let the dog shop for his own food
   b. not shop at all but feed him leftovers and tell him to think of all the starving Americans
   c. buy the most expensive, most heavily advertised food on the market shelf
   d. read the ingredients on the label

5. If you found out that you couldn't keep your dog because of an allergy, would you
   a. ask the vet to put him to sleep
   b. let him go, hoping that someone nice will find him
   c. give him to your mother, because she's such a soft touch
   d. move out of the house and let the dog stay
   e. do everything you can to find him a good home, calling the local humane shelter as the last extreme

6. If your dog bit a neighborhood child, would you
   a. beat the kid for being a pest
   b. bite the dog to let him know what it feels like
   c. blame the neighbors for the accident, charging that the child led the dog on, and threaten to sue for abuse
   d. introduce the dog to a dog trainer
   e. inform the child's parents and keep the dog confined, under observation for two weeks for signs of rabies

7. If your dog looked unkempt and dirty, would you
   a. ignore it, 'cause that's how dogs are
   b. tell him not to come home until he looked more presentable
   c. run him under the hose a couple of times as he runs through the yard
   d. take him to Vidal Sassoon
   e. give him a good brushing, and if he's still dirty, bathe and dry him thoroughly

8. If your female dog got out while in heat and had a whirl with the locals, would you
   a. buy a box of cigars
   b. wonder why your wife isn't as willing as your dog
   c. slap a paternity suit on the owner of the winning dog
   d. let the dog have her pups and give them to the kids to unload at school
   e. let the dog have her pups, find each of them a good home, and have her spayed

9. If your dog always jumped up on people, would you
   a. tell them they were lucky the dog hadn't bitten them
   b. assume a "dogs-will-be-dogs" attitude
   c. hit him on the head until he gets down
   d. enroll him in obedience school
   e. spend ten minutes a day teaching him not to jump up and discipline him firmly whenever he does

10. If you went away for a vacation, would you
   a. leave the dog at home with an open, ten-pound bag of dog kibble
   b. tell the dog to sponge off the neighbors for a couple of weeks
   c. leave the dog home and have one of the neighborhood kids check on him every couple of days

d. inspect several kennels recommended by your veterinarian and choose the cleanest and most effectively run

e. find a vacation retreat that allows pets and take the dog with you

SCORING AND WHAT YOUR SCORE MEANS

For each question score: a = 1, b = 2; c = 3, d = 4, e = 5. Then total your points.

40–50: You are a dog owner's dog owner and need no further coaching whatsoever.

30–40: You have the potential for being a satisfactory dog owner.

20–30: You're a schizophrenic type, but a few years of psychoanalysis and a thorough reading of every dog manual you can get your hands on might bring you around.

10–20: Get a cat.

Less than 10: You can't cope with yourself; your best bet would be to get a dog to take care of you.

☞THE DOG OWNEE'S APTITUDE TEST

So my furry friend, you've got a chance to be adopted by a very nice family. Are you worthy of a life of leisure beside a cozy fireplace? Here's a little quiz that will tell your prospective owner what to expect from you in key family situations.

Circle the correct answer to each of the following questions.

1. If you saw a slipper, would your instinct be to
   a. eat it
   b. bury it
   c. check to see if it's your size
   d. look at the label to see if it came from Gucci and then check to see if it's your size
   e. take it to your owner when he/she gets home from work

2. If an intruder entered your home, would you
   a. smile
   b. bite his ankle
   c. offer him a drink
   d. sniff to see if he's clean
   e. bark ferociously and hope that he goes away

3. If you went into the kitchen and found a piece of roast beef sitting unattended on the counter, would you
   a. eat it on the spot and bury the bone
   b. lick it all over and leave the room
   c. check to see if it's medium rare before eating it
   d. ignore it because of its high cholesterol count
   e. put it in the refrigerator so it won't go bad

4. If you saw a loose puppy wandering down the street, would you
   a. chase him into a neighbor's yard and beat him up in front of a bunch of kids
   b. check his tags before taking action to make sure his name is not too ethnic

    c. ask him what country club his owners belong to

    d. chase him home and stay there until his owner promises not to let it happen again

    e. invite him into your house

5. In the veterinarian's office, would you
   - **a.** shake uncontrollably, feign timidity, and bite the vet when he gets you on the table
   - **b.** whine during the examination and scream bloody murder when you get your injection
   - **c.** seduce the cute little bitch next to you
   - **d.** insist that the vet scrub down the examination table twice before placing you on it
   - **e.** remain calm and quiet, refusing to leave until the vet remembers that you also need a heartworm test

6. When you relieve yourself, do you
   - **a.** aim for someone's leg
   - **b.** scratch at the screen door until you make a hole that you can jump through
   - **c.** find a little-used corner of the house and take care of things quietly
   - **d.** refuse to go at all until the bathroom has been wiped down with Lysol
   - **e.** aim for a tree growing in soil deficient in uric acid

7. If you were given a doggie toy, would you
   - **a.** chew it to bits instantly
   - **b.** ignore it because you'd rather have something else—like a steak
   - **c.** check the price to see if it's worth wasting your time on
   - **d.** thank the donor very much but allow as how you've really outgrown that kind of stuff
   - **e.** play with it energetically for fifteen minutes, then put it away in your toy box

8. After you have played in a muddy area, do you
   - **a.** go into the house and shake the dirt all over the place
   - **b.** go into the front hall and roll on the rug to avoid carrying mud throughout the house
   - **c.** go into the house and jump on your owner's bed
   - **d.** refuse to come in until you have been bathed and dried
   - **e.** none of the above—you wouldn't be caught dead in mud

9. If you knew that it was suppertime and nothing seemed to be happening, would you
   - **a.** open the refrigerator and help yourself
   - **b.** go next door and raid the garbage cans
   - **c.** ring for room service
   - **d.** write an irate letter to the management
   - **e.** wait patiently, remembering that your time was your owner's time

10. When your owner takes you for a walk, do you
    - **a.** pull like crazy on your leash so that your owner has to hang on with all his might
    - **b.** bite him when he tries to put a leash on you
    - **c.** make him follow three steps behind you
    - **d.** make *him* wear the leash
    - **e.** walk (or trot) at his left side, keeping exactly abreast and in step

HOW TO SCORE AND WHAT YOUR SCORE MEANS

For each question score: a=1, b=2, c=3, d=4, e=5. Total your points.

Over 50: You're not as smart as you think you are—there are only 50 possible points.

40–50: You are an incredibly well-behaved and thoughtful animal and should probably be an owner, not an ownee.

30–40: You are quite fastidious, genteel, and care a great deal about the niceties of life. You will need to invoke a great deal of discretion when choosing an owner, because there are many around who will not understand you or appreciate your discriminating characteristics.

20–30: You have a very great sense of self and like to have things your own way. You, too, may have a problem finding the right owner. Remember, an owner, by his very nature, likes to be the upper hand.

10–20: Your canine instincts are strong and you could use a little help in the obedience department and are somewhat impervious to humans, but you're probably not going to have trouble finding an owner.

10 or below: You're a real dog.

☛WHAT A NAME REVEALS

Most people have preconceived impressions of people bearing certain names. Through acquaintances and personal experience we picture a certain image as soon as we hear a name spoken. This short quiz will let you see if you share the same impressions of certain names as 1,100 other people questioned in a recent poll.

1. Match the name to the appropriate adjective

1. diffident
2. aggressive
3. spoiled
4. manly
5. very good-looking
6. large, soft and cuddly
7. fat but sexy
8. thoughtful
9. temperamental but likeable
10. coarse
11. cheery, honest and proud
12. red and plodding
13. tall, wiry, elegant
14. plain
15. pretty
16. spiteful
17. sultry and surly
18. pretty but silly
19. masculine
20. sensual and selfish
21. hard, ambitious, domineering
22. childish

a. Anthony
b. Daniel
c. Edward
d. George
e. Harold
f. Mark
g. Paul
h. Richard
i. Robert
j. Roger
k. Thomas
l. Barbara
m. Emma
n. Florence
o. Gillian
p. Louise
q. Maureen
r. Nancy
s. Pamela
t. Patricia
u. Sally
v. Sarah

2. Attractive vs. Unattractive. Circle those names in the listing below that just *have to* belong to attractive people.

Norton	Richard
Nellie	Sophia
Louise	Anthony
Amanda	Gertrude
Carl	Sherry

3. Fat vs. Thin. Some names also imply to us physical characteristics. Next to the names below indicate which implies fat and which thin.

Bertha	Olga
Dominic	Barbara
Emily	Kenneth
Sally	Anthony
Ollie	Leo

4. Active vs. Passive. Which names below do you associate with an active, dynamic character? Which are probably the passive type?

Bridget	Mona	Sylvia	Deidre	Kirk
Rose	Bart	Cliff	Bobbie	Pansy
Johnny	Boyd	James	Percival	Sargeant
Dave	Prissy	Jody	Tobi	Valentine
Milton	Isadore	Agnes	Violet	Patty

5. Winners vs. Losers. Which of the following names have to be "winners" and convey positive "can't miss" qualities? How about the names of "sure losers"?

Elroy	Claude
Dean	Douglas
Gladys	Durward
Keith	Janet
Beverly	Pamela

ANSWERS

1.

1. i	7. l	13. a	19. n
2. d	8. c	14. t	20. v
3. f	9. o	15. p	21. s
4. b	10. e	16. r	22. u
5. h	11. g	17. q	
6. k	12. j	18. m	

2. Attractive: Richard, Sophia, Anthony, Sherry, Carl, Louise, Amanda
Unattractive: Gertrude, Nellie, Norton

3. Fat: Bertha, Dominic, Ollie, Leo, Olga, Barbara
Thin: Emily, Sally, Kenneth, Anthony

4. Active: Bridget, Johnny, Dave, Bart, Sylvia, James, Cliff, Jody, Deidre, Bobbie, Tobi, Kirk, Sargeant, Patty
Passive: Rose, Milton, Mona, Boyd, Prissy, Isadore, Agnes, Percival, Violet, Pansy, Valentine

5. Winners: Dean, Keith, Beverly, Douglas, Janet, Pamela
Losers: Elroy, Gladys, Claude, Durward

☛ WHAT'S YOUR PLANT PERSONALITY?

You'll find revealing facets of your *own* personality by answering these questions.

1. You water your plants
   a. too much
   b. just enough to get by
   c. rarely

2. You think about your plants
   a. constantly
   b. occasionally
   c. never

3. You obtain your plants from
   a. seeds
   b. cuttings from friends' plants
   c. stores

4. You have most of your plants in the
   a. living room
   b. kitchen
   c. bedroom

5. You grow plants mainly for
   a. the reward of growth
   b. decoration
   c. being in on the latest craze

6. You tend plants
   a. once a week
   b. every other day
   c. once a month

7. You prefer flowers that are
   a. oddly shaped
   b. small and delicate
   c. large and showy

8. You prefer foliage plants that are
   a. tall and dramatic
   b. small and compact
   c. in need of little care

9. You read and learn about plants
   a. occasionally
   b. constantly
   c. only when necessary

10. You grow plants from cuttings and off shoots because you are
    a. thrifty
    b. afraid of buying diseased or damaged plants
    c. interested in the novelty of this form of gardening

Excerpted from the book *Plant Language: What Your Plants Tell about You* by Jack Kramer. Copyright © 1979 by Jack Kramer. Reprinted by permission of Dell Publishing Co., Inc.

WHAT YOUR ANSWERS MEAN

1. **a.** You care too much. Stop drowning plants and smothering people.
   b. Thriftiness is admirable, but watch out, you have a stingy streak.
   c. Stick with people, they mean more to you than plants.
2. **a.** You're an expert worrier. Could there be something missing in your life?
   b. Varied interests probably make you a sought-after companion.
   c. Cool, calm, and collected, you try to be in control.
3. **a.** You have definite tastes, lead an orderly life and are very productive.
   b. You love attention and you're a little spoiled, but friends like you anyway.
   c. A cautious choice-maker, you stick to your decision.
4. **a.** A good sense of humor and never fussy, you're very hard to ruffle.
   b. You're sensitive to your surroundings, basically domestic, and love the home scene.
   c. You have an affinity for nature and an unusual capacity for pleasure.
5. **a.** You take great care in everything you do, and try to be an achiever.
   b. Your fussiness probably makes you hard to get along with.

c. Your constant status-seeking could make you an insincere friend.
6. **a.** Career-minded, well-organized and easygoing, you're a well-rounded person.
   b. Picky, picky—you just can't leave well enough alone.
   c. Overly self-confident, you won't admit your mistakes.
7. **a.** Always curious, you like the unusual and enjoy being different.
   b. Small flowers match your personality: you're neat and like perfection.
   c. You're not going to be ignored—ever!
8. **a.** You're flamboyant—probably an attractive dresser—and very sociable.
   b. Though not necessarily shy, you rarely display your emotions.
   c. You're not lazy—you just prefer not to take on too much responsibility.
9. **a.** You like doing things your own way.
   b. A strong maternal instinct can smother the people who are close to you.
   c. Easygoing is good, but watch out, indifference will hurt your relationships.
10. **a.** You love a good bargain, but don't get snagged by the impractical.
    b. You avoid risks and seek out the norm.
    c. You're a go-getter and love to be challenged, but bore easily.

☛ HOW TO RECOGNIZE A GOOD RELATIONSHIP WITH A MAN . . . AND A BAD ONE

When the emotional energy required to keep a marriage, love affair, or even a close friendship going outweighs the pleasure and intimacy gained from the relationship, it is time to do some clear-headed reevaluation. Every personal involvement has moments of stress that require a bit more support and patience on the part of one person or the other, but if you consistently give more than you receive, it may be time to call it quits. The problem is that when your are immersed in a relationship, it may be difficult to determine when the giving ends and the emotional draining begins. Sometimes, too, when you care deeply for a person, there is a tendency to hide the truth from yourself, camouflaging your dissatisfaction and ignoring your partner's.

Think about a man with whom you have an important relationship—a person you're close to, but who sometimes causes you to wonder, "Is it worth it?" With him in mind (he can be husband, lover, or friend), read the following situations. Your response to each one can tell you more about how you feel than you may consciously be willing to admit.

Appeared as "How to Recognize a Good Relationship and a Bad One" by Dianne Partie and Ann Frisch in *Mademoiselle*. Reprinted with permission of the authors. © 1977 Dianne Partie and Ann Frisch.

1. A good friend of yours has invited you to a dinner party. The man you're with is in a bad mood—hostile toward everyone and you in particular. This happens a lot when he's with your friends. Your typical reaction is to
   a. avoid him throughout the evening
   b. make an excuse to your hostess and leave early
   c. try to enjoy the party but let him know you are displeased

2. On gift-giving occasions you buy your friend (husband, lover)
   a. a useful household or personal gift that meets the social demand of the occasion
   b. a present that is frivolous, fun and more extravagant than he usually gets you
   c. a gift that approximates in value what he usually gets you

3. You've been waiting for over two hours. It has happened before, but this time you are even more upset. In he walks with a good excuse as usual. You
   a. accept his explanation even though your insides are churning
   b. tell him firmly but definitely that this is the last time you'll wait for him more than ten minutes
   c. get angry and really tell him off in your usual way

4. Lately, your friend (husband, lover) has been depressed, irritable and distant. You have asked him many times why he's in this mood. Your next tactic is to
   a. let him know you are a willing listener but go about your business
   b. wonder what you have done wrong and try to discover what it is
   c. meet the arguments head on since fighting is inevitable when he's in this mood

5. Unhappy with his successful accounting position, your friend (husband, lover) tells you he has decided to go to law school. You think he has made a mistake and your first impulse is to tell him that
   a. you will try to help him achieve his goal in whatever way you can
   b. he should give law a trial run by taking some night courses
   c. you think it is a stupid idea and a waste of time

6. Friendships, love affairs, and even marriages often prove to be of short duration these days. Your relationship is still going because
   a. in spite of serious differences, you hope the situation will improve
   b. you are usually prepared to make whatever compromises are necessary
   c. you care for each other and meet one another's needs

7. You and your husband (lover, friend) work for the same advertising agency. A big promotion makes your salary much higher than his, and he begins to make insinuating remarks about your abilities. You
   a. counter his flippancy with a serious question: ask him why he has so little respect for you
   b. explain to him firmly that the raise is well-deserved, since you have more experience and a better education than he does
   c. offer to loan him the money you know he has been needing, instead of treating yourself to a luxury you can now afford

8. Without consulting you, the man in your life has invited his college chum and new wife to join you in the country for a weekend. Since you and he had planned to spend a quiet weekend together, you are annoyed at his lack of consideration. You
   a. tell him you prefer not to postpone your previous plans
   b. try to overcome your annoyance and make the most of the weekend

c. tell him to cancel the invitation or you aren't going

9. When the two of you have a serious talk, it is almost always because
a. you want to have a closer understanding of each other
b. you have had another argument
c. he is dissatisfied with you

10. The qualities in you that you think are special and unique no longer seem to please the man in your life. You
a. decide that he will have to take you as you are
b. try to discover a new way of being a person he will like better
c. find yourself getting more and more upset by what you have always thought was his chauvinistic attitude

ANSWERS AND HOW TO SCORE

Find the answers you chose and total your score.

1. a. Avoidance indicates hidden anger. It would be a good idea to get your feelings out into the open. Maybe what you want is to end the relationship. 1 point
   b. Succumbing to his pressure tells you that his decisions definitely dominate. As long as you let yourself be bullied by his unpleasantness, the situation can never improve. 2 points
   c. Acknowledging the game lets him know you're sensitive to his feelings but are unwilling to be controlled by them. Make sure the discussion that follows an encounter like this leads to greater understanding. 3 points
2. a. This answer suggests that your relationship has moved into the begrudging, gift-giving class. There's a reason: it could be that you are angry or getting fed up. 1 point
   b. If this was your response, your emphasis may be too much on holding things together by virtue of your input. The most tangible example of over-giving, whether it is emotional, financial, or physical, is very often to be found in too-expensive gifts. 2 points
   c. You are probably a scrupulously fair person who is concerned with smooth running relationships. You are careful to give neither too much nor too little. Marriage, love affair, or friendship, you will strike a reasonable bargain. 3 points
3. a. You are helplessly trapped in the situation, afraid of ending the relationship and caught by dependency. Maybe you have had enough but refuse to let yourself know it. 2 points
   b. You have a distance still to go before you can say that this is a really good relationship. However, your firmness indicates that you are determined to establish an equal and frank association. 3 points
   c. This is the repetitive response of a person who has gone through it once too often. Why are you still so willing to sit and wait for him? It's time to quit or to change: you are the only one who knows which. 1 point
4. a. You are a good companion, willing to offer help without being overly controlling or overly dependent; you can be active or passive depending on what the situation calls for. 3 points
   b. Take a closer look at your behavior. Why are you so eager to take the blame? Why do you shoulder the brunt of his bad moods when chances are they probably have nothing to do with you at all? 2 points
   c. The sound of fireworks is in the air if you have chosen this. Impatient with his moods and no longer willing to put up with them, you are ready for battle whenever the opportunity presents itself—an early "time-to-call-it-quits" sign. 1 point
5. a. Ask yourself why you want to give so much when you don't honestly think he's made such a wise move. Deceiving yourself and him can only lead to an unhappy end. 2 points
   b. This answer suggests that you understand his need for a change but that you also have a sound awareness of the difficulties he may encounter. You are willing to offer suggestions and ideas but not a wholehearted approval which you honestly don't feel. 3 points

   c. Don't congratulate yourself for honesty if you chose this response. Like pride, unrestrained honesty sometimes comes before a fall. In this case, an opportunity to tell him your feelings about him may have masqueraded as an "honest" appraisal of the situation.

6. Each of these responses contains a key word which symbolizes the relationship.

   a. Your involvement is characterized by hope, but perhaps you have been hoping for too long. 1 point

   b. The woman who is too eager to please can easily get locked into a doormat routine—you have compromised too often. You can change, though, and if he can't take the change, maybe it's time to call it quits. 2 points

   c. Caring is an integral part of what should happen between men and women. You are probably doing just fine. 3 points

7. a. If you have chosen this direct approach, your relationship may be tumultuous, but apparently it can withstand an occasional confrontation. 3 points

   b. Aggressive defensiveness puts him in his place, which is, in your mind, somewhere beneath yours. Your lack of understanding reveals that you may already have pulled out of the relationship emotionally but lack the courage to say so. 1 point

   c. Bribery is, at best, a temporary solution, since your generosity has little to do with the real issues. If you think he can be placated in this way, there must be some reason why you have so little respect for him, and that is something to think about. 2 points

8. a. Straightforwardness suggests that there is a healthy equality between you. You are probably adaptable enough to go, if you must, but are not hesitant to state your preferences. 3 points

   b. Giving in may be the last resort in this particular situation, but if it is your very first response, beware. You are probably giving more than a healthy relationship can manage. 2 points

   c. Ultimatums are the red flags of any affair. If you can get cooperation only by threatening to pull out, you both may be happier if you do just that. 1 point

9. a. You share a common desire to build a stronger relationship if you chose this answer, and you know that sharing thoughts and feelings is the way to accomplish that goal.

   b. You can talk out many problems, but if argument follows argument in rapid succession, you are spending too much energy on a relationship that is going nowhere. You may, in fact, be using those constant scenes to add a spark of excitement to an otherwise monotonous life together. 1 point

   c. If this is your response, you are trying too hard to please. Either he is a chronic complainer or you are lacking in courage. Whichever, discussions are probably not working for you. 2 points

10. a. You are solidly independent, and you know that good relationships are based on mutual acceptance. 3 points

   b. Embarking on a personal revolution to please anyone implies a great deal of insecurity. If you truly believe that this is the only way to salvage the relationship, consider seriously whether or not it is worth saving (it probably isn't). 2 points

   c. You seem to have been coming to a decision a little at a time. This one is likely to be the final blow. 1 point

WHAT YOUR SCORE MEANS

10–16: Your relationship is on shaky ground. True, you still care enough to fight, but there is more to life than fighting, and those angry scenes can be damaging to your self-esteem if they continue for too long. Take a good look at what you want. If you opt for out, then make the break. If you decide to stay in, then put your heads together and try to figure out why things go wrong so often. Perhaps professional couseling will help.

17–23: You probably find yourself going more than halfway too much of the time. Nonstop giving is a danger signal in any relationship. Question your motives. What is there about you or this relationship that causes you to over-extend so often?

24–30: You have a sound, balanced relationship. You try to be an interested and sensitive partner and usually go halfway. This means you expect your partner to go halfway, too.

☞ WHAT HIS SLEEPING STYLE MEANS

Do you know why a man sleeps either in the nude, with his back to you, or curled up clutching a pillow? According to psychologists, all those little nocturnal quirks mean something. To see whether you're attuned to the true significance of a man's boudoir behavior, take this illuminating quiz. Select the answers that seem most accurate to you about men in general, not necessarily your man, then discover how shrewd you are—about the total man!

1. Whether your place or his, regardless of climate, if a man always wears pajamas to bed, what does this mean to you? It means
   a. the man is a traditionalist in most things
   b. he's not proud of his body
   c. he's health conscious and fears drafts

2. Whether you're bundling in a mountain aerie or on a tropical isle, your man sleeps in the nude. This means
   a. after cultivating those muscles, he's anxious to show them off
   b. he wants his body contact pure . . . and fast
   c. he thinks pajamas are for kids

3. Wearing underwear to bed means
   a. he was probably in the army or went to military school

   b. rushing into sex is not his style
   c. he has a modest streak

4. During sojourns at your place, he makes a point of suggesting satin sheets. This means
   a. he'd really rather be in bed with a one-night-stand blonde
   b. he has a secret desire to be really naughty
   c. he has a healthy interest in new sensations

5. His boudoir abounds in ultrasoft coverings: a goosedown comforter, feather pillows, a cocoonish mattress. Therefore
   a. he's a sensuous type who loves natural delights
   b. when shopping for bedding, a persuasive salesgirl prevailed
   c. he's allergic to synthetics

By William M. Fine for *Cosmopolitan* magazine, May 1979. Reprinted with permission of the author.

6. Tasteful designer sheets—brown and white pinstripes or burgundy red—adorn his inner sanctum. This shows that
   a. down to the smallest detail, this man is a chic sophisticate
   b. he's going through one of his trendy phases
   c. good design and an aesthetically pleasing setting are important to him

7. The telephone always has to be on his side of the bed because
   a. a nearby phone provides him with a feeling of authority, even security
   b. he's not terribly romantic
   c. he's in some line of work in which a telephone is crucial

8. Wearing his watch to bed means
   a. he's been influenced by James Bond; the watch adds panache
   b. he always likes to know what time it is, and fears missing early morning appointments
   c. he's fond of the watch

9. In the middle of the night, he tells you he's ravenous, indicating that
   a. having satisfied one appetite, he's ready to tend to another
   b. this busy person may not have eaten all day
   c. he believes food adds to the whole sensuous mood of love-making, and that you both should enjoy a snack

10. If a man sleeps all curled up, you imagine
   a. that's the way he snoozes most comfortably
   b. he's a placid sort, at peace with the world
   c. his fetal position indicates a certain amount of immaturity

11. A man who frequently clutches his pil-low to his chest when asleep is
   a. inclined to be anxious, even with you around
   b. a little boy still; he had a doting mother
   c. fantasizing a woman—could be you—in his arms

12. At night he thrashes around twisting the bedclothes because
   a. he is a light sleeper or borderline insomniac
   b. this lover may fear the outside world
   c. he's a restless man, always hard to please

13. He sleeps on his side, turned away from you because
   a. though he likes sex, sleeping solo is his habit
   b. he's a loner who craves solitude
   c. he suffers from a touch of claus-trophobia and prefers facing an open space

14. When a man sleeps on his side, but facing you, that means
   a. even when sleeping, he feels affec-tionate
   b. the added proximity to you makes him feel secure
   c. during the night, he'll probably want to make love again

15. His favorite nighttime position is face up, on his back because
   a. he's sure this way is best for his posture
   b. the chap's confident, with a strong character
   c. any other position makes him feel smothered

16. Sleeping on his stomach probably in-dicates
   a. he longs to return to semi-infancy
   b. during the night he rolls over and settles there for no particular reason

c. though he can be cuddly with a woman, he feels more in control this way

17. You can't help but be disturbed by his gentle but audible snoring and feel
   a. there's a small streak of thoughtlessness in his nature
   b. he's sleeping like a baby because of a pleasurable, exhausting evening
   c. a cold or congenital condition causes it

18. If he awakes during the night and wants to make love again, you assume
   a. you've found a healthily sexy mate
   b. you're more attractive to him than other women
   c. something may be worrying him and he seeks escape in sex

19. Your man is a definite night owl and never retires until well after midnight
   a. he's a restless libertine, prone to excess in other areas
   b. chatter and another brandy with you keep him blissfully awake
   c. sooner or later, he'll leave you

20. Turning in early is his preference because he's
   a. a homebody, tranquilly committed to the domestic scene
   b. a borderline recluse, lacking energy to exploit the evening hours
   c. bored; a few more years and he'll be thoroughly dull

HOW TO SCORE

Give yourself 5 points for each "correct" answer.

1. a	**6.** c	**11.** c	**16.** c
2. b	**7.** a	**12.** a	**17.** c
3. c	**8.** b	**13.** c	**18.** a
4. c	**9.** c	**14.** a	**19.** b
5. a	**10.** a	**15.** b	**20.** a

WHAT YOUR SCORE MEANS

80–100: You do know a lot about men, and what a boon to your relationship! (See, you really had him psyched out all the while!)

50–75: Your grasp of the male species is fairly good. You should have picked up plenty of pointers here to add to your intuitive knowledge.

Under 50: Men are a mystery to you. But, don't worry too much, for now that you realize how important it is to be heedful of your man's bedtime manners, you're well on the way to enlightenment!

☞IS YOUR HUBBY A REAL LADIES' MAN?

Have you ever wondered if your husband is a ladies' man? Or at least more of a ladies' man than he would like you to believe? Test his virility:

1. Even when just going to work, does he take unusual care with his appearance?
   a. usually
   b. sometimes
   c. rarely

2. Do you think his sports clothes are much too showy?
   a. very much
   b. perhaps
   c. not really

3. Does he shower and change his clothes even before going out on what he describes as casual errands?
   a. often
   b. occasionally
   c. rarely

4. At parties, does he spend more time talking to women than to men?
   a. usually
   b. occasionally
   c. rarely

5. At parties, does he usually like to get some pretty woman by herself?
   a. frequently
   b. sometimes
   c. not usually

6. When women are present, does he pay more attention to them than to you?
   a. very obviously
   b. not often
   c. seldom or never

7. Do you find he exaggerates?
   a. frequently
   b. sometimes
   c. not noticeably

8. Have any of your women acquaintances reported that he's made suggestive remarks to them?
   a. more than a few
   b. one or two
   c. none

9. Do you have the impression that other husbands view him with distrust?
   a. definitely
   b. possibly
   c. not especially

10. Do you think he works hard at trying to appear younger than he really is?
   a. very much so
   b. somewhat
   c. not especially

11. Does he seem to have an unusual number of women acquaintances?
   a. seems that way
   b. very possibly
   c. not especially

12. Does he seem interested in single women?
   a. definitely
   b. moderately
   c. not really

HOW TO SCORE

Score the following points for each of your answers, then total your score.
a = 2 points
b = 1 point
c = 0 points

WHAT YOUR SCORE MEANS

Over 20: This suggests a compulsive ladies' man. He's so attracted to the role, he doesn't worry about covering his tracks.

16–19: A ladies' man, but with more discretion.

11–15: Borderline. He's got the urge, but can be tamed.

Less than 7: This man is a gem. He's probably as human as the others, but you're number one with him.

☞ DOES YOUR MAN WANT A LIBERATED WOMAN?

Everyone talks about women's liberation, but how does your man really feel? Is he frightened of liberated women? Is he really attracted to them? Does he want you to be more liberated or would he prefer you to be more feminine? Is he content with you just the way you are? Find out by asking him to take this quiz based on celebrity interviews from Wendy Leigh's books.

1. Barry Newman says that he believes a woman belongs in the kitchen and should be waiting by the phone for him to call her. Do you:
   a. Agree completely
   b. Disagree; his attitude is old fashioned
   c. Feel that it depends on what the woman wants

2. Barbara Cartland says men still feel romantic and chivalrous toward women and that a woman should never compete with a man. Do you:
   a. Agree completely
   b. Disagree; women are clever enough to compete
   c. Feel that women can enjoy romance and be competitive as well

3. Richard Burton says that the first thing you do with most women is to tell them how beautiful they are. Do you:
   a. Agree
   b. Dislike women who want insincere compliments
   c. Feel that a woman sometimes needs compliments, but not always

4. Rossano Brazzi says that a man is stronger than a woman—he is the lion and she is the lamb. The man always feels he must control women, not because he is a dictator but because he is the man. Do you:
   a. Agree completely
   b. Disagree; a man can be weaker than a woman
   c. I think that there should be a balance

5. Rod Steiger says that intelligence is very important to him in a woman. Do you:
   a. Disagree; it doesn't matter at all
   b. Agree; I must have an intelligent woman
   c. Usually agree

6. Cheryl Tiegs says she likes a man who is gentle. Do you:
   a. Feel that gentleness is not masculine
   b. Try to be gentle
   c. Think a man should alternate between gentleness and toughness

7. Doc Severinsen says that he likes a woman who gives him freedom and is interested in domestic things. Do you:
   a. Agree
   b. Disagree
   c. Agree, but look for other attributes as well

8. Zsa Zsa Gabor says she always liked men who were stronger than she was and that when she meets a weak man she scares him to death. Do you:
   a. Want a woman who needs you to always be strong
   b. Dislike a woman who doesn't allow you to be weak
   c. Like a woman who lets me change

9. Omar Sharif says he likes a woman who makes him feel strong by being ultrafeminine. Do you:
   a. Agree; if a woman isn't feminine, I feel less than masculine
   b. Disagree; I like to feel weak sometimes
   c. Disagree; I feel strong or weak independent of a woman

10. Peter Frampton says that he likes a woman who takes over in a love relationship. Do you:
    a. Never agree
    b. Agree all the time
    c. Sometimes agree

11. Deborah Harry says that she likes a man who is a friend to her and doesn't always act as if men are superior. Do you:
    a. Disagree; I have male friends and don't need women as friends
    b. Agree; I want the woman I am with to be my friend
    c. I want her to be a friend but also retain some mystery

12. Glenda Jackson says that if a woman is dissatisfied with a relationship she should tell the man very soon. Do you:
    a. Disagree; a woman shouldn't be opinionated
    b. Agree; a woman should be totally honest
    c. Yes, but she should pick the moment very carefully

WHAT YOUR SCORE MEANS

If your man answered mostly *A* he is the ultimate M.C.P. and wants you to be the passive, pretty, feminine woman. Make sure you avoid having opinions or interests of your own, say "yes" to his every whim, avoid telling him what you want and don't ever say "no" to him. You are with the right man if what you want is to be totally protected, dominated and to be *his* own person.

If he answered mostly *B,* he wants a liberated woman and has very definite ideas about what women's liberation means. He wants you to be strong, intelligent, aware and alive. Make sure you display your equality and intelligence all the time. You are with the right man if you want a friend, someone who gives you freedom and never allows you to be weak.

If he answered mostly *C,* he wants a different woman. That is, a woman who is totally different every day. He wants you to be strong, weak, liberated and feminine. Make sure you remember to switch roles hourly and never bore him. You are with the right man if you can take the pace. Just make sure that he is as versatile as he expects you to be.

SMART CONSUMERISM

☞ HOW EFFECTIVE IS YOUR FAMILY BUDGET?

Four elements—insight, input, involvement and income—are the main tools for building a family budget. The quiz below will start you on your way.

Because families are made up of individuals, husband and wife should take this test separately. Note that individual answers don't count. It is the final sum that establishes each partner's view of money and his financial profile. Because there are no right or wrong attitudes toward money, there are no right or wrong answers. The purpose of the quiz is to explore your attitudes so you can establish the strategies that will work best for you.

1. I have managed the bulk of my own expenses since I was
   a. 16 to 18 **b.** 18 to 21 **c.** over 21

2. I have my own checking account
   a. now **b.** at one time **c.** never

3. I have my own savings account
   a. now **b.** at one time **c.** never

4. I have trouble balancing my checkbook
   a. never **b.** sometimes **c.** usually

5. I run out of money before the end of the month
   a. never **b.** sometimes **c.** usually

6. I have been bothered by a creditor demanding payment on an overdue bill
   a. never **b.** sometimes **c.** usually

7. I worry about money
   a. never **b.** sometimes **c.** usually

8. I have been refused credit
   a. never **b.** once **c.** more than once

9. I am in debt
   a. never **b.** sometimes **c.** usually

10. I spend more than I planned
    a. never **b.** sometimes **c.** usually

11. I can afford what I want
    a. usually **b.** sometimes **c.** never

12. I regret what I buy
    a. never **b.** sometimes **c.** usually

13. I save regularly
    a. usually **b.** sometimes **c.** never

14. I enjoy spending money
    a. never **b.** sometimes **c.** usually

Excerpted from the book, *The Family Budget Book.* Copyright © 1978 by Alice Priest. Published by Lorenz Press and used with their permission.

15. I feel as if I've thrown my money away
   a. never   **b.** sometimes   **c.** usually

16. My wife/husband thinks I'm a
   a. penny pincher   **b.** prudent spender   **c.** spendthrift

17. I think I'm a
   a. penny pincher   **b.** prudent spender   **c.** spendthrift

18. I like extravagances
   a. never   **b.** sometimes   **c.** usually

19. Lack of money is my biggest problem
   a. never   **b.** sometimes   **c.** usually

20. I buy on impulse
   a. never   **b.** sometimes   **c.** usually

21. I buy ahead
   a. usually   **b.** sometimes   **c.** never

22. I have to juggle my creditors
   a. never   **b.** sometimes   **c.** usually

23. There are important things I want that I will_____get
   a. probably   **b.** possibly   **c.** never

24. I would go into debt to take a vacation
   a. never   **b.** sometimes   **c.** usually

25. I review my net worth
   a. each year   **b.** sometimes   **c.** never

26. I count on future raises or bonuses to pay some of my bills
   a. never   **b.** sometimes   **c.** always

27. I write checks and then have to cover them
   a. never   **b.** sometimes   **c.** usually

28. I have had checks bounce
   a. never   **b.** sometimes   **c.** often

29. I estimate my expenses well
   a. usually   **b.** sometimes   **c.** never

30. My monthly rent or mortgage payments are_____of my monthly after-tax income
   a. less than 25%   **b.** 25%   **c.** more than 25%

HOW TO SCORE AND WHAT YOUR SCORE MEANS

Score 1 point for each *a*, 3 points for each *b,* and 5 points for each *c* answer. Total your scores separately and then find out what your comparative scores and individual ones mean.

Comparative Scores
If your mate's score and yours are within 20 points of one another, you are very fortunate. You can choose identical strategies, and, since you both view money similarly, there are likely to be few arguments over spending and saving. If your scores are between 20 and 40 points of each other, you will have to make some adjustments to each other's preferences. Trade-offs work well here. One person might agree to buy less expensive clothes, for example, to satisfy the partner's craving for saving. A spouse in turn could agree that the next raise would bring more safety-valve dollars for each.

Individual Scores
Below 70: Chances are that you are a very careful spender and that you value saving more than you value spending. Because you are inclined to be overcautious, you may lose money by avoiding even sensible investments that will protect you against inflation. You must learn to consider money a tool rather than an end in itself. On the bright side, you will probably never be in tight financial circumstances.

70–110: You have probably achieved a reasonable balance between saving, spending, and credit. Your biggest effort should go toward increasing your income by carefully monitoring interest rates, credit, dividends, and buying strategies.

110–150: You probably tend to hold money very lightly and regard saving as an unnecessary evil. Your strategies must be chosen with an eye toward fooling yourself. Payroll savings plans should be used to the maximum allowed. If your company can arrange deductions from payroll checks for health insurance, life insurance, and accident insurance, sign up now, even if it cuts into your life style. It will only bother you for the first few months. If your company has a credit union, join it. Limit your credit cards to one or two major gasoline cards and only one consumer credit card. When you make a major purchase, put as much money down as you possibly can. It will only hurt once. If you find that short-term debt—that is, money you owe that must be paid within three months—exceeds your allowance for credit in the budget, put all credit cards away and use only cash to pay for all purchases until you've brought debt into line. Vow never to pay finance charges at department stores or credit card companies or to borrow from finance companies. Their interest rates rank among the highest in the United States—1½ percent per month or 18 percent per year for most credit cards, and up to 30 percent at finance companies. No bank is allowed to charge this much for personal credit. So, even though interest charges are deductible from federal income tax, you should still borrow from places that charge the lowest rates.

The time to decide how money will be spent is before, not after, choices are forced on you. If you decide on how the rest of your money is to be distributed only after you have already made a major commitment, you have lost the first battle because you have closed off some of your options.

But don't despair. You may have lost a battle, but you haven't lost the war. Your joint goals at this point will be to regain your financial freedom in as short a time as possible. It may be that you'll need an extra income for a while, or you'll need to cut back stringently on discretionary spending for recreation, car use, or clothing. But the time will come when you'll have the financial reins back in your own hands again.

☞HOMEOWNER'S ENERGY AUDIT

Here's a quiz to show you why some of your home heating dollars may be going up the chimney.

Score

1. What is your thermostat setting?

If your thermostat is set at 68°F or less during daytime in winter, score 6 points; 5 points for 69°; 4 points for 70°. If your thermostat is set above 70°, score 0. ____

If you have central air conditioning, and you keep your temperature at 78°F in the summer, score 5 points; 4 points for 77°; 3 points for 76°; 0 for below 76°. If you have no air conditioning, score 7 points. ____

In winter, if you set your thermostat back to 60°F or less at night, score 10 points; 9 points for 61°; 8 points for 62°; 7 points for 63°; 6 points for 64°; 5 points for 65°. If your thermostat is set above 65° at night, score 0. ____

2. Is your house drafty?

To check for drafts, hold a flame (candle or match) about one inch from where windows and doors meet their frames. If the flame doesn't move, there is no draft around your windows and you score 10 points. If the flame moves, score 0. ____

If there is no draft around your doors, add 5 points. If there is a draft, score 0. ____

If you have a fireplace and keep the damper closed, or block the air flow when it is not in use, add 4 points. ____

If you do not have a fireplace, add 4 points. ____

If you leave the damper open when the fireplace is not being used, score 0. ____

3. How well is your attic insulated?

Check with your electric or oil company to determine the number of inches of ceiling insulation recommended for your zone (average is six to eight inches). If you already have the recommended thickness of insulation, score 30 points. ____

If you have two inches less insulation than you should, score 25 points. ____

If you have four inches less insulation than you should, score 15 points. ____

If you have six inches less than you should, score 5 points. ____

If you have less than two inches of insulation in your attic, score 0. ____

4. Is your floor insulated?

If you have unheated space under your

Adapted from *Sylvia Porter's Money Book* by Sylvia Porter. Copyright © 1975, 1976 by Sylvia Porter. Reprinted by permission of Doubleday & Company, Inc.

house and there is insulation under your floor, add 10 points; if there is no insulation, score 0. ____

If you have a heated or air-conditioned basement, or if there is no space under your house, score 10. ____

5. Do you have storm windows?
If you live in an area where the temperature frequently falls below 30°F in winter, and you use storm windows, score 20 points. If you do not have storm windows, score 0. ____

TOTAL SCORE ____

WHAT YOUR SCORE MEANS

90 or above: You already are an energy saver and are using energy more efficiently, on the average, than eighty percent of America.

Under 90: You are spending more money on energy than you need to. Check the quiz again to see where you lost the most points. Those are the areas in which you can make the greatest savings in your annual fuel bill while also improving the comfort, appearance, and resale value of your home.

☞ HOW TO RATE YOUR DOCTOR

It would be handy if doctors were like baseball players and you could tell the good ones from the bad ones by looking up their batting averages. But evaluating physicians demands far more sophisticated judgments, with ever more at stake for you. So how do you do it? To help you with the task, we present the following rating test.

Choose the answers that best describe your physician and his practice.

1. Type of practice:
   a. multi-specialty group practice
   b. one-specialty group practice
   c. formal association of physicians practicing in separate locations
   d. loose association of physicians practicing in one location
   e. solo-practice physician

2. Hospital affiliation:
   a. full-time staff of a university-affiliated hospital
   b. part-time staff of a university-affiliated hospital
   c. staff member of a large community hospital (more than 250 beds) not affiliated with a university
   d. staff member of a small community hospital (fewer than 250 beds) not affiliated with a university
   e. no hospital privileges

3. Credentials:
   a. Board certified in a specialty that requires periodic recertification
   b. Board certified in a specialty that does not require periodic recertification
   c. Board eligible to become certified in specialty
   d. Board eligible at one time (no longer eligible to become certified)
   e. practicing physician—never board eligible

4. How did you select your doctor?
   a. recommended by intern, resident, and/or staff nurse
   b. recommended by other physician(s)
   c. recommended by other patient(s)
   d. recommended by a medical society
   e. no recommendation (selected from phone book)

5. School-affiliated internship and/or residency.
   Yes   No

6. Keeps good medical records and updates your medical history.
   Yes   No

7. Participates in continuing education programs sponsored by national or regional medical societies.
Yes   No

8. Personable and efficient office personnel.
Yes   No

9. Makes house calls.
Yes   No

10. Accepts Medicare and Medicaid patients.
Yes   No

11. Member of the local medical society.
Yes   No

12. Desk-side or bed-side manner:
    a. warm personality, good rapport with patients
    b. average personality, helpful attitude

HOW TO SCORE

Let's tally your doctor's qualifications and performance record. While there are no incorrect answers, certain ones are worth more. Assign the following points to each response and establish a total score.

1. a–5, b–4, c–3, d–2, e–1
2. a–5, b–4, c–3, d–2, e–1
3. a–5, b–4, c–3, d–2, e–1
4. a–5, b–4, c–3, d–2, e–1
5. Yes–4, No–0
6. Yes–4, No–0
7. Yes–4, No–0
8. Yes–3, No–0
9. Yes–2, No–0
10. Yes–2, No–0
11. Yes–1, No–0
12. a–3, b–1

WHAT YOUR SCORE MEANS

36–44: Outstanding. You've found your own Marcus Welby, M.D.

31–35: Excellent

21–30: Good

11–20: Fair

1–10: Poor. Take your body elsewhere!

☛ HOW MUCH DID YOU PAY FOR THAT?

Like all other traditional masculine and feminine roles in today's society, the roles married men and women play in spending the family income are also changing. Not long ago women were the only grocery shoppers, while the man of the household maintained the family car. Today, spending responsibilities are determined more by a person's interests, availability, and often their bargain hunting expertise.

The quiz that follows is a lot of fun and will help you better understand your family's spending patterns. Take it with your spouse for added enjoyment.

Have one person read aloud the following list of consumer goods and services. Each should record their estimate of what it would cost to buy these today. Note also who usually purchases each item.

	Cost		Cost
1. pound of lean hamburger	——	**10.** door mat	——
2. package of 20 two-ply plastic trash bags	——	**11.** queen-size bedspread	——
		12. laundry basket	——
3. three-pound bag of onions	——	**13.** five-quart mixing bowl (aluminum)	——
4. one-pound can of ground coffee	——		
5. quart of bleach	——	**14.** terry cloth dish towel	——
6. bottle of after-shave lotion	——	**15.** vacuum cleaner	——
7. tube of sun-screen lotion	——	**16.** lampshade	——
8. gallon of anti-freeze	——	**17.** pair of good snow tires	——
9. twenty-pound bag of wild bird seed	——	**18.** glass for a 12″ x 24″ window pane	——

	Cost		Cost
19. top-line router tool	——	**31.** pair of women's leather boots	——
20. linear foot of 1″ by 12″ clear pine	——	**32.** leather handbag	——
21. top line canoe	——	**33.** good quality, 100% wool sports jacket	——
22. aluminum back-packing frame	——	**34.** good leather belt	——
23. bottled-gas camp stove	——	**35.** wash, cut, and blow-dry for woman	——
24. set of socket wrenches	——	**36.** tune-up on the car	——
25. football	——	**37.** annual home-owners insurance premium	——
26. boy's hockey stick	——		
27. children's pajamas	——	**38.** annual water bill	——
28. pair of little girl's kneesocks	——	**39.** rent on a racquet-ball court for one hour	——
29. women's ski jacket	——		
30. women's 100% wool sweater	——		

ANSWERS AND WHAT YOUR SCORE MEANS

You'll have to check with your spouse or local newspaper advertising to see how close you were to current prices. Chances are, your best estimates were on those goods and services you yourself purchase. The most enjoyable way to score this test is by reading your answers together with your spouse. Some responses from each of you may very well be ridiculous. The point of this little exercise is not merely proving who knows more about spending but to provide an understanding of your spouse's spending requirements. This could help you recognize some overall family budgeting problems.

LOVE, SEX, AND MARRIAGE

☞ IS SEX AS DELICIOUS FOR YOU AS IT COULD BE?

A great deal of beautiful sexual feeling goes to waste because culture and parents teach that strong and uninhibited sexual feelings are bad and deserving of guilt. As a result, most people literally block off feelings of sexual pleasure from their bodies. This process is technically known as "body armoring." The degree to which you armor your body against sexual feeling determines the amount and variety of sexual enjoyment you can experience. Take the following test and see if you are depriving yourself of sexual pleasure.

1. Do you avoid looking into your partner's eyes while making love?
   Yes   No

2. Are you sexually attracted to partners who have a hard, sculptured look and appear aloof and cool?
   Yes   No

3. As you are approaching an orgasm do you do any of the following: clench your fists, bite down on your tongue, grind your teeth, furrow your brow or hold your breath?
   Yes   No

4. Does your body tense when your partner begins to climax?
   Yes   No

5. Do you often experience genital pain during intercourse, especially as you are about to climax?
   Yes   No

6. Do you feel guilty about allowing your partner to caress, fondle, and pet you without responding in kind?
Yes   No

7. Do you often feel inclined to giggle and laugh during lovemaking?
Yes   No

8. Are there areas of your body, genitals especially, that become very ticklish during lovemaking?
Yes   No

9. Do you sometimes get cramps in your legs and feet while making love?
Yes   No

10. As you feel yourself about to climax, are you capable of delaying or cutting off the orgasm?
Yes   No

HOW TO SCORE AND WHAT YOUR SCORE MEANS

Give yourself one point for each No answer. Then find your score in the appropriate category below.

10: Unarmored. You allow your sexual feelings to burst forth unrestrained. You feel that sexuality is a vital part of your life and want to obtain the most pleasure you can from your body. Guilt has no place in your sex life. You are easily aroused, love wild sensations, and enjoy your sensuality to the fullest.

8–9: Relatively unarmored. You're in the ball game and winning, no doubt about it. But something is keeping you from letting go all at once and enjoying the ecstasy of total loss of control in the sex act. Let go! Give in! You have nothing to lose but your armor and nothing to gain but joy.

5–7: Somewhat armored. You are allowing guilts and fears about having a good time sexually to interfere with your pleasure. You too often let thinking take the place of feeling. If you fall into this category you are in great danger of being a sexual hypocrite. You are always talking about how sexually free you are, but underneath you have nagging fears and doubts about your inadequacy.

2–4: Heavily armored. You are riddled with guilt about your sexual desires and expend most of your energy trying to suppress sexual feelings. You find many excuses for avoiding intercourse, usually using physical complaints such as "headache," "too tired," "cramps." You won't start enjoying sex to the fullest until you find out why you want to deprive yourself of pleasure.

0–1: Completely armored. When was the last time you felt anything? You have armored your body against sexual pleasure to the point where you do not even consciously recognize that you have sexual feelings and needs. You are a volcano of sexual energy contained within a hard, smooth shell of cool. You value intellect and dignity above all else. If you do engage in sexual relations, it is a mechanical pursuit, and you pride yourself on not becoming emotionally involved. Better find out why you are so afraid of your own sexuality before that volcano erupts!

☞ THE INTIMATE HOURS

Here is how the Intimate Hours Program works. First of all, there are no right or wrong answers to the fifty questions nor high or low scores. Couples who answer the questions must feel assured of complete privacy; no one but the two people directly involved are supposed to see the answers. Try to be alone—just the two of you. If possible, let the children sleep over at a friend's; or if that can't be arranged, make sure they're tucked in bed for the night. Turn off the telephone or take it off the hook. In a private setting, a man and woman can focus completely on each other.

You and your husband should sit down together to complete the questions. Either write your answers on the program itself, or just talk about your responses—whichever is easier and more enjoyable. It is important that you try to go through the entire program once, without interruption, instead of dealing with only a few questions at a time. Don't stop for lengthy discussion about any single question the first time around. Mark the questions that are especially interesting to either of you, then go back and talk about them. You need not be limited by the possible answers listed; they are there for convenience only. Add any answers you wish. You may also find that one question suggests other questions to you; that's fine, too, but be sure you and your mate discuss those as well.

Remember, give yourself plenty of time. Providing and receiving pleasure is what the program is all about: These are your Intimate Hours.

1. Does your mate enjoy making love as much as you do?
   a. always
   b. often
   c. sometimes
   d. rarely
   e. never

2. Does your mate want to make love as often as you do?
   a. yes
   b. no
   c. don't know

3. The most satisfactory lovemaking occurs when
   a. you and your mate reach orgasm simultanteously
   b. the woman reaches a climax first
   c. the man reaches climax first
   d. the woman has an orgasm, but the man does not
   e. the man reaches a climax, but the woman does not

4. Do you prefer making love
   a. in bright light

b. in soft light
c. in shadowy light
d. in total darkness
e. regardless of lighting conditions

5. If you have a TV set in your bedroom, do you turn it off
  a. before beginning any sex play
  b. after beginning sexual activity
  c. leave it on during sexual activity

6. There is something in sex that intrigues you or your mate, but that you have never engaged in.
  a. true
  b. false
  c. there was, but no longer
  d. don't know

7. If you make a purely affectionate move toward your mate, does that quickly arouse his/her desire for sexual intercourse
  a. too often
  b. often
  c. sometimes
  d. rarely
  e. never

8. How much time do you spend with your mate in foreplay?
  a. too much time
  b. not enough time
  c. enough time

9. Would you prefer that the entire sex act with your mate took (on the average)
  a. less time than it does now
  b. about the same time it does now
  c. more time than it does now?

10. It is more important for you/your mate to
  a. have one or more orgasms during sex
  b. be assured that you/your mate is loved during sex

c. be assured that you/your mate is loved after sex
d. be caressed and fondled after sex.

11. Presuming that your mate has an orgasm before you, is he/she still interested in activity stimulating you to orgasm?
  a. always
  b. often
  c. sometimes
  d. rarely
  e. never

12. A woman can sometimes feel used after sex, due to her mate's inattention to her after he has had an orgasm. Have you ever experienced this in your relationship?
  a. always
  b. often
  c. sometimes
  d. rarely
  e. never

13. When you do something that pleases your mate sexually, does he/she indicate his/her pleasure?
  a. verbally
  b. nonverbally
  c. not at all

14. Do you think that once a person has been aroused sexually, he/she
  a. always wants or needs an orgasm
  b. sometimes wants or needs an orgasm
  c. never needs an orgasm
  d. probably enjoys sex with or without an orgasm

15. Do you prefer making love
  a. in the morning
  b. in the afternoon
  c. in the evening
  d. at night, after dinner

e. late at night

f. time does not matter

16. Do you find your mate sexier when he/she goes to bed
    a. completely covered by gown or pajamas
    b. wearing tops only
    c. wearing bottoms only
    d. no difference

17. Does your mate like to see you naked?
    a. always
    b. often
    c. sometimes
    d. rarely
    e. never

18. You most prefer making love with your mate
    a. when neither of you has been drinking
    b. when you have been drinking, but your mate has not
    c. when your mate has been drinking, but you have not
    d. when both of you have been drinking

19. You prefer sex most
    a. in your own home
    b. in a hotel or motel
    c. in a resort
    d. in a romantic place

20. Do you think that, sexually, your mate is
    a. too aggressive
    b. aggressive enough
    c. passive
    d. too passive

21. During intercourse, you and your mate generally use
    a. only one favorite position
    b. only a couple of positions
    c. several positions
    d. many different positions

22. You know just how to arouse your mate sexually, and can do so
    a. always
    b. often
    c. sometimes
    d. rarely

23. What are your mate's three most erogenous zones—those areas of his/her body where contact is most likely to arouse him/her? (Fill-in)
    a.
    b.
    c.

24. Are your mate's erogenous zones the same today as they were when you were first married?
    a. yes, all of them
    b. most of them
    c. some of them
    d. one of them
    e. none of them
    f. don't know

25. What kind of literature, photos, films, sounds or aromas stimulate your sexual desires?
    a. romantic stories
    b. pornography
    c. art or underground films
    d. certain kinds of music
    e. sexy love stories
    f. erotic art
    g. incense
    h. none of the above
    i. other

26. Which of the items listed immediately above diminishes your sexual desires?
    a.
    b.
    c.
    d.
    e.
    f. none of them

27. After an unpleasant discussion or argument with your mate, do you go to bed angry and use sex as a way of making up?
   a. always
   b. often
   c. sometimes
   d. rarely
   e. never

28. Deviations from, or experimenting with, any methods of sex other than coital intercourse are
   a. perverted
   b. dirty
   c. interesting
   d. stimulating
   e. essential to marital sexual enjoyment

29. If the telephone rings while you are engaged in sex with your mate
   a. you ignore it
   b. you answer it
   c. if it is for you, you answer it briefly and hang up
   d. if it is for your mate, he/she answers it briefly and hangs up
   e. you/your mate answer it for whatever length that conversation would normally take

30. It is more important that the wife keep her figure to remain sexually appealing to the husband than it is for the husband to maintain his physique in order to remain sexually appealing to her.
   a. definitely
   b. probably
   c. possibly
   d. definitely not

31. If you found sex with your mate unsatisfactory for a considerable time, would or should you
   a. give your mate some sex books to read as a hint
   b. suggest changes
   c. become more assertive

   d. put up with the unsatisfactory sex
   e. avoid sex on various pretexts whenever you could
   f. compensate by masturbating
   g. find more satisfactory sex elsewhere
   h. tell your mate directly and openly that his/her sexual performance bothers you

32. When your mate wants to make love, he/she generally approaches you
   a. romantically
   b. seductively
   c. pleasantly
   d. in a matter-of-fact manner
   e. in the same way every time
   f. demandingly, as if it is your duty to have sex whenever your mate wishes
   g. saying or doing nothing other than hoping you want sex at the same time he/she does

33. When you or your mate want to show appreciation or love for the other, how often do you attempt a super sexual performance?
   a. always
   b. often
   c. sometimes
   d. rarely
   e. never

34. Do you or does your mate withhold sex to get even for some real or imagined wrong?
   a. always
   b. often
   c. sometimes
   d. rarely
   e. never

35. How do you avoid your mate's sexual advances when you are not in the mood?
   a. claim headache or other physical illness
   b. distract him/her with another conversation

c. drink alcohol
d. go out
e. go to sleep
f. complain about money
g. show anger
h. bring up children's problems
i. watch TV
j. read
k. other _____

36. Arguments between you and your mate are generally resolved
   a. very quickly
   b. in a fairly short time
   c. slowly
   d. only after a very long time
   e. frequently they are not resolved— just shelved

37. Are you as conscientious now about your personal grooming habits when you go to bed with your mate as you were when you first went together?
   a. always
   b. often
   c. sometimes
   d. rarely
   e. never

38. When you got married, did you expect there would be periods of time— cycles—when your sexual activity with your mate would be substantially better than at other times, and obviously, times when it would be much worse?
   a. yes
   b. yes, but didn't anticipate either the extremes or the duration of the cycles
   c. no

39. Does your mate tend to regard sex
   a. very seriously
   b. too seriously
   c. with a little humor
   d. with a great deal of humor
   e. too lightly

40. Do you think that your sexual fantasies should remain secret and totally private?
   a. always

b. some of them
c. no, they should be shared

41. Sexual fantasies
   a. enhance your enjoyment of sex
   b. diminish your enjoyment of sex
   c. destroy your enjoyment of sex
   d. have no effect on your enjoyment of sex

42. Is there something in sex that your mate once attempted with you that you did not like, rejected, or discouraged that you would like to try now?
   a. quite a few things
   b. a couple of things
   c. one thing
   d. nothing

43. Is one of you the dominant partner in lovemaking and one the submissive?
   a. always
   b. usually
   c. no

44. Would you like to reverse these roles on occasion?
   a. yes
   b. no

45. Do you prefer that sex with your mate
   a. be planned for a particular time, almost like a date
   b. be totally spontaneous

46. Do you look forward to making love?
   a. regularly
   b. sometimes
   c. no, prefer spontaneous, unplanned sex

47. Do you tell your mate that you enjoy sex with him/her?
   a. frequently
   b. occasionally
   c. rarely
   d. never

48. Do you and your mate say "I love you" with what you consider sufficient frequency?
   a. yes
   b. no

49. Closely following orgasm, does your mate prefer to
   a. hold you
   b. talk
   c. turn on TV
   d. go to sleep
   e. other _____

50. Following orgasm, would you prefer that your mate
   a. held you
   b. talked
   c. turned on TV
   d. went to sleep
   e. other _____

☛ TEST YOUR MAN'S LOVE RATING VS. LEADING CELEBRITIES

This special test let's you compare your Romeo's ideas on women, sex, and love with the love secrets of famous national stars. Try these questions on your husband, lover, or friend, and see how he rates as a Casanova.

1. Zsa Zsa Gabor says a woman can't learn to be sexy and attractive. Do you think you could help a woman to be more sexy and attractive?
   a. No, I wouldn't want to change her.
   b. Yes, I could help her to learn to please me.
   c. Yes, I could.
   d. No. I could teach her to be more free, though.

2. Michael Caine says there is no way you can tell if a woman is sexy by just looking at her. Do you agree?
   a. No, but I don't think about sex when I first meet a woman.

   b. No. I can always tell by the shape of her mouth.
   c. Yes. Even if she isn't, there is always some hope.
   d. Yes. There is no relationship between appearance and sexiness.

3. Doc Severinsen says beauty doesn't make a woman sexier or less sexy. How do you feel?
   a. If a woman is beautiful, then I always find her sexy.
   b. I would rather have a beautiful woman than a sexy woman, and sexy women aren't always more beautiful.

By Wendy Leigh. Reprinted by permission from *The Star*, News Group Publications, Inc.

c. Beautiful women are too vain to be really sexy.

d. I agree with Doc Severinsen.

4. Oliver Reed says he finds a woman sexy if she is a willing slave. Do you agree?

a. No, relationships should be romantic.

b. Yes, as long as she is active as well.

c. No, I am equally interested in her desires.

d. Yes, sometimes.

5. Elliot Gould says it's great if a woman asks for what she wants in a relationship. Do you agree?

a. No, I dislike a woman who is too forward.

b. No, I know all about a woman's desires when I meet her.

c. Yes, but with actions not words.

d. Yes, I like her to tell me her desires.

6. Barbara Cartland says that men nowadays are terrified that they won't be good lovers. What do you think your partner's standards are; what kind of lover does she long for?

a. A man who loves her.

b. A man who takes her out to expensive dinners and doesn't go out with other women.

c. A man who is very physical.

d. A man who offers variety and experiments sexually.

7. James Caan says he thinks love makes a women sexy and attractive. What do you think?

a. Yes, love is essential to relationships.

b. Yes, I find a woman is sexy and attractive to me if she loves me. But it doesn't matter if I love her.

c. No, but I like it if a woman really desires me.

d. No, sometimes a woman is sexier and more attractive if I don't love her.

8. Vidal Sassoon says that Marlene Dietrich is his fantasy woman. Who is your fantasy woman?

a. Olivia Newton-John.

b. Suzanne Somers.

c. Farrah Fawcett.

d. Faye Dunaway.

9. Omar Sharif says he doesn't particularly like slim women. How do you feel?

a. I like women to be small and dainty.

b. I like women who look like models.

c. I like women who are athletic.

d. I like all types of women.

10. Barry White says women of nineteen are as sexy as women of forty-five. What age group do you find most attractive?

a. 16–20

b. 20–30

c. 30 upwards

d. all ages

11. Cloris Leachman says women don't need to know tricks in order to be sexy and attractive. What do you think?

a. Women should learn to be mysterious.

b. Women should learn to look dazzling.

c. Women should look natural.

d. Women should learn the trick of changing their image and looking different.

12. Isaac Hayes says he prefers women who are shy and standoffish. How do you feel?

a. I like women who are shy and feminine.

b. I like women who don't talk too much.

c. I like women who are flirtatious and encouraging.

d. I like women to be aggressive some times, and standoffish at others.

13. Richard Burton says a woman is sexy and attractive if you can talk to her

and laugh after making love. Do you agree?

a. I think relationships should be mystical and not discussed.

b. I don't like women who chatter.

c. I like a woman to communicate the way she feels about me.

d. I like a woman to communicate all her desires.

14. Joe Namath says his mother doesn't allow him to talk about sex. What is your reaction to this test?

a. I found it embarrassing and dangerous to the romance of relationships.

b. I know how I feel about relationships and don't need to discuss my feelings.

c. It was fun, I wish I knew everything my partner thought about me.

d. It was helpful. It enabled me to express my feelings to my partner about our relationship.

HOW TO SCORE AND WHAT IT MEANS

Tally the number of a, b, c, or d answers and read below to discover your Casanova's rating.

Mostly a's: He is Prince Charming who needs you to be his Cinderella. He respects his mother, adores his sisters and hates women to be his equal. When you first met, he wined and dined you, declared that he adored you, and showered you with presents. This man wants a woman who follows wherever he leads; who knits, sews, adores hearts and flowers, devours romantic novels, and never really exists as an independent woman. In fact, you will probably find out that he doesn't really want a woman at all—merely a fairy princess.

Mostly b's: He is a macho man who wants a status woman. He isn't really a lover at all and would much rather talk to men, tell lockerroom stories and watch baseball on TV. He wants you to be a cook in the kitchen, a status symbol in the living room, and a Barbie Doll in love. He will never be your partner. He may respect you, but he won't want to spend much time with you. He will compliment you on your model looks, and when he walks into a room with you, loves everyone to stare in admiration and envy. Just remember, this man only wants you for the status you bring him, not for yourself.

Mostly c's: He is a Casanova who wants every woman to react like a cheerleader. He loves pleasing you, so long as you keep telling him how pleased you are. He'll want to hear about all the other men in your life, especially if you tell him that he is more masculine and attractive than any of them. And he'll never stop telling you about all the women he has known, the women he wants to know, and, above all, the millions of women who are desperate to get to know him. He thinks he is a Valentino, Rubirosa, and Warren Beatty all rolled into one. Everything will be fine, as long as you keep on saying yes and never ever stop applauding.

Mostly d's: He is a liberated man who wants a liberated woman. He knows and loves everything about women. He is able to move from romance to sex, from wildness to tenderness, from domination to worship, and all in one day. One minute he will act like your father, the next like your son. He will bring out all your wickedness and help you to enact all your most far-out fantasies. He will titillate you, explore you, and exhaust you. Just make sure that his responsiveness to love is matched by his responsiveness to life—that he relates to all of you and not just to you as the dream modern woman.

☞ MARITAL CHECKUP: A QUIZ FOR COUPLES TO TAKE TOGETHER

Just as a medical checkup shows the condition of our body, sometimes we need a marriage checkup to determine the condition of our relationship. To take this quiz, each partner should number from 1 to 35 on a separate piece of paper. Check only those questions that apply to your feelings or behavior, or fill in the blanks where indicated. After you have both completed the answers, read the analysis of your replies.

1. When my spouse and I are separated for a few days, I miss him/her terribly, but when we're together again I wonder why I felt so very lonely during the time we were apart.

2. I have never told my spouse a lie.

3. I often wonder whether I would have been happier married to someone else.

4. It hurts me when I see other people take advantage of my spouse.

5. My spouse is a better parent than I am.

6. When my spouse and I go out to a restaurant alone, we seem to find it hard to find things to talk about.

7. My spouse and I never fight.

8. I don't like to burden my spouse with my personal troubles, so when I have problems at work or with other people, I make sure that I keep them to myself.

9. I feel lucky that my spouse chose me, since he/she is more desirable than I am.

10. My spouse and I have no secrets from each other—we tell each other everything.

11. I don't like most of my spouse's friends, but because I love him/her, I force myself to go out with them socially.

12. When I see that my spouse is upset, I give him/her advice that I think helps him/her solve those problems.

13. Three activities that I like to do with my spouse are _____, _____, and _____.

Excerpted from "How Healthy Is Your Marriage?" by Sally Wendkos Olds, *Ladies' Home Journal*, January 1978. Reprinted by permission of Julian Bach Literary Agency. Copyright © 1978 by Sally Wendkos Olds.

14. I can't imagine what living with my spouse ten years from now will be like.

15. I need to protect my children from my spouse's unfair treatment of them.

16. It takes the romance out of our sexual relationship if I tell my partner what I like during lovemaking.

17. I feel a husband and wife should never spend a night away from each other if they can possibly help it.

18. Whenever we have a bad fight, I think that we might break up.

19. Since it's embarrassing to admit to my partner when I've made a stupid mistake, I usually avoid talking about my errors.

20. I often have the feeling that my spouse's job or the children are more important to him/her than I am.

21. Our fights usually start over something small (like the eggs being overcooked or one of us being late), but then they have a tendency to escalate until our really deep angers with each other come out.

22. If my spouse knew my secret fears, he/she would think less of me, so I try to keep them to myself.

23. The three things that worry my partner the most are _____, _____ and _____. The three things that worry me the most are _____, _____ and _____.

24. I have never once questioned my wisdom in choosing my spouse.

25. I think sex is vastly overrated.

26. I know what my spouse is going to say about most topics so well that I could almost finish his/her sentences myself.

27. I don't like it when I have to go to a party without my spouse.

28. I would rather be with my spouse doing nothing than be involved in an interesting activity without him/her.

29. Because I think a little mystery keeps a relationship exciting, there are certain feelings and experiences I don't tell my spouse.

30. Our sexual relationship is so exciting that I have never fantasized about making love with anyone else.

31. Once the vows of fidelity have been broken, no matter what, the marriage is irreparably damaged.

32. My partner and I have worked out our own separate jobs in running our marriage, and it works out best when we each stay in our own sphere and away from each other's.

33. I don't like to hurt my partner's feelings, so I usually don't say anything when he/she does little things that annoy me.

34. I look forward to the next stage in our marriage—when we will have children, when the children are all in school, or when they are grown and out of the house.

35. We hardly ever fight, but when we do, it often takes us days to overcome the bitterness between us.

HOW TO SCORE AND WHAT YOUR SCORE MEANS

The Perfect Marriage. Questions 2, 7, 10, 24, 27, 28 and 30 explore some of the myths many people have about what a healthy marriage should be. What are these myths? That the perfect marriage fills all the emotional needs of both spouses, rendering relationships and activities outside the marriage unnecessary; that it is free of conflicts; that the perfect marriage is an all-encompassing blend of two personalities fused into one entity.

A marriage like this is apt to suffocate a couple. It leaves no breathing space for either partner. It leaves no room for marriage as a joining of two individuals who wish to share a life yet still retain their own personalities, values, and goals. It leaves no room for the growth that can sprout from the points of stress within a relationship.

If you check five or more of questions 2, 7, 10, 24, 27, 28 and 30, you may want to look more closely at your expectations of marriage. Are they unrealistic? Are you repressing normal conflicts? Are you ignoring the seeds of future trouble?

Companionship. Questions 1, 6, 11, 13, 17, 27 and 28 examine your ability to enjoy each other's company. Since many studies show that the primary reason people marry is for companionship, problems in this area can upset marital satisfaction.

If you checked questions 1 or 6, or if you could not complete 13, you may be feeling lonely within your marriage.

If you checked questions 17, 27 or 28, you may be overdoing the companionate side of marriage, submerging your identity and becoming overly dependent on your spouse.

Communication. Questions 2, 7, 8, 10, 16, 18, 19, 21, 22, 23, 29, 33 and 35 delve into the crucial area of the way you and your spouse share your thoughts and feelings. If you checked questions 8, 16, 19, 21, 22, 29, 33 or 35, take a close look at the brakes you've put on what you're willing to share. So often we want understanding from our partner, yet we think, "If he loved me, he'd know how I feel." But even lovers are not mind readers.

When we keep silent about important matters, resentments often seethe beneath a deceptively calm surface, only to erupt in destructive marital storms.

In response to 23, if each of you correctly names two out of the spouse's three greatest worries, you are probably in close emotional touch.

On the other hand, if you checked 2 or 10, ask yourself why you need to tell all. People sometimes speak hurtful words in the name of truth. Before you confide a touchy issue to your mate, ask yourself why. Do you want to relieve a guilty conscience? To test love? Or are you trying to bring into the open an issue that has been dividing you?

In general, it is healthy to speak out early about resentments, hurts, and irritations before these feelings fester. When it is hard to sort out what to share and what to keep private, it is often helpful to seek professional guidance.

Commitment. How firm is your resolve to make your marriage work? To overcome obstacles, settle conflicts, work toward shared goals, build a future together?

If you checked questions 3, 14 or 18, and did *not* check 34, you may want to assess your sense of commitment to your partner. It is only natural, of course, to have *some* questions about whether you've made the right decisions in the past and are headed in the right direction for the future. It's normal to wonder occasionally, "Would I have been happier if I had married someone else?" But when these doubts surface constantly, they rob you of a sense of security in your future and turn minor problems into dread forebodings of disaster.

Sexuality. If you checked 30, you are probably repressing harmless thoughts experienced by virtually everyone. If you checked 31, you may be in the grip of a belief that can shatter the covenant between you more than the experience of infidelity itself. Extramarital sex can have a variety of meanings, depending on the particular circumstances in which it occurs. It always needs to be looked at, but it need not be seen as a sign that a marriage is over.

Mutual Respect. A successful marriage rests on a cornerstone of mutual respect. You feel confident that your spouse can manage his own life well, that he is an individual in his own right, and that he upholds his end of the relationship. Questions 4, 12, 15, 17, 22, 25, 26, 30, 31, 32 and 35 are all measures of the respect you bear to each other.

If you checked questions 4, 12, 15 or 26, ask yourself whether you really admire your spouse. If you feel you have to protect him from being taken advantage of, that he needs your advice in handling problems, or that he's not an effective parent, what does that say about your opinion of his coping skills?

Question 32 relates to your ability to let your spouse step out of his or her original marital role. Interaction becomes strained when one partner is threatened by changes in the other. When you can't let your partner be flexible, you are reacting to him not as he is, but as you have created him in your mind.

Self-Esteem. Questions 5, 9, 19, 20, 22, 27 and 28 bring out your feelings about yourself. How we feel about ourselves affects the ties we form with others. If you checked five or more of these questions, you seem to be undervaluing yourself and your contributions to the marriage.

Just as a family doctor might recommend that you consult a specialist because of some troubling symptom, you may decide that an issue raised by your marital self-examination is too difficult for you and your spouse to handle by yourselves. If so, you may want to call upon a professional marriage couselor. In many cases, a therapist is able to reduce a problem that had seemed particularly overwhelming. At other times, a counselor can help two individuals handle as positively as possible the difficult decision to separate. Either way, the counselor's support can help both partners to better understand themselves, each other, and the dynamics of their relationship.

☞ WHAT YOU DON'T KNOW ABOUT YOUR SPOUSE

No matter how long you have been married—or how happily—there is plenty you don't know about your spouse. And knowing your mate's background, habits, and preferences is important—for knowing is a sign of caring.

Here's a quiz for you and your spouse. Take turns completing the test, then correct each other's paper, giving one point for each correct answer.

1. What's your mother-in-law's maiden name?

2. What book has your spouse read most recently?

3. Can you list every pet your spouse has owned, including childhood family pets?

4. Which parts of the newspaper does your spouse read first?

5. For whom did your spouse vote in the last presidential election?

6. What is your spouse's shoe size?

7. Did your spouse collect anything as a child? What?

8. If your spouse had to name the most attractive thing about his/her body or face, what would it be?

9. Has your spouse ever bought a lottery ticket?

10. Who is your spouse's number one friend?

11. In a restaurant, what salad dressing does your spouse usually order?

12. Does your spouse remember where you went on your first date together?

13. What household chore does your spouse hate most?

14. Does your spouse weigh him/herself at least once a week?

15. Name any one of your spouse's former teachers.

16. How did your spouse learn to drive a car?

17. What was your spouse's first job? (Including part-time jobs as a youngster.)

18. Who is your spouse's favorite relative, outside the immediate family?

By Dan Carlinsky. Reprinted by permission of the author.

19. Who is the *least* favorite?

20. What was your spouse's grade average in high school?

21. If your spouse could choose any car in the world, which would it be? (A bonus point if you know the color.)

22. How often does your spouse wash his/her hair?

23. How old was your spouse on his/her first date?

24. What's your spouse's favorite flavor of ice cream?

25. If your spouse was limited to one TV show a week, what's the one he/she couldn't do without?

26. What's your spouse's favorite restaurant?

27. What piece of furniture in your house would your spouse most like to replace?

28. Did your spouse have his/her own record player in high school?

29. Can your spouse recite the number on his/her car license plate?

30. What does your spouse think is the most common cause of fights in your house?

WHAT YOUR SCORE MEANS

Above 26: Very impressive.

20–25: Not bad, but pay more attention.

Below 25: Better consider a cram course; you're not tuning in.

☞ THE GENERAL APTITUDE TEST BATTERY

This general battery of tests measures your overall aptitude and was developed by the United States Employment Service in 1947. Since that time many schools and organizations, both public and private, have found it to be the best validated multiple aptitude test battery in existence for use in vocational guidance.

There are four main categories in this examination: (1) Name Comparison, (2) Computation, (3) Three Dimensional Space, (4) Vocabulary. You should work on each section independently, allowing yourself exactly six minutes on each section. Try to answer all questions since scoring is based on the number of *correct* answers. You are better off answering a question that is uncertain rather than leaving it blank. There is only one right answer to each question.

Part 1—Name Comparison

Instructions

In this section you will be determining if names given are the same or different. Here are two examples:

a. S.G. Barton—S.G. Barton S   D

The two names are *exactly* the same. You should circle the S.

b. Harry Steiner—Harry Stiener S   D

These two names are different, so you should circle the D.

Do the following exercises in the same way. Circle S if they are the *same* or the D if they are *different*. You have 6 minutes.

1. Ace Bros.—Ace Bros.   S   D
2. Saunders Co.—Saunders Co.   S   D
3. E. O. Ulrick—E. O. Ulrich   S   D
4. USL Batteries—USL Batteries   S   D

From the U.S. Department of Labor, Manpower Administration.

5. Kosack & Co.—Kosack & Co.   S   D
6. Jos. A. Jones—Jos. A. Jones   S   D
7. Zirkle Co.—Sirkle Co.   S   D
8. Galea Co.—Galea Co.   S   D
9. Philip Carey—Phillip Carey   S   D
10. Lewis Co.—Louis Co.   S   D
11. A. Daigger Co.—A. Dagger Co.   S   D
12. Blackistone, Inc.—Blackstone, Inc.   S   D
13. Cohen, A. & Co.—Cohen, A. & Co.   S   D
14. Amer. Vacuum Co.—Amer. Vacuum Co.   S   D
15. Herzmark & Safer—Herzmack & Safer   S   D
16. Keneth Leizear—Kenneth Leizear   S   D
17. Hamilton Nat'l Bank—Hamilton Nat'l Bank   S   D
18. Menehan's Drugs—Menehan's Drugs   S   D
19. Pierce Transfer Co.—Pierce Transfer Co.   S   D
20. Ransdel—Ransdel   S   D
21. Bierton Brothers—Beirton Brothers   S   D
22. Edelin John A.—Edelin John A.   S   D
23. Shight Wagon Mfg. Co.—Shight Wagon Co.   S   D
24. Forshyth's Soles—Forsyth's Soles   S   D
25. Acme Iron Works—Acem Iron Works   S   D
26. B. R. Acker Corp.—B. R. Acker Corp.   S   D
27. Embrey & Wood, Inc.—Embrey Wood, Inc.   S   D
28. K. Frazier Agency—K. Frazer Agency   S   D
29. How Co., Inc.—Howe Co., Inc.   S   D
30. Jaye Binghampton—Jaye Binghamton   S   D
31. Terminix Co.—Terminix Co.   S   D
32. L. Fritter & Son.—L. Frither & Son   S   D
33. Atlas Mfg. Co.—Atlas Mfg. Co.   S   D
34. Belfield S. C.—Bellfield S. C.   S   D
35. Heidenreich Bros.—Heidenriech Bros.   S   D
36. Payne & Waechter—Payne & Waechter   S   D
37. Al Simone—Al Simone   S   D
38. J. Harding & Co., Inc.—J. Harding & Co., Inc.   S   D
39. Harry Poretsky—Harry Portesky   S   D
40. A. W. Lee Inc.—A. W. Lee Inc.   S   D
41. Prima Agency—Prime Agency   S   D

42. Frick Co.—Frich Co.   S   D

43. Dumayer—Dunayer   S   D

44. R. C. Freas Company—R. C. Freas Company   S   D

45. Copenhaver—Copenhawer   S   D

46. Leeth Bros., Inc.—Leith Bros., Inc.   S   D

47. Beuchlers Ltd.—Beuchler Ltd.   S   D

48. Royal Electric Co.—Royal Electric Co.   S   D

49. Wyn-Deen Travel Co.—Wyn-Deen Travel Co.   S   D

50. Nat'l Museum—National Museum   S   D

51. S. Abrams—S. Abrams Co.   S   D

52. F. J. Detorie Roofing—F. J. Detoree Roofing   S   D

53. Veal Bros.—Veal Bros.   S   D

54. Pa. Products Co.—Pa. Products Co.   S   D

55. Griffit Co.—Griffitt Co.   S   D

56. J. S. Le Feure—J. S. Le Feuer   S   D

57. Aetna, Inc.—Etna, Inc.   S   D

58. E. E. Fox Co.—E. E. Fox Co.   S   D

59. R. W. Bohrer Ltd.—R. W. Bohrer Ltd.   S   D

60. Cary, Inc.—Chary, Inc.   S   D

61. Sheaffer's—Shaeffer's   S   D

62. DuPont Works, Inc.—DuPont Works, Inc.   S   D

63. Robey & Tom—Robey & Tom   S   D

64. McGrady Mfg. Co.—McGrady Mfg.   S   D

65. Frances Mateoux—Francis Mateoux   S   D

66. World Tourists, Inc.—World Tourist, Inc.   S   D

67. Wood Conversion Co.—Wood Conversion Co.   S   D

68. S. H. Hinest Co., Inc.—S. N. Hinest Co., Inc.   S   D

69. Vita Health Food Co.—Vita Health Food Co.   S   D

70. Bates Co.—Bates Co.   S   D

71. Berrall & Locraft—Berrall Locraft   S   D

72. Carlyle Apts.—Carlyln Apts.   S   D

73. Bee Hive Express Co.—Bee Hive Espress Co.   S   D

74. Ferndale's Home—Ferndale's Home   S   D

75. Morton Steiner—Morton Stiener   S   D

76. Soper A. F. & Co.—Soper A. F. & Co.   S   D

77. Fred S. Gichner—Fred S. Gichner   S   D

78. Amer. Gas Light Co.—Amer. Gas Light, Inc.   S   D

79. G. E. Norris—G. E. Morriss   S   D

80. Phillips & Bird Co.—Phillipps & Bird Co.   S   D

81. Prest-O-Lite—Prest-O-Light   S   D

82. Nat'l Roofing Co.—Nat'l Roofing Co.   S   D

83. Mt. Valley Co.—Mt. Valley Co.   S   D

84. Dr. H. A. Locke's—Dr. H. A. Lock's   S   D

85. Samuel Pierce—Samuel Peirce   S   D

86. Capital Cigar Co.—Capital Cigar Co.   S   D

87. Men's Shop—Men's Shop   S   D

88. Geo. C. Gallaudet—Geo C. Galludet   S   D

89. Alto. Apts.—Alto. Apts.   S   D

90. Austin V. G.—Austin V. G.   S   D

91. G. W. Irvings Jr.—G. W. Irvings Jr.   S   D

92. Claire Manor—Clair Manor   S   D

93. Hufnagel Coal Co.—Hufnagel Coal Co.   S   D

94. A. B. Shade Co.—A. B. Shade Co.   S   D

95. Pernt-Craft—Pernt-Craft   S   D

96. A. A. A. Machine Co.—A. A. A. Machine Co.   S   D

97. Billers Corp.—Biller Corp.   S   D

98. Nat'l Trade Mark Co.—Nat'l Trade Mark Co.   S   D

99. Southern Sales Co.—Southern Sale Co.   S   D

100. Lowdermilk Wm. H. & Co.—Lowdermilk Wm. H. & Co.   S   D

101. Garwood—Garwood   S   D

102. Jno. Fayed Co.—Jno. Fayed & Co.   S   D

103. Warner-Fruhaf—Warner-Fruhaf   S   D

104. Stones Co.—Stones Co.   S   D

105. Cahoon, Inc.—Cahoon, Inc.   S   D

106. Bazzuro Co.—Bazurro Co.   S   D

107. Ruarke Co.—Ruarke Co.   S   D

108. Stuart's—Stuart's   S   D

109. Naples House—Maples House   S   D

110. L. H. Hazleton—L. H. Hazlton   S   D

111. M. M. Coleman—M. M. Coleman Co.   S   D

112. Uniform Shop, Inc.—Uniform Shop, Inc.   S   D

113. Nat'l Office Co.—Nat'l Office Co.   S   D

114. Owen R. Edmonston—Owen R. Edmonton   S   D

115. James A. Fribush—James A. Friebush   S   D

116. Armour Liquor Shop—Armour Liquor Shop   S   D
117. Best Della Lowry Co.—Best Della Lowry Co.   S   D
118. J. Wm. Leest's Sons—J. Wm. Leest Sons   S   D
119. Fostter Bros. Mfg. Co.—Foster Bros. Mfg. Co.   S   D
120. Dome Oil—Dome Oil   S   D
121. Schwindt N. N. & Sons—Schwind N. N. & Sons   S   D
122. Blick Coal Co.—Blick Coal Co.   S   D
123. Capitol Bedding Co.—Capital Bedding Co.   S   D
124. Pumphrey Warne—Pumphrey Warne   S   D
125. Ridgely & Hicks—Ridgeley & Hicks   S   D
126. Noland Co., Inc.—Nolan Co., Inc.   S   D
127. Eulysses Hone—Eulyses Hone   S   D
128. Louis W. Labafish—Louis W. Labfish   S   D
129. Desl's Art—Desl's Art Co.   S   D
130. Astoria Mfg. Co., Inc.—Astoria Mfg. Co., Inc.   S   D
131. Fred Lapier—Fred Lapien   S   D
132. Uline-Ice Co., Inc.—Uline-Ice Co., Inc.   S   D
133. Steven & Son—Steven & Sons   S   D
134. Benj. Posner—Benj. Posner   S   D
135. Smith Bros., Inc.—Smith Bros. Co.   S   D
136. April Showers Co.—April Showers Co.   S   D
137. The Modes—The Modes   S   D
138. Tokheim Dealers—Tokheim Dealers   S   D
139. Toledo Scale Co.—Toledo Scale Co.   S   D
140. Pon-Ton Co.—Pon-Ton Co.   S   D
141. Essence Co. Ltd.—Essence Co. Ltd.   S   D
142. John L. Dufief—John L. Dufeif   S   D
143. Meisel Tire Co., Inc.—Meissel Tire Co., Inc.   S   D
144. Colsom-Merriam Co.—Colsom-Merriam & Co.   S   D
145. Langohr Theodore L.—Langhor Theodore L.   S   D
146. Slehman's Ltd.—Slehman's Ltd.   S   D
147. Fox & Pir—Fox & Pir   S   D
148. Bay Ridge Inn, Inc.—Bay Ridge Inn, Inc.   S   D
149. Scaighter—Scaighler   S   D
150. Steinere Co.—Steinere & Co.   S   D

STOP HERE! Now, go on to the next section.

Part 2. Mathematical Computation

Instructions

The following test includes exercises in arithmetic. Follow the mathematical operation indicated and select the correct answer. If the answer does not appear in the choices given, circle "E, none of these." You can do all your figuring on scratch paper. You have 6 minutes to complete this test.

1. ADD (+)

3
4

A   3
B   5
C   6
D   7
E   none of these

2. SUBTRACT (−)

7
4

A   2
B   3
C   5
D   8
E   none of these

3. MULTIPLY (×)

2
4

A   5
B   7
C   8
D   10
E   none of these

4. SUBTRACT (−)

63
41

A   22
B   25
C   27
D   29
E   none of these

5. DIVIDE (÷)

3 $\overline{)27}$

A   9
B   11
C   12
D   13
E   none of these

6. SUBTRACT (−)

19
9

A   9
B   10
C   11
D   14
E   none of these

7. DIVIDE (÷)

4 $\overline{)168}$

A   37¾
B   39
C   41¼
D   42
E   none of these

8. ADD (+)

1
8
3

A   5
B   9
C   11
D   12
E   none of these

9. MULTIPLY (×)

15
4

A   20
B   40
C   50
D   60
E   none of these

10. DIVIDE (÷)

5 $\overline{)35}$

A   5
B   6
C   7
D   8
E   none of these

11. ADD (+)

16
17
20

A   53
B   60
C   62
D   69
E   none of these

12. SUBTRACT (−)

832
21

A   791
B   801
C   810
D   811
E   none of these

13. DIVIDE (÷)

6 $\overline{)42}$

A   4
B   6
C   8
D   9
E   none of these

14. SUBTRACT (−)

120
32

A   88
B   89
C   90
D   98
E   none of these

15. DIVIDE (÷)

9 /297

A 33
B 35
C 36
D 41
E none of these

16. ADD (+)

697
13

A 684
B 700
C 710
D 711
E none of these

17. MULTIPLY (×)

93
4

A 332
B 354
C 366
D 372
E none of these

18. DIVIDE (÷)

6 /186

A 28
B 29
C 30
D 31
E none of these

19. SUBTRACT (−)

4345
917

A 3398
B 3428
C 3434
D 3538
E none of these

20. MULTIPLY (×)

43
7

A 291
B 301
C 308
D 318
E none of these

21. SUBTRACT (−)

109
37

A 32
B 46
C 62
D 65
E none of these

22. MULTIPLY (×)

634
6

A 3794
B 3804
C 3812
D 3854
E none of these

23. SUBTRACT (−)

89213
764

A 88317
B 88359
C 88432
D 88449
E none of these

24. ADD (+)

563
877
89

A 1429
B 1439
C 1519
D 1529
E none of these

25. MULTIPLY (×)

58
9

A 512
B 522
C 527
D 552
E none of these

26. ADD (+)

878
552
97

A 1527
B 1534
C 1567
D 1593
E none of these

27. DIVIDE (÷)

11 /132

A 11
B 12
C 13
D 22
E none of these

28. MULTIPLY (×)

7246
3

A 21628
B 21728
C 21738
D 21748
E none of these

29. DIVIDE (÷)

7 /644021

A 9203
B 92003
C 92030
D 92041
E none of these

30. MULTIPLY (×)

749
4

A 2996
B 2999
C 3026
D 3093
E none of these

31. SUBTRACT (−)

520763
2591

A 517175
B 518012
C 518162
D 518172
E none of these

32. ADD (+)

1824
617
533

A 2974
B 2977
C 2984
D 3074
E none of these

33. MULTIPLY (×) A 608176
                     B 608212

  76034   C 608264
      8   D 608272
                     E none of these

34. SUBTRACT (−) A 7409
                     B 7419

  71304   C 70408
   .895   D 70409
                     E none of these

35. ADD (+)   A 87313
                     B 88218

  84546   C 88306
   1732   D 88318
   2040   E none of these

36. DIVIDE (÷)   A 1299
                     B 12707

  7 /90363   C 12894
                     D 12907
                     E none of these

37. MULTIPLY (×) A 463050
                     B 463055

  15435   C 466040
    30   D 466135
                     E none of these

38. SUBTRACT (−) A 41399
                     B 42309

  131141   C 42399
   89742   D 50399
                     E none of these

39. MULTIPLY (×)

                     A 40564
                     B 40664

  782   C 50664
   52   D 51674
                     E none of these

40. ADD (+)

                     A 2972
                     B 2984

  1942   C 2990
   539   D 3012
   621   E none of these

41. MULTIPLY (×) A 37496
                     B 38496

---

  872   C 38226
   43   D 39296
                     E none of these

42. SUBTRACT (−) A 3371469
                     B 3371498

  4065947   C 3374696
   694478   D 3376469
                     E none of these

43. DIVIDE (÷)   A 22713
                     B 24713

  5 /1103565   C 110713
                     D 120713
                     E none of these

44. ADD (+)   A 85972
                     B 86264

  21307   C 86432
   9865   D 86882
  52270   E none of these
   327
  2663

45. DIVIDE (÷)   A 1405
                     B 14005

  60 /840300   C 14015
                     D 14050
                     E none of these

46. MULTIPLY (×) A 4846118
                     B 4856118

  47609   C 4857318
   102   D 4866118
                     E none of these

47. ADD (+)   A 2927
                     B 2947

  123   C 2967
   64   D 2987
  741   E none of these
    5
  819
    7
   78
    1
  965
   42
   89
    7
    6

48. DIVIDE (÷)

13 / 263718

A 2028
B 2029 1/13
C 20186
D 20276
E none of these

49. ADD (+)

13209
8977

A 75361
B 85381
C 86376
D 86381

61140
497
2558

50. DIVIDE (÷)

17 / 344913

E none of these

A 2289
B 20146
C 20269
D 20289
E none of these

STOP HERE! Now, go on to the next section.

Part 3. Three-Dimensional Space Relationships

Instructions
Here are some exercises in finding objects made from pieces of metal. Look at this example below:

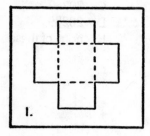 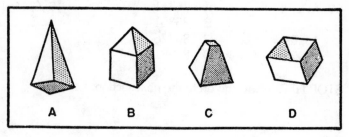

At the left is a drawing which represents a flat piece of metal. The dotted lines show where the metal is to be bent. At the right are drawings of four objects. Notice that only object D can be made by bending the metal piece in figure 1. You would circle the letter D under the correct object. Here's another example:

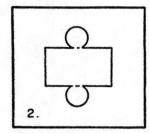 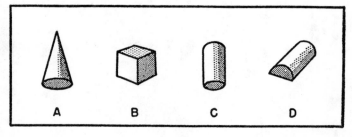

At the left is another drawing of a flat piece of metal. Only object C can be made from figure 2, this time by both rolling and bending the metal. Therefore, you would circle letter C under the object.

More exercises like these follow. In each exercise only one object can be made from the flat piece pictured, either by bending or rolling, or both. Circle the letter under the correct finished object. You have 6 minutes to complete this section.

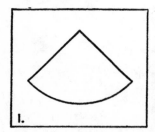 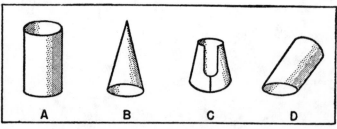

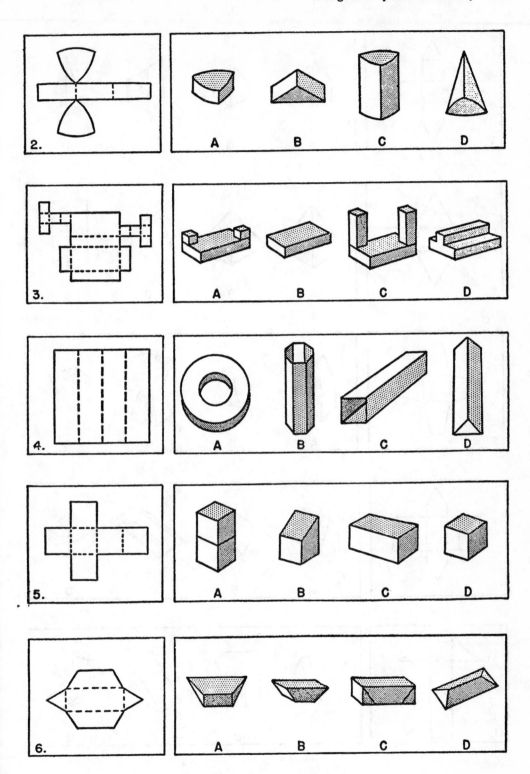

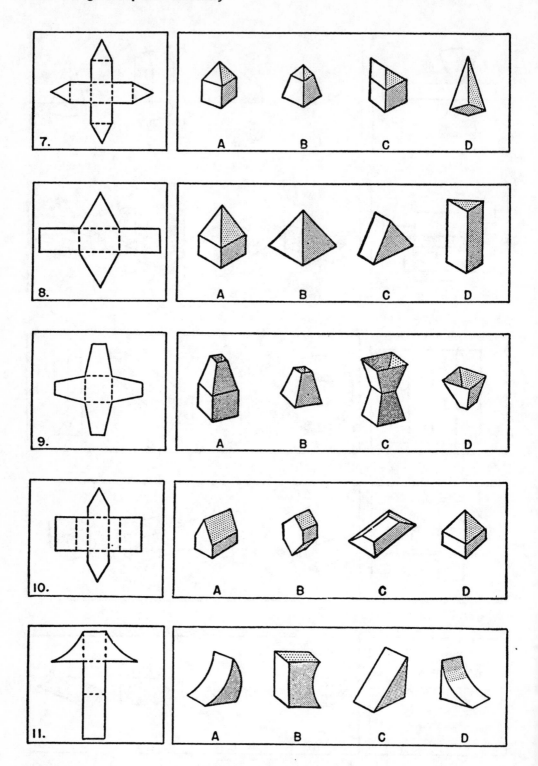

7.   A   B   C   D

8.   A   B   C   D

9.   A   B   C   D

10.   A   B   C   D

11.   A   B   C   D

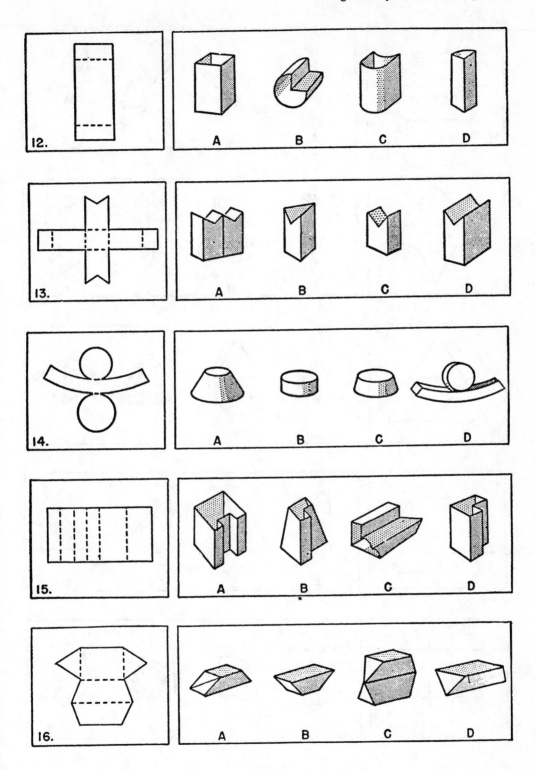

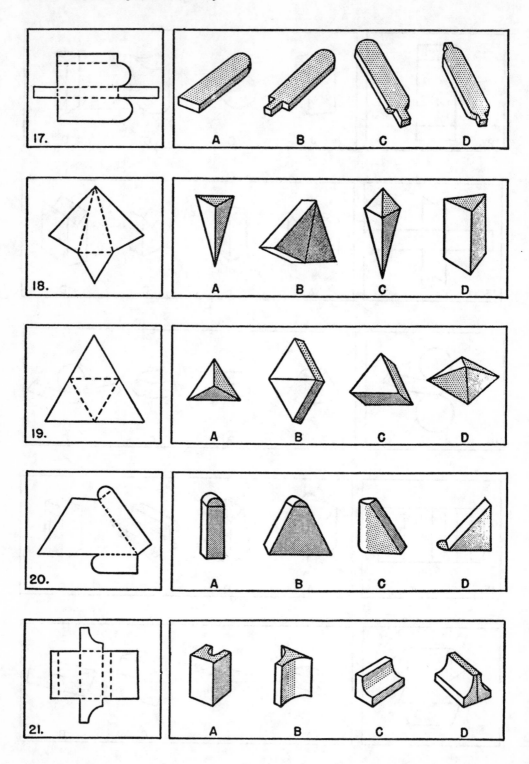

22.   A   B   C   D

23.   A   B   C   D

24.   A   B   C   D

25.   A   B   C   D

26.   A   B   C   D

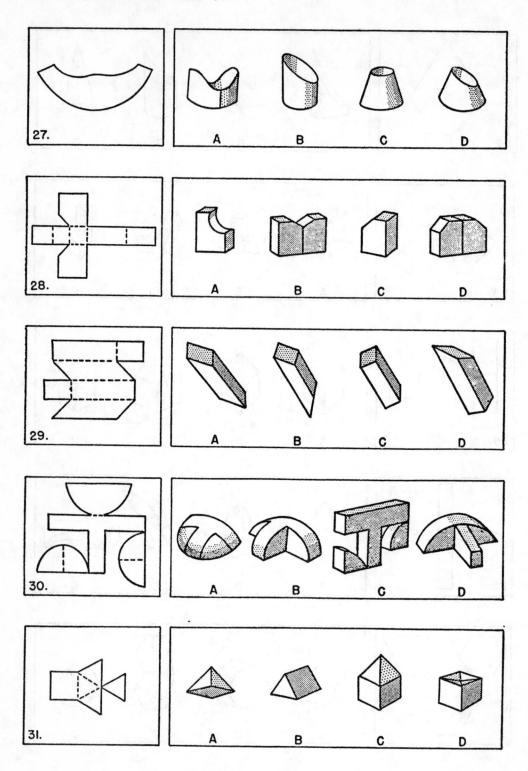

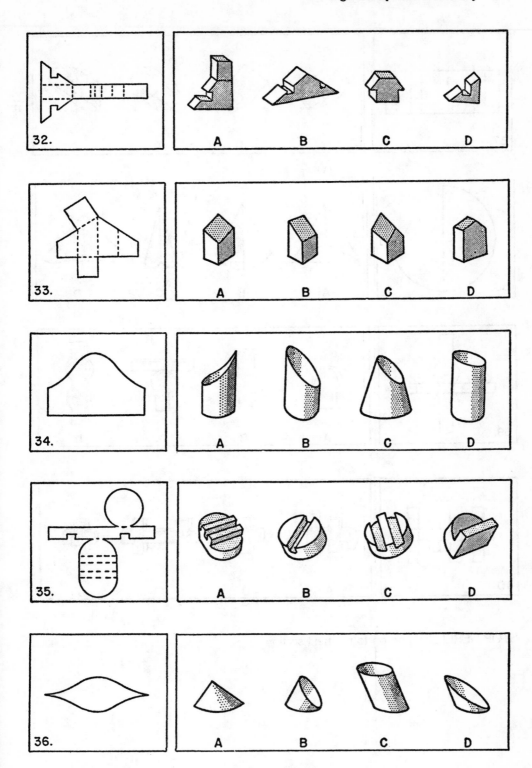

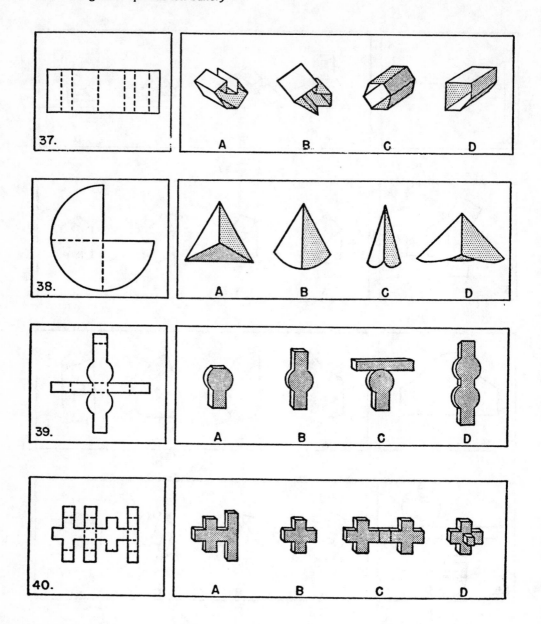

STOP HERE! Now, go on to the next section.

Part 4. Vocabulary

Instructions
Here are some exercises in finding the two words which are most nearly the *same* in meaning or *opposite* in meaning.
Look at this example:
1. a. big   b. large   c. dry   d. slow
Big and *large* have the *same* meaning. The letter for *big* is *a* and the letter for *large* is *b*. You would circle both *a* and *b*. Here's another example:

2. a. dreary   b. loyal   c. ancient
d. disloyal
Loyal and *disloyal* have *opposite* meanings. The letter for *loyal* is *b*, and the letter for *disloyal* is *d*. Here you would circle both *b* and *d*.

The following exercises are just like these. In each case, circle the correct letters that indicate the *two* words that are nearly the *same* in meaning or *opposite* in meaning. You have 6 minutes to complete this section.

1. a. few	**b.** exact	**c.** bright	**d.** many
2. a. remember	**b.** imagine	**c.** read	**d.** forget
3. a. leave	**b.** deter	**c.** enter	**d.** rest
4. a. expedient	**b.** costly	**c.** expensive	**d.** final
5. a. prescription	**b.** habit	**c.** association	**d.** custom
6. a. longing	**b.** knowledge	**c.** desire	**d.** power
7. a. strong	**b.** erect	**c.** frail	**d.** small
8. a. distant	**b.** resounding	**c.** distended	**d.** close
9. a. poison	**b.** toxin	**c.** poultice	**d.** pillory
10. a. measure	**b.** gouge	**c.** inflate	**d.** gauge
11. a. borrow	**b.** receive	**c.** lend	**d.** steal
12. a. angry	**b.** unhappy	**c.** enraged	**d.** deleterious
13. a. domestic	**b.** rural	**c.** urban	**d.** polite
14. a. potion	**b.** poison	**c.** venom	**d.** disease
15. a. consult	**b.** decline	**c.** conserve	**d.** destroy
16. a. moist	**b.** parched	**c.** wrinkled	**d.** sandy
17. a. verbal	**b.** abridged	**c.** expurgated	**d.** shortened
18. a. lustrous	**b.** calm	**c.** comfortable	**d.** serene
19. a. remote	**b.** continental	**c.** homely	**d.** distant
20. a. debatable	**b.** legal	**c.** illicit	**d.** cursory
21. a. slanting	**b.** smooth	**c.** round	**d.** sleek
22. a. kindliness	**b.** diplomacy	**c.** personality	**d.** tact
23. a. disobey	**b.** cease	**c.** digest	**d.** desist
24. a. uninhabited	**b.** populated	**c.** inhibited	**d.** rural
25. a. sour	**b.** saccharine	**c.** bizarre	**d.** salient
26. a. compassion	**b.** charm	**c.** distress	**d.** sympathy
27. a. dense	**b.** wet	**c.** tepid	**d.** lukewarm
28. a. fragmentary	**b.** convulsive	**c.** spasmodic	**d.** peripatetic
29. a. dogmatic	**b.** pedantic	**c.** positive	**d.** political
30. a. pace	**b.** part	**c.** scroll	**d.** role

31. a. devastate	**b.** sanction	**c.** disapprove	**d.** satiate
32. a. praise	**b.** love	**c.** appraise	**d.** laud
33. a. garner	**b.** dedicate	**c.** decorate	**d.** garnish
34. a. straight	**b.** adroit	**c.** exquisite	**d.** clumsy
35. a. hieroglyphics	**b.** dramatics	**c.** chronicles	**d.** annals
36. a. ally	**b.** villain	**c.** adversary	**d.** conqueror
37. a. apathy	**b.** temperance	**c.** enthusiasm	**d.** attachment
38. a. territorial	**b.** terrestrial	**c.** celestial	**d.** centennial
39. a. capricious	**b.** tolerant	**c.** whimsical	**d.** provincial
40. a. orator	**b.** prophet	**c.** counselor	**d.** seer
41. a. refugee	**b.** renegade	**c.** deserter	**d.** tramp
42. a. secret	**b.** benign	**c.** malign	**d.** malleable
43. a. tangible	**b.** tentative	**c.** exceptional	**d.** definitive
44. a. profuse	**b.** meager	**c.** prognostic	**d.** mawkish
45. a. audacious	**b.** mischievous	**c.** cautious	**d.** arduous
46. a. principle	**b.** principal	**c.** precept	**d.** preface
47. a. nuptial	**b.** nugatory	**c.** connubial	**d.** martial
48. a. betrayed	**b.** fiscal	**c.** despotic	**d.** arbitrary
49. a. vindictive	**b.** strident	**c.** retiring	**d.** extroverted
50. a. manifest	**b.** elaborate	**c.** evident	**d.** decorous
51. a. caustic	**b.** imaginary	**c.** military	**d.** trenchant
52. a. imitate	**b.** mitigate	**c.** emanate	**d.** alleviate
53. a. unsound	**b.** transcendent	**c.** similar	**d.** analogous
54. a. carol	**b.** poem	**c.** carousal	**d.** dirge
55. a. abstruse	**b.** disarming	**c.** profound	**d.** profuse
56. a. lateral	**b.** remote	**c.** latent	**d.** hidden
57. a. humorous	**b.** auspicious	**c.** portentous	**d.** audacious
58. a. laconic	**b.** verbose	**c.** truthful	**d.** stentorian
59. a. altruistic	**b.** selfish	**c.** affable	**d.** reserved
60. a. misanthrope	**b.** philanthropist	**c.** actuary	**d.** anthropologist

STOP HERE. Now let's see how you scored.

ANSWERS

Part 1. Name Comparison

1. S	**9.** D	**17.** S	**25.** S
2. S	**10.** D	**18.** S	**26.** S
3. D	**11.** D	**19.** S	**27.** D
4. S	**12.** D	**20.** S	**28.** D
5. S	**13.** S	**21.** D	**29.** D
6. S	**14.** S	**22.** S	**30.** D
7. D	**15.** D	**23.** D	**31.** S
8. S	**16.** D	**24.** S	**32.** D

33. S	**63.** S	**93.** S	**123.** D
34. D	**64.** D	**94.** S	**124.** S
35. D	**65.** D	**95.** S	**125.** D
36. S	**66.** D	**96.** S	**126.** D
37. S	**67.** S	**97.** D	**127.** D
38. S	**68.** D	**98.** S	**128.** D
39. D	**69.** S	**99.** D	**129.** D
40. S	**70.** S	**100.** S	**130.** S
41. D	**71.** D	**101.** S	**131.** D
42. D	**72.** D	**102.** D	**132.** S
43. D	**73.** D	**103.** S	**133.** D
44. S	**74.** S	**104.** S	**134.** S
45. D	**75.** D	**105.** S	**135.** D
46. D	**76.** S	**106.** D	**136.** S
47. D	**77.** S	**107.** S	**137.** S
48. S	**78.** D	**108.** S	**138.** S
49. S	**79.** D	**109.** D	**139.** S
50. D	**80.** D	**110.** D	**140.** S
51. D	**81.** D	**111.** D	**141.** S
52. D	**82.** S	**112.** S	**142.** D
53. S	**83.** S	**113.** S	**143.** D
54. S	**84.** D	**114.** D	**144.** D
55. D	**85.** D	**115.** D	**145.** D
56. D	**86.** S	**116.** S	**146.** S
57. D	**87.** S	**117.** S	**147.** S
58. S	**88.** D	**118.** D	**148.** S
59. S	**89.** S	**119.** D	**149.** D
60. D	**90.** S	**120.** S	**150.** D
61. D	**91.** S	**121.** D	
62. S	**92.** D	**122.** S	

Part 2. Mathematical Computation

1. D	**14.** A	**27.** B	**40.** E
2. B	**15.** A	**28.** C	**41.** A
3. C	**16.** C	**29.** B	**42.** A
4. A	**17.** D	**30.** A	**43.** E
5. A	**18.** D	**31.** D	**44.** C
6. B	**19.** B	**32.** A	**45.** B
7. D	**20.** B	**33.** D	**46.** B
8. D	**21.** E	**34.** D	**47.** B
9. D	**22.** B	**35.** D	**48.** E
10. C	**23.** D	**36.** E	**49.** D
11. A	**24.** D	**37.** A	**50.** D
12. D	**25.** B	**38.** A	
13. E	**26.** A	**39.** B	

Part 3. Three Dimensional Space Relationship

1. B	**4.** C	**7.** A	**10.** A
2. A	**5.** D	**8.** C	**11.** D
3. A	**6.** D	**9.** B	**12.** B

13. C	20. C	27. D	34. B
14. C	21. C	28. C	35. B
15. D	22. B	29. A	36. B
16. D	23. D	30. B	37. B
17. A	24. D	31. A	38. D
18. A	25. A	32. D	39. A
19. A	26. B	33. A	40. B

Part 4. Vocabulary

1. a–d	16. a–b	31. b–c	46. a–c
2. a–d	17. b–d	32. a–d	47. a–c
3. a–c	18. b–d	33. c–d	48. c–d
4. b–c	19. a–d	34. b–d	49. c–d
5. b–d	20. b–c	35. c–d	50. a–c
6. a–c	21. b–d	36. a–c	51. a–d
7. a–c	22. b–d	37. a–c	52. b–d
8. a–d	23. b–d	38. b–c	53. c–d
9. a–b	24. a–b	39. a–c	54. a–d
10. a–d	25. a–b	40. b–d	55. a–c
11. a–c	26. a–d	41. b–c	56. c–d
12. a–c	27. c–d	42. b–c	57. b–c
13. b–c	28. b–c	43. b–d	58. a–b
14. b–c	29. a–c	44. a–b	59. a–b
15. c–d	30. b–d	45. a–c	60. a–b

WHAT YOUR SCORE MEANS

Go back over each section and count the total number of answers you had correct in each section. The maximum raw scores for each section are as follows:

Name Comparison: 150
Mathematical Computation: 50
Three Dimensional Space: 40
Vocabulary: 60

The total number you answered correctly in each section is your raw score. Below is a chart outlining the various categories tested in this aptitude examination. By taking your raw score from each section and comparing it to the minimal normal score in each area, you will see your occupational strengths and weaknesses. The degree of variance from the minimum (either above or below it) will show you how superior or inferior your aptitude is in each area.

Use your raw score from section:	Your raw score	To find your aptitude in:	Minimum acceptible raw score is
1		Clerical Perception	43
2		Numerical Computation	41
3		Spatial Reasoning	21
4		Verbal Reasoning	23

☞ SCIENCE APTITUDE

Here's a science aptitude test that has been in use for more than thirty years and was designed to discover science talent on the high school level. Of the many thousand students taking the test, none has made a perfect score. See if you can profess expert knowledge of the life and physical sciences by answering everything correctly.

1. To what does the word Cassiopeia refer?
   a. a constellation in the northern latitudes
   b. a large flightless bird of the Pacific
   c. one of the earliest used of all spices
   d. the mineral (SnO_2), the principal ore of tin

2. Which of the following is *not* a bone?
   a. femur
   b. humerus
   c. thalamus
   d. tibia

3. All mechanical energy is either
   a. electrostatic or potential
   b. electrostatic or radioactive
   c. kinetic or potential
   d. kinetic or radioactive

4. Which of these fits least with the other three?
   a. larynx
   b. pharynx
   c. thorax
   d. trachea

5. Which of the following is the most frequent use of blood typing?
   a. aid to physicians in selecting proper antigenic sera for patients
   b. establishment of non-paternity in cases of litigation
   c. insurance of compatibility of blood of donor and donee in blood transfusions
   d. prediction of length of life

6. Which of the following planets has the greatest number of known satellites?
   a. Mars
   b. Pluto
   c. Saturn
   d. Uranus

7. When wheel A turns counterclockwise
   a. B turns clockwise and C clockwise
   b. B turns clockwise and C counterclockwise
   c. B turns counterclockwise and C clockwise
   d. B turns counterclockwise and C counterclockwise

8. If a situation in which all A is C and all B is C changes to one in which all A is B and all B is C, then
   a. all A is C
   b. all B is A
   c. all C is A
   d. all C is B

9. Which of the following is *not* one of the three great classes or organic compounds in cells?
   a. carbohydrates
   b. fats
   c. proteins
   d. salts

10. The word sternum refers to the
    a. breast bone
    b. dorsal side
    c. lower tip of the spine
    d. pelvic girdle

11. What is the biological science which deals with the relations of organisms and the environment, including relations to other organisms?
    a. botany
    b. ecology
    c. helminthology
    d. zoology

12. Bryophytes are forms of
    a. animal life
    b. minerals
    c. plant life
    d. stars

13. Containers, A, B, and C are of the same height and diameter. A and C are half filled and B three-quarters filled with a normal salt (NaCl) solution. Which contains the least water?
    a. A
    b. B
    c. C
    d. All contain equal amounts

14. Which of the following terms does *not* apply to all of following: manatee, dugong, whale, and seal?
    a. aquatic
    b. herbivorous
    c. mammalian
    d. multi-cellular

15. Which of the following is an element?
    a. salicylate
    b. salientia
    c. samarium
    d. sanidine

16. In this sketch of a horizontal section of the eyeball, A indicates the
    a. cornea
    b. fovea
    c. iris
    d. retina

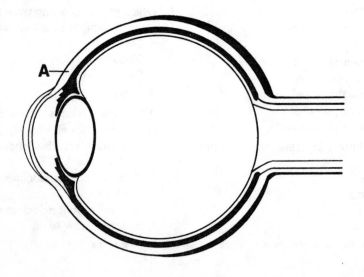

ANSWERS

1. a	**5.** c	**9** d	**13.** b
2. c	**6.** c	**10.** a	**14.** b
3. c	**7.** b	**11.** b	**15.** c
4. c	**8.** a	**12.** c	**16.** a

Tally the number of right answers.

WHAT YOUR SCORE MEANS

14–16: Mr. Wizard.

11–13: Donate your brain to science.

8–10: Time to buy a new chemistry set.

Less than 8: Check your pulse.

☞ TEST YOUR TYPING SPEED

This is a timed typing test, used by the United States Civil Service Commission to determine typing speed and accuracy for GS-2, clerk-typists, and GS-3, clerk-stenographers. You are allowed five minutes to type as many lines of the following two-paragraph test as possible. If you finish both paragraphs before the time is up, double space and begin the exercise again.

You should space, paragraph, spell, punctuate, capitalize and begin and end each line precisely as shown in the exercise (do not include the columns of numbers in the margins). Make no erasures, insertions, or other corrections as you type. Errors are penalized whether or not they are corrected, so it is best to keep typing.

Keep in mind that the Civil Service has minimum standards in both speed and accuracy, and that above these standards, accuracy is twice as important as speed.

Typing Test

Set a timer for five minutes and begin typing the following exercise at once.

1	Because they have often learned to know types of archi-	— 52(7)
2	tecture by decoration, casual observers sometimes fail to	— 54(7)
3	realize that the significant part of a structure is not the	— 56(8)
4	ornamentation but the body itself. Architecture, because	— 59(8)
5	of its close contact with human lives, is peculiarly and	— 61(9)
6	intimately governed by climate. For instance, a home built	— 64(9)
7	for comfort in the cold and snow of the northern areas of	— 66(10)
8	this country would be unbearably warm in a country with	— 68(10)
9	weather such as that of Cuba. A Cuban house, with its open	— 71(11)
10	court, would prove impossible to heat in a northern winter.	— 73(11)
11	Since the purpose of architecture is the construction of	— 76(12)
12	shelters in which human beings may carry on their numerous	— 78(12)
13	activities, the designer must consider not only climate con-	— 80(12)[2]
14	ditions, but also the function of a building. Thus, although	— —
15	the climate of a certain locality requires that an auditorium	— —
16	and a hospital have several features in common, the purposes	— —
17	for which they will be used demand some difference in struc-	40(3)[1]—

From the U.S. Civil Service Commission, "Stenographer, Typist, Clerk and Office Machine Operator Federal Office Assistant Examination."

18	ture. For centuries builders have first complied with these	42(4) —
19	two requirements and later added whatever ornamentation they	44(5) —
20	wished. Logically, we should see as mere additions, not as	47(6) —
21	basic parts, the details by which we identify architecture.	49(6) —

HOW TO SCORE

Two columns of blanks and numbers are arranged on the right side of the test. The first column is used for scoring the first 21 lines typed. The second column is used to score any lines which you were able to type a second time before the five minutes were up.

Typing speed: The numbers in the columns which are *not* in parentheses show the gross number of words per minute typed. In other words, if you reached line 20 during the five minute time period, you were typing at a rate of 47 words per minute. If you typed fewer than 17 lines in five minutes, your speed was under 40 words per minute, and you would be ineligible for Civil Service positions rated GS-2, clerk-typist, or GS-3, clerk-stenographer.

Typing accuracy: The numbers which are enclosed by parentheses in the columns show the maximum number of typing errors permitted in the exercise up to that line, for GS-2, clerk-typist, and GS-3, clerk-stenographer. In other words, if you reached line 20 during the five minute test period, you would be permitted a maximum of 6 typing errors. If you typed faster, and reached line 4 a second time, you would be permitted 8 errors in the total exercise. All of the following are considered errors:

1. Words or punctuation marks incorrectly typed. (A spacing error following a word or punctuation error is not counted).
2. Inconsistent margins or paragraph indentation.
3. Line, or portion of a line, typed over other material or typed with all capitals.
4. A series of consecutive words omitted, repeated, inserted or transposed. Individual word or punctuation errors should also be counted within such a series, but the total number of errors should not exceed the number of words mistyped.

If you managed to type beyond line 13 for a second time, do not count any errors made in the second typing of lines 14 through 21. You were typing at 80 words per minute, which is considered a speed score of 100.

☛ SPELLING BEE

Select the correct spelling of the word that means:

1. talkative
a. loqaecious   **c.** locquacious
b. loquacius   **d.** loquacious

2. one of the original thirteen colonies
a. Massachussets **c.** Massachussetts
b. Massachusetts

3. pertaining to an original state
a. primitive   **c.** primetive
b. primative

4. an incident
a. occurrence   **c.** occurence
b. ocurrence   **d.** occurrance

5. to commend to the attention of another as worthy
a. reccommend   **c.** recommend

b. reccomend   **d.** recomend

6. a discussion in which disagreement is expressed
a. argument   **c.** argewment
b. arguement

7. incapable of being avoided
a. inevatible   **c.** inevitible
b. inevitable

8. to disclose or reveal; make known
a. devulge   **c.** divuldge
b. divulge

9. from far away
a. long-distance **c.** longdistance
b. long distance

10. a flowering plant growing in an uncultivated state
a. wildflower   **c.** wild flower
b. wild-flower

ANSWERS

1. d	**4.** a	**7.** b	**10.** a or c
2. b	**5.** c	**8.** b	
3. b	**6.** a	**9.** a	

Tally the number of correct answers.

WHAT YOUR SCORE MEANS

10: Excellent

9: Very Good

7-8: Average

6 or under: Better keep a dictionary by your desk!

☞ RATE YOUR VOCABULARY

Select the correct definition for the following words:

1. dandiprat
   a. finger-exerciser for pianists, invented in 1835
   b. a small diving bird
   c. a pouched mouse
   d. a little fellow, insignificant or contemptible

2. minim
   a. a mining tool
   b. apothecaries measure, roughly equivalent to one drop of water
   c. a person who hates authority
   d. a watchtower, enclosed balcony or bay window, offering a panoramic view

3. strepent
   a. noisy, loud
   b. smooth, even, regular, steady
   c. grammatically correct
   d. mildly ridiculing

4. pouze
   a. an extra-large suitcase
   b. a universal scholar or thoroughly educated person
   c. refuse from cider-making
   d. a ceramic pot with a horizontal handle

5. diacritical
   a. staying closed at maturity
   b. distinguishing, marking a distinction
   c. unlucky, making unlucky
   d. existing between stars and their planets

6. animalcule
   a. the animal as distinct from the spiritual nature of man
   b. the soul, or true innerself
   c. of or relating to animal life, as distinct from plant life
   d. a microscopic or minute organism

7. laconic
   a. slow, lazy
   b. terse, concise, succinct
   c. ecclesiastical
   d. inclined to weep

8. cantilever
   a. a poem composed to lament the dead
   b. a projecting beam, supported only at one end
   c. any of several large, edible flatfishes
   d. a luminous ring or disk of light

9. freemartin
   a. a member of a religious organization devoted to prayer

b. a freed vassal
c. a member of a weavers guild
d. a sterile cow, born as a twin of a bull

10. casque
a. a small case or chest

b. a law based on precedent
c. a helmet or other armor for the head
d. a flush joint in a wood floor

ANSWERS

1. d	**4.** c	**7.** b	**10.** c
2. b	**5.** b	**8.** b	
3. a	**6.** d	**9.** d	

Tally the number of correct answers.

WHAT YOUR SCORE MEANS

8–10: Excellent
6–7: Very Good
4–5: Average
1–3: Better bone up!

☞GRAMMATICAL SKILLS

Select the word in parentheses which completes the sentence most grammatically.

1. Mr. Cox is the man (who, which) helped me.

2. Although (it's, its) improving (it's, its) service, the Quick-Mart will never be as good as the Fast Way.

3. My sister and (I, me) go to the library at least once a week.

4. We purchased a larger (amount, number) of hamburger buns for the picnic.

5. The president was (altogether, all together) right when he told the students to petition only after they were (altogether, all together) on their demands.

6. (Being as, Because) it was my birthday, I wanted to celebrate.

7. I (can't hardly, can hardly) keep from screaming when the traffic is bad.

8. I (imply, infer) from your comments that you are not interested in bidding on this property.

9. In (principle, principal), I agree with you.

10. I cannot hope to (affect, effect) a change in attitude in a mere two weeks.

ANSWERS AND EXPLANATIONS

1. Who. Use "who," rather than "which" (or "that") when referring to persons.
2. It's; its. "It's" is a contraction of "it is," and "its" is the possessive of "it."
3. I. "I" is used when the noun is the subject of the verb; "me" when it is the object.
4. Number. "Amount" is used to refer to things in bulk, or mass; "number" to refer to countable objects.
5. Altogether; all together. Use "altogether" to mean thoroughly or completely, and "all together" to mean in a group, or collectively.
6. Because. "Being as" is considered substandard English.
7. Can hardly. "Can't hardly" is a double negative.
8. Infer. A writer or speaker "implies." A reader or listener "infers."
9. Principle. "Principle" means fundamental truth and "principal" is the chief official or main element.
10. Effect. "Affect" means to influence or pretend. "Effect" means to bring about.

Tally the number of correct answers.

WHAT YOUR SCORE MEANS

9–10: Excellent

8: Very Good

6–7: Average

under 6: Better bone up!

PARENTING: RATE YOUR POTENTIAL AND ENDURANCE

☞ IS PARENTING YOUR BAG?

The decision to have a child is one of the most important and difficult ones women and men make, yet very few are prepared for the job of parenthood. It may be more rewarding than other jobs, but it is also more demanding. And, unlike other professions, parenthood is permanent.

The following questionnaire is designed to shed light on your emotional maturity and financial resources—two important considerations in parenthood. It is a guide to self-knowledge to help you see what kind of parent you will be. If you are already a parent, don't fear finding out you are "wrong" for the job. You may gain reassuring knowledge about basic qualities for successful parenting that you possess but may not be fully utilizing.

This questionnaire won't tell you whether or not to become a parent, but it should tell you a few things that will be useful in making the decision to have a family now, or postpone the event for a while. In addition, you are likely to learn something about your attitudes, values, and priorities.

Group A

1. I know where I'm going in life.
True   False

2. What I'm doing in life matters.
True   False

3. My age is
  a. under 21
  b. 21–25
  c. 25–29
  d. 30 or over

4. My marriage has lasted
  a. two or more years
  b. four or more years
  c. six or more years

5. I have lived away from my parents for more than two years.
True   False

6. I rely on my parents for occasional loans.
True   False

7. My spending habits are sensible.
True   False

8. I've never really thought about my goals.
True   False

9. I can intelligently discuss how the world will change in the next twenty-five years.
True   False

Group B

10. I don't believe in savings or stocks.
True   False

11. My spouse and I live comfortably.
True   False

12. We could live on half our income.
True   False

13. I enjoy being stylishly dressed.
True   False

14. I yearn for luxuries that I can't afford.
True   False

15. I don't comparison shop for small items.
True   False

16. My economic future looks fairly secure.
True   False

17. I enjoy being able to spend $10 on impulse.
True   False

18. We have more than $2,000 in savings.
True   False

19. We like to save a set part of our income.
True   False

20. I don't enjoy the theater or spectator sports unless I have good seats.
True   False

21. I would love to travel extensively.
True   False

22. I know how we spent last year's income.
True   False

23. I like to wear something new to every party.
True   False

24. If I were handed $2,000 in cash, I would want to (choose one)
   a. take a trip
   b. buy something expensive
   c. invest in high-interest bonds
   d. buy land

e. buy gifts for friends or family
f. use the money for home furnishings
g. contribute to a worthy cause
h. use the money for maternity costs
i. use the money for continuing education for me or my spouse

Group C

25. I love to sleep late.
True   False

26. I am rarely sick in bed for more than a day.
True   False

27. I am prone to small maladies.
True   False

28. I'm not too tired at night to enjoy some activity.
True   False

29. I sometimes feel I may go to pieces.
True   False

30. I take most things in stride, not getting upset easily.
True   False

31. When I have a cold, I
   a. keep going easily
   b. find it's a struggle to keep going
   c. use it as a reason to stop working
   d. love to pamper myself and be pampered

32. I can go without sleep for days.
True   False

33. I am a high-strung person.
True   False

34. I enjoy at least one outdoor sport regularly.
True   False

35. Possessions are relatively unimportant to me.
True   False

36. I prefer eating out to dinner at home.
True   False

37. A child would cramp our present living quarters.
True   False

38. Our home is decorated to our satisfaction.
True   False

39. I have unconsciously arranged our home with the eventual presence of a child in mind.
True   False

40. I find my home stifling and don't like staying home.
True   False

41. I find my home pleasant, but I am unhappy when circumstances keep me home.
True   False

42. My favorite possessions are of
a. real value
b. sentimental value
c. real and sentimental value

43. A child is more important than possessions.
True   False

44. Ours is not a children's neighborhood.
True   False

45. If we had a baby, I would make one room of our home "off limits" to toddlers.
True   False

HOW TO SCORE

Find the point value of your answers below and total your score for each group. The answers marked "U" are unscorable.

Group A	Group B	Group C	
1. T–6	**10.** F–2	**25.** F–1	**40.** F–1
2. T–10	**11.** T–2	**26.** T–2	**41.** F–2
3. a–0	**12.** T–2	**27.** F–1	**42.** U
b–10	**13.** F–2	**28.** T–2	**43.** U
c–15	**14.** F–2	**29.** F–3	**44.** F–2
d–20	**15.** F–1	**30.** T–1	**45.** F–1
4. a–2	**16.** T–1	**31.** a–1	
b–4	**17.** F–1	**32.** T–1	
c–6	**18.** T–2	**33.** F–2	
5. T–1	**19.** T–1	**34.** U	
6. F–1	**20.** F–1	**35.** T–1	
7. T–2	**21.** F–2	**36.** F–1	
8. F–6	**22.** T–3	**37.** F–2	
9. T–4	**23.** F–1	**38.** U	
	24. h–4	**39.** T–2	

WHAT YOUR SCORE MEANS

The questionnaire, which was based on an ongoing study for the Consortium on Parenthood Aptitude, attempts to determine whether you have three basic resources in a sufficient degree to get you off to a good start as a parent: maturity, money, and good health and home.

Group A questions 1–9 reveal your level of maturity. Total possible maturity points are 56. Your points on these questions _____.

Rate your score according to this scale:

0–14: Low

15–22: Low average

23–40: Average

41–48: High

49–56: Very high

Group B questions 10–24 reveal your level of affluence, attitudes about money, your priorities for spending it, and any self-indulgent habits. Total possible money points are 27. Your points on these questions _____.

Rate your score according to this scale:

0–4: Low

5–11: Low average

12–17: Average

18–23: High

24–27: Very high

Group C questions 25–45 test for good health and home environment. Total possible home and health points are 26. Your points on these questions _____.

Rate your score according to this scale:

0–4: Low

5–10: Low average

11–16: Average

17–22: High

23–26: Very high

Parents who are satisfied with the experience of raising children indicate the importance of becoming less materialistic during a child's early years. Everyone has possessions they value, so it makes sense to child-proof your home and be prepared to put things you love out of reach of young children.

☞ WHAT KIND OF PARENT ARE YOU?

Recently, Yankelovich, Skelly and White, Inc., a big national polling organization, set out to study how Americans are raising their children today. After preliminary samplings, they decided that, for the purposes of analysis, they could break families down fairly neatly into two groups: the new breeds and the traditionalists.

As a parent, you may wonder which label the pollsters would have assigned to you had you been one of the 2,102 people with children under age thirteen they questioned. The test below will provide a good clue. Of the following statements abstracted from the survey commissioned by General Mills, check only those that most closely correspond to your own views.

1. Parents should sacrifice to give their kids the best.
2. Saving money is not an important value to you.
3. You're concerned that your child be outstanding.
4. Boys and girls should be raised alike.
5. The most important characteristics in a child are, in order: • good manners • responsibleness • good sense and judgment • respect for elders.
6. In contrast to question 5, you believe the most important characteristics in a child are, in order: • good sense and judgment • responsibleness • good manners • independence.
7. It's up to the man to be the main family provider.
8. The offspring who should go to college are the ones who are the best students, regardless of sex.
9. People who want no children are basically selfish.
10. It's okay for parents to have a pal-like relationship with their children.

HOW TO SCORE AND WHAT YOUR SCORE MEANS

If you tended to check more even-numbered statements, according to survey criteria, you're new breed, along with 43% of other parents. If the reverse is true, and you generally checked the odd-numbered statements, you're a traditionalist, along with a 57% majority.

By Geraldine Carro. Appeared in the July 1977 *Ladies' Home Journal*. © 1977 LHJ Publishing, Inc. Reprinted with permission of *Ladies' Home Journal*.

In summing up their report entitled, "Raising Children in a Changing Society," the pollsters observed that new-breed parents are more self-oriented than child-oriented. Better educated and richer than the traditionalists as a group, they place less importance on marriage, religion and saving money. They believe in equal rights for parents and children, are less strict, and believe that boys and girls should be raised alike.

In comparison, traditionalists feel marriage, religion, saving money, and hard work are still very important; they are both stricter with their children and more willing to make sacrifices for them.

The traditionalists, however, have changed, too. While they believe that boys and girls should be raised differently, this attitude is breaking down in practice. And while they value marriage highly, they don't believe unhappily married parents should stay together for the children's sake.

☞ PARENTS' DRUG AWARENESS QUIZ

This quiz is designed to probe your knowledge about drug abuse. By drug abuse, we mean the deliberate use of any chemical substance for nonmedical purposes which results in the impaired physical, mental, emotional, or social health of the user.

Some questions have more than one answer. It's not so important that you get the right answers. What is important is that you start thinking about the impact drug abuse has on all our lives and how it could plague you and your family.

Circle the correct answer(s) to each of the questions.

1. During which period(s) was drug abuse a problem in the United States?
   a. during the Civil War
   b. in the 1950s
   c. in the 1960s
   d. all of the above

2. Which age group has the highest percentage of drug abusers?
   a. 10–17
   b. 18–25
   c. 26–35
   d. 36–60
   e. 61 and over

3. How do most drug users make their first contact with illicit drugs?
   a. through "pushers"
   b. through their friends
   c. accidentally
   d. through the media

4. Which of the following is the most commonly abused drug in the United States?
   a. marijuana

   b. alcohol
   c. cocaine
   d. heroin

5. Which drug poses the greatest health hazard to the most people in the United States?
   a. cigarettes
   b. heroin
   c. codeine
   d. LSD
   e. caffeine

6. Which of the following is not a narcotic?
   a. heroin
   b. marijuana
   c. morphine
   d. methadone

7. Which of the following is not a stimulant?
   a. amphetamine
   b. caffeine
   c. methaqualone
   d. methamphetamine

8. Which of the following drugs does not cause physical dependence?
a. alcohol
b. morphine
c. peyote
d. secobarbital
e. codeine

9. Which of the following poses the highest *immediate* risk to experimenters?
a. inhalants
b. marijuana
c. nicotine
d. LSD

10. Overall, why is intravenous injection the most dangerous method of using illicit drugs?
a. because the drug enters the system so rapidly
b. because nonsterile equipment and solutions can cause serious complications
c. because users usually get a larger amount of the drug by this method
d. a and c only
e. a, b and c

11. When does a person who uses heroin become physically dependent on it?
a. immediately (first time)
b. after four or five times
c. after prolonged use (20 times or more)
d. different for each person

12. When people become dependent on heroin, what is the primary reason they continue to take it?
a. experience pleasure
b. avoid withdrawal
c. escape reality
d. gain acceptance among friends

13. Which of the following has (have) been used effectively to treat drug abusers?
a. methadone maintenance
b. detoxification (medically supervised drug withdrawal)
c. drug-free therapy
d. psychotherapy
e. all of the above

14. Which of the following are social costs of drug abuse?
a. loss of employee productivity
b. increased possibility of auto accidents
c. depletion of already scarce drug abuse services
d. b and c only
e. a, b, and c

15. What is the most unpredictable abused drug on the street today?
a. PCP
b. heroin
c. LSD
d. alcohol

HOW TO SCORE

1. d. All of the above. Drug use is as old as history, and certain periods of U.S. history are associated with special drug abuse problems. During the Civil War, for example, morphine was used as a pain killer. Morphine's addictive properties were not well understood, and many soldiers became dependent on it.

Throughout the century, there were periodic "drug scares" created by the use of cocaine at the turn of the century, heroin in the 1920s, marijuana in the 1930s, and heroin again in the 1950s. The 1960s saw a social explosion of drug use of all kinds from LSD to heroin and marijuana.

In the 1970s, phencyclidine (PCP), a psychedelic of the 1960s, has reappeared on the street and is causing concern because of its bizarre effects. And new compounds, marketed as "room deodorizers" are being inhaled for a "high."

2. b. 18–25
3. b. Through their friends.
4. b. Alcohol. Many people in the United States have trouble with alcohol, and estimates show that about 10 million are dependent on the drug.
5. a. Cigarettes. Approximately 300,000 deaths annually from coronary disease, other heart disease, lung cancer, respiratory disease, and other types of cancer have been linked to cigarette smoking.
6. b. Marijuana. In the past, marijuana was legally classified as a narcotic, but it isn't now. Marijuana's psychopharmacological effects (the way a drug works on a person's mental and physical system) differ from the effects of narcotics.
7. c. Methaqualone. Methaqualone is a nonbarbiturate sedative-hypnotic called a "lude" or "soaper" on the street. But it, like the stimulant drugs, is also a drug of abuse.
8. c. Peyote. Physical dependence on mescaline (the active ingredient of the peyote cactus) or other hallucinogens has not been verified.
9. a. Inhalants. Sniffing aerosols or other volatile substances can result in immediate death.
10. e. The danger of contracting hepatitis or other infection is often overlooked by drug users who inject with nonsterile equipment.
11. d. Different for each person. Although the time it takes for a person to become physically dependent on heroin varies, we do know that repeated use ultimately causes physical dependence. Some people become physically dependent after using heroin as few as three or four times.
12. b. Avoid withdrawal. When people stop taking heroin after they have become physically dependent, they develop withdrawal symptoms: vomiting, muscle spasms, profuse sweating, insomnia, and other physical conditions. If they once again begin to take the drug, withdrawal symptoms disappear.
13. e. All of the above. All have been used successfully, both individually and in combination, to treat drug abusers.
14. e. Hours lost from productive work, increased traffic accidents caused by driving under the influence of drugs, and dollars spent on treatment and law enforcement programs—these are the social costs we all pay, one way or another, for drug abuse.
15. a. Phencyclidine (PCP, "angel dust"). Phencyclidine is an unpredictable and highly dangerous drug. Its use has been associated with bizarre and violent behavior, with accidents, and with psychotic episodes.

WHAT YOUR SCORE MEANS

If you score high, you are probably in a better position to identify a potential drug problem, deal more effectively with drug abuse, or prevent it. A low score indicates that you should spend a little time familiarizing yourself with the drug problem. It's in the best interests of your entire family. For information write:
National Institute On Drug Abuse, 5600 Fishers Lane, Rockville, MD 20857.

☞ HOW FIT ARE YOUR KIDS? TEST I

A poor reaction to exercise is usually a sign of a low level of fitness rather than of disease. This test can help to identify children with low levels of fitness and, in some instances, may reveal signs of health problems which warrant medical investigation.

1. **Flexed Arm Hang (girls):** Arm and shoulder strength
   Equipment: A stopwatch and a sturdy bar, comfortable to grip and adjustable in height (height of bar should be approximately the same as the child being tested).
   Starting Position: Using an overhand grip, the child hangs with chin above bar and elbows flexed. Legs must be straight and feet free of floor.
   Action: Hold position as long as possible.
   Rules: Timing should start as soon as child is in position and released from any support other than her own. Timing should stop when the child's chin touches or drops below the bar. Knees must not be raised and kicking not permitted.

   To pass at ages 10–17: 3 seconds
2. **Pullups (boys):** Arm and shoulder strength
   Equipment: A bar of sufficient height, comfortable to grip.
   Starting position: Grasp the bar with palms facing forward; hang with arms

and legs fully extended. Feet must be free of floor.
   Action:
   Count 1: Pull body up with the arms until the chin is higher than bar.
   Count 2: Lower body until arms are fully extended. Repeat as many times as possible.
   Rules: The pullup must be smooth, not a snap movement, legs must be kept straight and not kicked. One pullup is completed and counted each time the child raises his chin above the bar.

   To pass at ages 10–13: 1 pullup
         14: 2 pullups
         15: 3 pullups
         16: 4 pullups
         17: 5 pullups
3. **Situps (boys and girls):** Abdominal strength
   Equipment: None. However, a mat or other soft (grass) surface preferred.
   Starting position: Child lies on back with knees flexed, feet about one foot apart. The hands, with fingers laced, are grasped behind the head. A partner holds the performer's ankles and keeps

Adapted from "Youth Physical Fitness," prepared by the President's Council on Physical Fitness and Sports.

his heels in contact with the floor while counting each successive situp.

Action:

Count 1: Sit up and turn the trunk to the left, touching right elbow to left knee.

Count 2: Return to starting position.

Count 3: Sit up and turn trunk to the right, touching left elbow to right knee.

Count 4: Return to starting position.

Repeat the required number of times. One complete situp is counted each time the child returns to the starting position.

To pass at age:	Boys	Girls
10	25	20
11	26	20
12	30	20
13	38	20
14	45	20
15	49	19
16	50	18
17	45	18

4. Squat Thrust (boys and girls): Agility

Equipment: A stopwatch or a watch with a sweep second hand.

Starting Position: Child stands erect.

Action:

Count 1: Bend knees and place hands on floor in front of feet. Arms may be between, outside or in front of knees.

Count 2: Thrust legs back until the body is perfectly straight from shoulders to feet (pushup position).

Count 3: Return to squat position.

Count 4: Return to standing position.

Rule: The child should be instructed how to do a correct squat thrust and encouraged to do as many as possible within a ten-second time limit. The child must come to an erect standing position at the completion of each squat thrust.

To pass:

Girls ages 10–17: 3 squat thrusts in ten seconds

Boys ages 10–17: 4 squat thrusts in ten seconds

☞ HOW FIT ARE YOUR KIDS? TEST II

Although similar to the previous test, this youth fitness test has been officially adopted by the President's Council on Physical Fitness and Sports as part of its motivational and evaluation program. The test consists of a battery of seven achievements designed to measure various components of physical fitness of girls and boys aged ten to seventeen. Results of the complete set give an overall picture of the fitness of the child. The youth fitness test is the only fitness test for which national norms have been developed and is the basis for the Presidential Physical Fitness Award.

The achievements and the physical components which they measure are:

1. pullups (boys): arm and shoulder girdle strength
flexed arm hang (girls): arm and shoulder girdle strength
2. situps: abdominal and hip flexor strength
3. shuttle run: speed and change of direction
4. standing broad jump: explosive power of leg extensor muscles
5. 50-yard dash: speed
600-yard run-walk: cardiovascular endurance

1. Pullups (boys)
Equipment: A bar, of sufficient height, comfortable to grip.
Starting Position: Grasp the bar with palms facing forward; hang with arms and legs fully extended. Feet must be free of floor.
Action:
1. Pull body up with the arms until the chin is placed over the bar.
2. Lower body until the elbows are fully extended.
3. Repeat the exercise as many times as possible.
Rules:
1. The pull must not be a snap movement.
2. Knees must not be raised.
3. Kicking the legs is not permitted.
4. The body must not swing.
5. One complete pullup is counted each

Adapted from "Youth Physical Fitness," prepared by the President's Council on Physical Fitness and Sports.

time the child places his chin over the bar

1. Flexed Arm Hang (girls)

Equipment: A stopwatch and a sturdy bar, comfortable to grip and adjustable in height (height of bar should be approximately the same as the child being tested).

Starting Position: Using an overhand grip, the child hangs with chin above bar and elbows flexed. Legs must be straight and feet free of floor.

Action: Hold position as long as possible.

Rules: Timing should start as soon as child is in position and released from any support other than her own. Timing should stop when the child's chin touches or drops below the bar. Knees must not be raised; kicking is not permitted.

2. Situps (boys and girls)

Equipment: A stopwatch and a mat or other soft (grass) surface preferred.

Starting Position: Child lies on back with knees flexed, feet about one foot apart. The hands, with fingers laced, are grasped behind the head. A partner holds the performer's ankles and keeps his heels in contact with the floor while counting each successful situp.

Action:
1. Sit up and turn the trunk to the left, touching right elbow to left knee.
2. Return to starting position.
3. Sit up and turn trunk to the right, touching left elbow to right knee.
4. Return to starting position.
   Repeat as many times as possible during a one minute period. One complete situp is counted each time the child returns to the starting position.

3. Shuttle Run

Equipment: Two blocks of wood, 2" x 2" x 4" (blackboard erasers may be used) and stopwatch. Mark two short parallel lines 30 feet apart. Place the blocks of wood behind one of the lines.

Starting Position: Child stands behind the line opposite the blocks ready to run.

Action: On the signal, "Ready, go!" the child runs to the blocks, picks up one, returns and places it behind the starting line. (He does not throw or drop it.) He then runs and picks up the second block and carries it back across the starting line.

Rules:
1. Allow two trials.
2. Disqualify any trial in which the block is dropped or thrown.
3. Record the better of the two trials in seconds to the nearest tenth.

4. Standing Broad Jump

Equipment: Any level surface and tape measure.

Starting Position: Child stands with the feet comfortably apart, with toes just behind the takeoff line. Preparatory to jumping, child should have knees flexed and should swing the arms backward and forward in a rhythmical motion.

Action: Jump, swinging arms forcefully forward and upward, taking off from the balls of the feet.

Rules:
1. Allow three trials.
2. Measure from the takeoff line to the heel or any part of body that touches the surface nearest the takeoff line.
3. Record best of three trials in feet and inches to the nearest inch.

Note: It may be convenient to anchor the tape measure to the surface at a right angle to the takeoff line and have the child jump along the tape. The scorer stands to the side with a stick, touches the stick to the point where the child lands, and observes the mark to the nearest inch.

5. Fifty-Yard Dash

Equipment: Stopwatch.

Starting Position: Child stands behind the starting line. The starter takes a position at the finish line with a stopwatch. He raises one hand preparatory to giving the starting signal.

Action: When the starter brings his hand down quickly to his thigh, the child leaves his mark. As the child crosses the finish line, the time is noted and recorded.

Rules:

1. The score is the lapsed time between the starter's signal and the instant the child crosses the finish line.
2. Record the time in seconds to the nearest tenth.

6. 600-Yard Run-Walk (ages 10–17)

Options:

Ages 10–12: 1-mile or 9-minute run

Ages 13 or older: 1½-mile or 12-minute run

Equipment: Stopwatch and running area with designated starting and finish lines.

Starting Position: Child stands behind starting line.

Action: On the signal, "Ready, go!" the child starts running the 600-yard distance (walking only if necessary), or either of the above options.

Rules:

1. Walking is permitted, but the object is to cover the distance in the shortest possible time.
2. Record the time in minutes and seconds.
3. Course should be laid out on level ground.

Note: It is possible to test several children at the same time. Have the children pair off before the start of the test. One of the partners runs, while the other stands near the timer. The timer calls out the time continuously, until the runners have all crossed the finish line. Each child near the timer listens for, and remembers, his partner's time as the latter finishes.

SCORES REQUIRED TO PASS TEST

						BOYS				
Age	Situps (flexed leg)	Pullups	Standing Broad Jump	50-Yard Dash	600-Yard Run-Walk	Ages 10–12 1-mile or 9-min. run*		Ages 13 and over 1½-mile or 12-min. run*		Shuttle Run
	1 MIN.					*TIME*	*YARDS*	*TIME*	*YARDS*	
10	42	5	5′8″	:7:7	2:11	7:06	2081			:10.4
11	43	5	5′10″	:7.4	2:09	6:43	2143			:10.1
12	45	6	6′1″	:7.1	2:0	6:20	2205			:10.0
13	48	7	6′8″	:6.9	1:54			9:40	3037	:09.7
14	50	9	6′11″	:6.5	1:47			9:40	3037	:09.3
15	50	11	7′5″	:6.3	1:42			9:40	3037	:09.2
16	50	11	7′9″	:6.3	1:40			9:40	3037	:09.1
17	49	12	8′0″	:6.1	1:38			9:40	3037	:09.0

*Options. For 600-yard run-walk.

Age	Situps (flexed leg)	Flexed-Arm Hang	Standing Broad Jump	50-Yard Dash	600-Yard Run-Walk	Ages 10–12 1-mile or 9-min. run*		Ages 13 and over 1½-mile or 12-min. run*		Shuttle Run
	1 MIN.					TIME	YARDS	TIME	YARDS	
10	38	:24	5'5"	:7.8	2:30	8:33	1801			:10.9
11	38	:24	5'7"	:7.5	2:25	8:02	1824			:10.5
12	38	:23	5'9"	:7.4	2:21	7:28	1847			:10.5
13	40	:21	6'0"	:7.2	2:16			14:00	2232	:10.2
14	41	:26	6'3"	:7.1	2:11			14:00	2232	:10.1
15	40	:25	6'1"	:7.1	2:14			14:00	2232	:10.2
16	38	:20	6'0"	:7.3	2:19			14:00	2232	:10.4
17	40	:22	6'3"	:7.1	2:14			14:00	2232	:10.1

*Options. For 600-yard run-walk.

☞ A MOTHER'S QUIZ: WILL YOUR DAUGHTER MARRY A MAN LIKE YOU?

What kind of man will your daughter marry? Though there are hundreds of variables which will determine her decision, the kind of mother you are will have a lot to do with it. And the quiz which follows is designed to give you a rough idea of the qualities you have which may influence her choice. Answer each question by circling the correct letter:

A = Always;
O = Often;
S = Seldom;
N = Never.

Part 1

1. Do you force your daughter to eat everything on her plate?
A O S N

2. Are you late for appointments?
A O S N

3. Is your daughter's room messy?
A O S N

4. Do you let your daughter select her own clothes when you shop?
A O S N

5. Can you easily choose just one Christmas present for your daughter?
A O S N

6. Do you insist on scheduled bedtimes?
A O S N

7. Do you take away privileges as a punishment?
A O S N

8. Does your husband pay the household bills?
A O S N

9. Do you approve of your daughter's friends?

A O S N

10. Do you insist on playing games by the official rules?

A O S N

11. Do you overrule your daughter if she wants to watch a TV show you don't approve of?

A O S N

12. If your daughter sets the table wrong, do you reset it?

A O S N

Part 2

1. Are you at home when your daughter returns from school?

A O S N

2. Do you think pets are good for children?

A O S N

3. Are you openly demonstrative with your family?

A O S N

4. Does your daughter eat dinner with you?

A O S N

5. Can you easily choose just one Christmas present for your daughter?

A O S N

6. Do you invite your daughter into bed with you in the morning?

A O S N

7. Do you think it's all right to cry?

A O S N

8. Is your daughter allowed to keep secrets from you?

A O S N

9. Can you pretend to believe your daughter when she weaves a harmless fantasy?

A O S N

10. Are you embarrassed if a casual acquaintance kisses you by way of saying hello?

A O S N

11. Do you have trouble sleeping through the night?

A O S N

12. Do you carry a picture of your daughter with you?

A O S N

Part 3

1. Are you afraid to be alone in the house?

A O S N

2. Do you share breakfast time with your daughter?

A O S N

3. Do you feel you must have some time by yourself and some time alone with your husband?

A O S N

4. At the end of the day, are you too tired to play with your daughter?

A O S N

5. Does your daughter like to dress up for special occasions?

A O S N

6. Are there days when you would prefer not to see your daughter at all?

A O S N

7. Are there things you're just not good at?

A O S N

8. After an ordinary week, do you look forward to the weekend with the children?

A O S N

9. Are you comfortable eating alone in a restaurant?

A O S N

10. Are you annoyed when your daughter wakes you up in the middle of the night?

A O S N

11. Do you do minor household repairs?

A O S N

12. Is your daughter able to entertain herself?

A O S N

HOW TO SCORE

Find the point values of your answers and total your score for each section of the test.

Part 1

	Always	Often	Seldom	Never
1.	4	3	2	1
2.	1	2	3	4
3.	1	2	3	4
4.	1	2	3	4
5.	4	3	2	1
6.	4	3	2	1
7.	4	3	2	1
8.	1	2	3	4
9.	1	2	3	4
10.	4	3	2	1
11.	4	3	2	1
12.	4	3	2	1

Part 2

	Always	Often	Seldom	Never
1.	4	3	2	1
2.	4	3	2	1
3.	4	3	2	1
4.	4	3	2	1
5.	1	2	3	4
6.	4	3	2	1
7.	4	3	2	1
8.	4	3	2	1
9.	4	3	2	1
10.	1	2	3	4
11.	1	2	3	4
12.	4	3	2	1

Part 3

	Always	Often	Seldom	Never
1.	1	2	3	4
2.	1	2	3	4
3.	4	3	2	1
4.	4	3	2	1
5.	1	2	3	4
6.	4	3	2	1
7.	1	2	3	4
8.	1	2	3	4
9.	4	3	2	1
10.	4	3	2	1
11.	4	3	2	1
12.	4	3	2	1

WHAT YOUR SCORES MEAN

Part 1 Dominance and Submissiveness

Over 35: You're the dominant member of the family and you like to have your own way.

25–35: You know what you want and you set rules and regulations for your children. At the same time you're flexible and able to understand other points of view.

Under 25: You play a fairly submissive role in your family and let others make the decisions.

If you have a good, healthy relationship with your daughter, she will see your dominance or your flexibility as a positive quality, and she will choose a husband to whom she can relate in much the same way she relates to you.

- If she feels that you are too authoritarian, she may seek from a husband what she feels she never got from you—submission—and establish a marriage in which she is the dominant partner.
- If you have been possessive of your daughter, she might find herself attracted to a man who wants to "take her over," since that's a situation she's familiar with.
- If you have been very indecisive in your relationship with your daughter, she may be painfully shy and dependent on others for her sense of self. If she's wise she will choose a husband who admires her openly and builds her self-confidence.

Part 2 Warmth and Responsiveness

Over 35: You are an extremely warm and affectionate person and you have no trouble expressing love.

25–35: You are loving and warm, but you're probably not given to effusive physical displays of affection.

Under 25: You're a reserved person, and you usually have everything under control.

Displays of love and affection help to instill a sense of self-worth in a daughter, but whether you're effusive or reserved, if your daughter is confident of your love, she will choose a husband who loves her just as much as you do—or more.

- If you are extremely devoted to your daughter, your love may have a smothering effect on her, making it difficult for her to see herself as a separate individual. If she is too dependent on your love and approval, she may simply choose a husband to whom she can transfer her dependency without ever gaining the self-confidence to stand on her own two feet.
- If your daughter feels that you are cold and unapproachable, she may unconsciously find remote, distant men who are appealing and mysterious. Or if she perceives your reserve as unhappiness, she may be drawn to subdued, suffering men who seem particularly needy.
- If your lack of warmth or attention make your daughter feel inadequate, her best choice is a husband who finds her more than adequate and who is very open about expressing affection.

Part 3 Independence and Drive

Over 35: You are very self-sufficient, and the odds are that you have a successful career outside the home.

25–35: You are an independent woman, and you probably don't feel confined by traditional feminine roles.

Under 25: You're not driven, and you are willing to have others take on decision-making responsibility.

Daughters of working mothers have been shown to be highly independent and self-sufficient themselves, and if you are content with your life—as a working mother or a full-time mother—your daughter will be able to make her own decisions, and she will choose a husband who admires her individuality and her abilities.

- If your daughter feels neglected because of your self-sufficiency or inadequate because of your success, she may choose a similarly driven husband who substitutes material success for warmth and attention.
- If you are very submissive and unable to teach your daughter to be independent, she may be drawn to weak men who make her feel strong by comparison.
- If your daughter feels inadequate, either because of your success or your shyness, she will be happiest with a husband who respects her and encourages her talents.

LAW AND BUSINESS

☞HOW WELL DO YOU KNOW THE LAW?

How much do you really know about the law? Take this test and find out. There are ten basic questions covering many of the same legal topics that are on every bar exam. The rules are simple. The questions are all multiple choice or true or false. There is only *one* correct answer to each of the multiple choice questions.

Helpful hint: forget about everything you've ever seen in TV courtroom dramas.

1. Donna D., a hard-working secretary from Flatbush, N.Y., met Tom S., a Hustle champ, at the local disco. The couple dated for about three months and then Donna, deeply in love, withdrew all her savings and bought Tom a $7,000 sports car as a birthday present. Six weeks later, Tom stunned Donna by proposing. They had never even discussed marriage, but Donna accepted gladly. Tom gave her a $500 engagement ring.

    The couple discoed happily until Donna spotted her Hustle king tooling around town with a blond. She immediately called off the engagement. Tom is now demanding the ring back. Donna wants the car returned to her.

    Donna will have to

    a. be more wary of Hustlers

    b. give up the ring, but only when Tom gives her the car

    c. give up the ring, forget about the car and chalk it up to experience.

2. Vinnie C. and Al M. were arrested for a brutal murder. The cops immediately read them the famous Miranda warnings: "You have the right to remain silent. Anything you say may be used against you in a court of law. You have a right to have an attorney present during questioning. If you can't afford an attorney, one will be appointed free of charge."

    Vinnie told the police that he was waiving his rights and that he didn't want an attorney. He then confessed to the crime. Al, however, refused to answer questions

From the *Sunday News Magazine*, March 4, 1979, by Arthur Browne. Copyright © 1979 New York News, Inc. Reprinted by permission.

and said he wanted his lawyer. An hour later his attorney arrived at the station house, told police not to question Al, and instructed Al to remain silent. Late that night a detective stopped by Al's cell merely to check on his well being.

"You don't look too good," the detective remarked.

"I don't feel well," Al replied. "I want to get something off my chest."

At that point the detective once again read Al the Miranda warnings.

"I don't care about all that," Al said, "and I don't want anything more to do with that shyster lawyer."

Al then confessed.

Which one of the following statements is true?

a. Only Vinnie's confession can be used in court against him.

b. Only Al's confession can be used in court against him.

c. Both confessions can be used in court.

d. Neither confession can be used in court.

3. George J. was a struggling artist living in SoHo and surviving hand-to-mouth. After a human interest story appeared about George in the newspaper, a wealthy patron of the arts sent him a $50,000 check through the mail with a note that read, "Just a gift to make life a bit easier." George happily cashed the check and deposited it in his own bank account. All went well until the Internal Revenue Service, suspicious about a sudden boost in George's life style, called him in for an audit. George had always paid his taxes to the penny, but he suddenly realized he had never paid any income tax on the $50,000 gift. He is now seeking a good tax lawyer.

George doesn't owe the IRS a cent.   True   False

4. Heavy snow and freezing rain created treacherous conditions on the streets and sidewalks during the night, but by dawn the storm was over. At noon Richard M. emerged from his house to find that his Queens Village neighbors had already cleaned their sidewalks, but he decided he wouldn't even look at a snow shovel. Later that day, police slapped Richard with a summons for not shoveling his walk. An hour later, with the snow still untouched, a passerby slipped on Richard's walk and broke his leg.

Which one of the following statements is true?

a. The passerby can successfully sue Richard M. for negligence.

b. The passerby can successfully sue the city for negligence.

c. The passerby will lose if he sues either Richard M. or the city.

d. The city police don't have the power to issue summonses for not shoveling snow.

5. Eddie M. had long been a thorn in the side of narcotics detectives. A major drug dealer, he ran his operation out of a Manhattan bar, but he had never once been busted. That is, until the cops got an anonymous phone tip that a cache of Mexican brown heroin was stashed in a suitcase in the bar's backroom. That night after closing, two detectives climbed through a window, searched the bar and found the narcotics. They decided not to bust Eddie right away, however, hoping to bag his buyer too. The next day the cops watched Rick K. enter the bar empty-handed and emerge with the suitcase. A few minutes later Eddie and Rick were busted. The heroin was seized.

Which one of the following statements is correct?

a. Rick and Eddie are both going to jail for a long time.
b. Rick and Eddie will both get off scot free.
c. The heroin can be used as evidence to convict Rick but not Eddie.

6 & 7. Johnny T. wanted to add a new room to his house in the Bronx. Against his better judgment he hired Fitzy, his brother-in-law from Brooklyn, to do the job for $3,000. When the work was finished, Johnny paid Fitzy in full, but then discovered the room leaked and none of the windows opened. Fixing the mess would cost $1,000 more. Furious, Johnny demanded at least that much money back. When Fitzy responded, "What are you going to do, make a federal case out of this?" Johnny yelled back, "Yeah, that's just what I'm going to do." He hurried off to the federal courthouse determined to rake his brother-in-law over the legal coals.
Johnny will be able to sue Fitzy in federal court. True   False
Assuming that Johnny can sue in federal court, federal law is bound to be tougher on a guy like Fitzy than state law. True   False

8. Martin G. was an eccentric, elderly widower with two grown ne'er-do-well sons. When the boys were infants, Martin's lawyer drew up a will leaving everything to them, but a year before he died Martin angrily tore up the will in front of witnesses. The day after his death, the shredded will was found in Martin's bank safe deposit box along with a sheet of paper bearing two type-written sentences that said only:

"I leave half of my estate to my faithful butler and half to my faithful nurse, who both cared for me so well for so long. I leave nothing to my sons because they are bums."

Below that was only Martin's signature. The torn will and the sheet of paper were rushed directly from the bank to Surrogate's Court. The sons, up to their ears in gambling debts, are claiming Martin's one-million-dollar estate.

Which one of the following statements is correct?
a. The butler and nurse won't get anything because there was no formal reading of the will.
b. The sons will split everything.
c. The butler and nurse will split everything.
d. The sons, the butler and the nurse will split the estate four ways.

9. After years of living in a cramped apartment, Barb and Dave F. finally found their dream house on Long Island. They signed a standard contract of sale with the house's owner, Mr. Nice, to buy the place for $60,000 and gave him a $6,000 down payment. The closing was set for June 1, but there was one problem: Their lease expired on May 1. Mr. Nice refused to move up the closing, but agreed to let Barb and Dave move in a month early. They moved in on May 1. On May 15—two weeks before Barb and Dave were going to take title—the house was struck by lightning and burned to the ground. Barb and Dave are now demanding their $6,000 back.
Complete the following sentence.
Barb and Dave
a. can successfully demand their money back.
b. can force Mr. Nice to rebuild the house and sell the new place to them.
c. will only lose their $6,000.

d. will have to give Mr. Nice $54,000, the remainder of the purchase price, if he demands it

10. Gretchen K. was suing her doctor for malpractice because he left a sponge inside her after a routine appendectomy. The judge told the jury that they could award Gretchen compensation only if they found the doctor guilty of malpractice beyond a reasonable doubt.

The judge doesn't know what he is talking about.   True   False

ANSWERS

Score one point for each correct answer.

1. c. Generally, once a gift has been given and accepted in good faith, there is no legal way to force its return. That is why Donna will not be able to force Tom to return the car. In New York, however, the law does not view an engagement ring as such a simple gift. Section 80-B of the state's Civil Rights Law provides that, when the sole motive for making a gift is a "contemplated marriage which has not occurred," the party who gave the gift can recover it. And that applies regardless of who was at fault in causing the breakup.

2. a. The Miranda warnings were developed by the United States Supreme Court as a means of preventing the police from violating a criminal defendant's Fifth Amendment right against self-incrimination as well as his Sixth Amendment right to counsel. Vinnie knowingly and voluntarily waived his Miranda rights. His confession is perfectly admissible in court. Al also waived his rights, but, oddly, his confession can't be used against him. Once an attorney enters the picture, a criminal defendant is no longer legally capable of waiving his right to counsel unless his lawyer is present when he makes the waiver.

3. True. Everyone knows that the IRS wants to tax every possible cent of income. And that's exactly what the tax code calls for. But the code also lists exceptions—types of income that will not be taxed—and among the exceptions are gifts, no matter how large. Donors of sizeable gifts, however, must pay a gift tax on their largesse.

4. c. Even though the police can and do issue summonses for not shoveling snow, the responsibility for keeping the streets and sidewalks clean and safe always belongs to the city. The law won't hold a property owner liable for not doing a job that really should have been done by the city. In cases such as this the courts have ruled that before the city will be held liable it must have a "reasonable time" to get the shoveling done itself—much longer than just the day that lapsed here between the time the snow stopped falling and the time the accident occurred.

Richard M., incidentally, was lucky that he never touched the snow. If he had started shoveling and had done a bad job of it, he could have given the passerby good ground for suit. Doing a bad job of shoveling is negligence. Leaving the snow alone is not.

5. b. The Fourth Amendment to the United States Constitution protects the public, including criminals, from unreasonable searches and seizures. The search of Eddie's bar was unconstitutional because the police entered the premises without a search warrant based on probable cause. The fact that the police did find heroin does not retroactively justify invading Eddie's rights.

Since the search was unlawful, Eddie can prevent it from being used as evidence against him. The cops didn't violate Rick's rights by searching Eddie's bar. But because they never would have known to arrest Rick had they not done the unlawful search, a corollary to the exclusionary rule called the "fruit of the poison tree doctrine" comes into play. Under the doctrine, the results of an unlawful act by police can be suppressed. Here that includes Rick's arrest.

6. False. Johnny should sue in the New York City Civil Court. To sue in federal court, you generally must be suing for more than $10,000 and you must also meet either of the two following criteria: (1) All the opposing parties to the suit must live in different states; or (2) The suit must deal with a "federal question," such as the interpretation of the United States Constitution.

7. False. Federal courts decide suits such as this according to the law of the state in which their court is located. That means that if you sue in a federal court in New York, the judge will apply New York law, but if you filed the same suit in New Jersey, New Jersey law would govern. Johnny should get the same results, then, no matter what court he sues in in New York.

8. b. There is no such thing as a reading of a will, therefore answer *a* is meaningless. The butler and the nurse still lose out, however, and despite their father's wishes, the sons take all. By tearing up his old will in front of witnesses, Martin revoked it. His attempt to replace it with the sheet of paper in the safe deposit box failed, however. Wills must be executed under a set of rigid technical rules designed primarily to prevent fraud. Generally, the rules require that a will must be in writing and signed in the presence of two witnesses, who also sign the document. Since there were no witnesses to the signing of the sheet of paper, it will not be given effect as a will. The law will be forced to distribute Martin's estate as if he died without a will. Regardless of what he wanted, the law states that, in this situation, Martin's sons will inherit everything simply because they are his closest surviving kin.

9. d. In New York, if a house burns down before a would-be buyer takes title to it, the buyer can generally back out of the deal and demand a refund of his down payment if he didn't cause the fire. But if the buyer has possession of the house when the fire occurs, the general rule doesn't apply. In that case, he won't be able to get a refund and can also be compelled to pay the full purchase price for a pile of ashes.

10. True. Everyone knows that a jury has to find someone guilty beyond a reasonable doubt before he can be convicted of a crime. But malpractice is not a crime. It is a civil matter. In civil matters, which also include things like negligence, libel and slander, and breach of contract, the jury does not find someone guilty. Instead, it finds the defendant "liable" to pay compensation for his actions. Also, the standard of proof in civil matters is not "beyond a reasonable doubt." Rather, a jury only needs a "fair preponderance of the evidence" to find a defendant liable. In other words, if fifty-one percent of the evidence says so, the jury can find him liable. The judge should have told the jury they could award Gretchen compensation if they found the doctor liable by a fair preponderance of the evidence.

WHAT YOUR SCORE MEANS

8–10: What's your fee for a simple divorce?

3–7: Consider law school.

0–3: Get yourself a lawyer.

☞ WOULD YOU MAKE A GOOD PROSECUTING ATTORNEY?

Here's a quiz to help you find out if you would make a good prosecuting attorney. Just mark what you consider the right answer to each question, then compare your answers to the correct ones at the end of the quiz.

1. A killer, adjudged insane and committed to an institution, recovers his sanity. Would you
a. insist upon trying him
b. let him go free

2. The case hinges upon whether lie detector tests have as much legal status and validity as fingerprints. Would you
a. maintain that they do
b. admit that they don't

3. The body of a person believed murdered two years ago has never been found, but there is ample evidence of the crime. Would you
a. go on with the trial
b. drop the case

4. The question arises whether a murder suspect was irresistibly drawn back to the scene of the crime. Would you say this is
a. usually true
b. not as a rule

5. A man has been charged with a misdemeanor for refusing to help police make an arrest. Would you
a. contend the charge is reasonable
b. tell the police to forget it

6. There's been a wave of embezzlement by trusted employees. Would you expect to find that more of the culprits are
a. men
b. women

7. Police ask if it is all right for them to use underworld tipsters to crack an important case. Would you say
a. yes
b. nothing doing

8. The question arises: "Are there more

married or single women in jail these days?" Would you say

a. more married women

b. more single women

ANSWERS

1. b. Prosecutors know that juries usually acquit a defendant who was unquestionably insane when he murdered.

2. b. Although lie detector tests are valuable, they do not have the judicial recognition given to fingerprinting.

3. a. Even if there is no body, it can sometimes be established that a murder took place.

4. b. Except for a few sadist slayers, killers avoid the scene of the crime.

5. a. The man may have committed a misdemeanor.

6. a. Male embezzlers outnumber females by more than three to one, according to the FBI.

7. a. Even federal authorities pay for tips leading to convictions.

8. b. According to the United States Bureau of Prisons, there are more single and divorced women in prison.

☞ DO YOU HAVE WHAT IT TAKES TO START YOUR OWN BUSINESS?

Considering that most of the 600,000 new business ventures started in America each year fail, that's a mighty important question for those who have visions of achieving the American dream. The Entrepreneurship Institute, a non-profit organization dedicated to assisting and encouraging entrepreneurship, has developed this questionnaire to help you determine whether you have the qualifications to succeed in your own business.

Answer the questions for yourself.

1. Do I have a close relative who is or was in business for him/herself?
   Yes   No

2. Have I ever worked for a small firm where I had close contact with the person who started it?
   Yes   No

3. Did I ever work for a small division of a larger firm where I had close contact with the top manager?
   Yes   No

4. Is my work experience in a variety of functional areas, such as marketing, finance, and production?
   Yes   No

5. Have I ever had my employer reject my "better mousetrap" idea?
   Yes   No

6. Am I between the ages of thirty and forty?
   Yes   No

7. I like to do things, rather than plan things.
   Yes   No

8. I have lived in three or more cities in my life.
   Yes   No

9. I have been fired before.
   Yes   No

10. (If I am married:) My spouse is supportive of my work.

Yes   No

11. What generally happens to me is something I make happen, not something that is due to luck, good and otherwise.

Yes   No

12. If I had to make a choice between working for a firm which I do not own for twice the money I make now, and running my own firm at my present compensation, I would choose to start my own firm.

Yes   No

13. When a problem comes up that everyone around me says is unsolvable, I usually try to figure out ways to solve it.

Yes   No

14. As a child, I sold lemonade or had a paper route or similar activities.

Yes   No

15. I get along well with other people.

Yes   No

16. My subordinates respect me and work hard for me, even if they don't necessarily like me.

Yes   No

ANSWERS AND WHAT YOUR SCORE MEANS

Compute your total score by counting one point for *every* yes answer.

13–16: Get going on your business plan—you have the earmarks of entrepreneurship.

10–12: Think twice before taking the plunge.

6–9: The pension you'll get can always be invested by others.

0–5: Have you considered the fact that there are over 200,000,000 Americans who are not entrepreneurs?

1. The available data show that the majority of entrepreneurs had a father or close relative in business for themselves. The importance of a role model in entrepreneurship is well documented. To make being in business for yourself credible, it is considered important that you see people in action who have also started firms. Strangely, studies on this variable show that a close relative entrepreneur will frequently discourage entrepreneurship in another relative, so don't be dismayed if everyone around you tells you how tough it is and why you shouldn't do it.

2-3. Persons who work in small firms or in small divisions of larger firms get more varied experiences than those who work in very large firms or large divisions of large firms. Because those who work in the smaller firm environment usually get more opportunities to work closely with the top management and/or founders of those firms, their experience pertinent to entrepreneurship is more varied and useful. When you work for such firms, you come to realize that the top manager/entrepreneur is human, and that they make mistakes. One frequently gets the attitude from such experiences that, "If they can do it, so can I."

4. The more functional area experiences, the better. An entrepreneur is a jack-of-all-trades, at least initially. The entrepreneur needs to be conversant with the total functions of the enterprise, and cannot generally afford experts at first. Even if you are wealthy and can afford the experts, you need to understand their functions and how they fit together. This is best gained through education and experience. If you have worked in marketing and finance and know the other important functional areas pertinent to the business you want to start, this is a decided plus for your goal of starting your own firm.

5. More companies are started for negative reasons than for positive ones, and the rejection of

your idea for the "better mousetrap" is a common negative reason. Large corporations frequently do more to unwittingly encourage entrepreneurship by discouraging creativity than they know. Their reasoning is valid to them—a $5,000,000 market is too small for a $500,000,000 company—but not to you, the entrepreneur. Your "pet rock" may be all right as an independent business, but not within your existing firm.

6. If you are between thirty and forty, that's probably good. These are peak years for energy, vitally necessary for the hard work ahead of you. They also are peak years for having the variety of experience and education that can help you through the difficult first years. Age can give an edge over younger entrepreneurs. At the same time, entrepreneurs in their thirties are not necessarily as accustomed to the comfortable life style that happens in later years, and can do without a bit more readily. If you are younger or older than this, don't get too upset—we find the entrepreneurial population is evenly distributed, with some people forming their first corporation even in their sixties.

7. Most entrepreneurs like to do, not read, write, think or plan. Entrepreneurs are people of action. This does not mean that you cannot be successful if you like to plan. Indeed, the odds favor a planning approach, but also require action. If you are one of those fortunate persons who is at home both planning and acting, consider yourself a prime candidate for entrepreneurship.

8. Mobility is a key factor in the decision to start a company. This is related to flexibility, a necessity in the beginning stages of a firm. An openness and receptivity to new ideas and situations can be enhanced by variety, and movement frequently forces this flexibility. In high-technology company formations studied, a very large majority of the firms were started by persons who moved around a great deal. Entrepreneurship is also related to being the "new man in town"—the lack of roots and ties found among immigrants and minorities.

9–16. Give yourself a point for every "yes" response. The wider the variety of experience you have and the more determined you are to tackle "insoluble" problems, the better your chances of success.

☛CLAWING YOUR WAY TO THE TOP

Have you seriously considered the cost of getting ahead? The cost to hour health? To your peace of mind? To your private life? Have you measured the gains against the losses? Here is a quiz to determine whether you are the sort of person who should—or shouldn't—claw your way to the top.

1. Day-to-day happiness is extremely important to me.
   a. agree strongly
   b. agree moderately.
   c. disagree moderately
   d. disagree strongly

2. I can dissemble pretty well when I have to.
   a. agree strongly
   b. agree moderately
   c. disagree moderately
   d. disagree strongly

3. I am envious of friends who are now more successful than I am.
   a. agree strongly
   b. agree moderately
   c. disagree moderately
   d. disagree strongly

4. I am terribly concerned about what people think of me.
   a. agree strongly
   b. agree moderately
   c. disagree moderately
   d. disagree strongly

5. I think it's a good idea always to "look busy" at the office.
   a. agree strongly
   b. agree moderately
   c. disagree moderately
   d. disagree strongly

6. I would not be overjoyed to give up a windowless office that was cool and comfortable for a hot, uncomfortable, corner office with a window.
   a. agree strongly
   b. agree moderately
   c. disagree moderately
   d. disagree strongly

7. It is much simpler to answer one's own phone rather than let a secretary do it.
   a. agree strongly
   b. agree moderately
   c. disagree moderately
   d. disagree strongly

8. I have an expensive life style, and I don't want to give it up.
   a. agree strongly
   b. agree moderately

c. disagree moderately
d. disagree strongly
9. I am leery of making sacrifices for anything unless I can be assured of positive results.
a. agree strongly
b. agree moderately
c. disagree moderately

d. disagree strongly
10. Leisure activities bore me; I would
much rather be at the office.
a. agree strongly
b. agree moderately
c. disagree moderately
d. disagree strongly

HOW TO SCORE

Award yourself the following number of points for each answer.

1. a–0, b–1, c–2, d–3
2. a–3, b–2, c–1, d–0
3. a–3, b–2, c–1, d–0
4. a–3, b–2, c–1, d–0
5. a–3, b–2, c–1, d–0

6. a–0, b–1, c–2, d–3
7. a–0, b–1, c–2, d–3
8. a–3, b–2, c–1, d–0
9. a–0, b–1, c–2, d–3
10. a–3, b–2, c–1, d–0

WHAT YOUR SCORE MEANS

0–10: If you tried to climb too high on the corporate ladder you would be likely to fall off and break both your legs. Very probably, you already know this about yourself. You are too straightforward, too uncalculating and too much yourself to want to make the necessary compromises to get ahead. Your main ambition is to be happy and fulfilled. You have interests outside your work. You are, according to Michael Maccoby's breakdown of organizational types, a "craftsman," not a "gamesman" or "jungle fighter."

11–30: You have a certain amount of ambition, which is healthy but not overwhelming. There are certain sacrifices that you are not prepared to make to bring about your goals. You are at a disadvantage when you try to compete with the more political people in your company. You can't lie as well as they can, you are careless about your corporate image, and in the middle of a boring meeting, you sometimes find your mind drifting to thoughts of mountain climbing in the Himalayas or the tennis match you won against the club champion. If you try to climb too high on the corporate ladder, you may not notice when one of your co-workers starts sawing away at the very rung upon which you are perched.

20 to 30: You are a corporate infighter and very good at it. Such activity fits your temperament and psychology. It is you everyone else has to watch out for. Whatever rung you are on now, you are going higher.

INSTANT PSYCHOLOGICAL ANALYSIS

☞PSYCHO QUIZ: HOW NEUROTIC ARE YOU?

Dr. Sherman Feinstein, a psychiatrist at the Psychosomatic and Psychiatric Institute of Michael Reese Hospital and Medical Center in Chicago, defines neurosis quite simply: You hurt, or you can't function, but there seems to be no reason why. We all suffer incapacitating emotions at times. When should we seek help? These questions, suggested by Dr. Feinstein, may help you decide.

Section I.

1. Do you worry about becoming seriously ill?
a. frequently
b. sometimes
c. seldom or never

2. A friend has invited you on a first-time camping trip you think you'd enjoy. Would the thought of all the things that could happen, even remote dangers, make you refuse the invitation?
a. probably
b. probably not

3. Does being alone at home make you nervous?
a. frequently
b. sometimes
c. seldom or never

4. Do you ever have a nagging sense of danger, even though your logic tells you you're safe?
a. frequently
b. sometimes
c. seldom or never

5. If your husband or child was thirty minutes late in coming home, would you begin to fear he had come to some harm?
a. probably
b. probably not

Section II.

1. Have you ever said no to a chance for a relationship because you were sure the other person would hurt you?
a. frequently

b. sometimes
c. seldom or never

2. Do you feel unloved and unlovable?
   a. frequently
   b. sometimes
   c. seldom or never

3. If you suffered a significant loss (the death of a loved-one, the loss of a career) more than a year ago, are you still deeply grieved by that loss?
   a. yes
   b. no

4. Do you feel unworthy of your achievements or the friendships you enjoy?
   a. frequently
   b. sometimes
   c. seldom or never

5. Do you need to drink or take drugs in order to keep from feeling bored?
   a. frequently
   b. sometimes
   c. seldom or never

6. Have you ever seriously thought about making a radical change in the way you live—such as becoming a nun, joining a commune, moving to Europe?
   a. frequently
   b. sometimes
   c. seldom or never

7. Have you ever contemplated suicide?
   a. frequently
   b. sometimes
   c. seldom or never

8. Though you seem to be in good physical condition, do you suffer from constant fatigue, inertia, or, in contrast, do you feel very agitated much of the time?
   a. frequently
   b. sometimes
   c. seldom or never

9. Your boss unexpectedly calls you into his office, and you sense that it's important. Are you more likely to guess you're about to fired or given a promotion?
   a. fired
   b. promotion

Section III.

1. You are yelled at for a mistake you didn't make. You
   a. get mad and counterattack
   b. become so anxious you feel paralyzed, unable to say a thing
   c. try to talk things out calmly and clear the air

2. You are yelled at for a mistake you did make. You
   a. get mad and counterattack
   b. stay calm and accept the blame

3. Over the radio you hear about an enormous traffic jam on the expressway, and, sure enough, your husband comes home late. You
   a. get mad at him anyway, because he's spoiled the evening
   b. get mad because he didn't phone you to say he'll be late
   c. give him a kiss and warm up his dinner

Section IV.

1. Is there a specific situation that always frightens you for which no amount of persuasion allays the fear.
   a. yes
   b. no

2. If you fear a specific situation when you are in it, does the mere thought of being in that situation also make you afraid?
   a. yes
   b. no

3. Are you unable to relax and be relatively free of fear in specific situations (such as flying or crowds) that make you nervous?
   a. yes
   b. no

4. Has a recent change in your life made it impossible for you to avoid a specific situation you dread?
a. yes
b. no

5. Does a specific situation continue to frighten you even though no harm comes to you when you're actually in that situation?
a. yes
b. no

Section V.

1. Do you dwell on things you should have done but didn't, or things you did but shouldn't have?
a. frequently
b. sometimes
c. seldom or never

2. Do you have routines, habits, or rituals that you follow every day, without which you feel uncomfortable, ill at ease, or afraid?
a. yes
b. no

3. When something worries you, is there some trick you use to help you feel better, even though it doesn't solve the problem? (For example: would you raid the refrigerator when you lost a job, or scrub a clean floor if you had a fight with a friend?)
a. yes
b. no

4. When you are confronted by a situation or object that evokes a strong emotional response, do you react to your feelings unthinkingly? (For example: actually shuddering if you touch dirt, or breaking out in a cold sweat and feeling you have to get away when in a crowd?)
a. yes
b. no

5. If you had left the house and were on the road, several miles away, would you turn back and go home because you thought you just might have left the stove on?
a. yes
b. no

Section VI.

1. How often should the man in your life express his feelings for you with words or tokens such as flowers?
a. frequently
b. sometimes
c. seldom or never

2. If you had a pleasant lunch with a girl friend in the city, would you suddenly feel abandoned or anxious when she had to leave and you had to continue the afternoon's activities alone?
a. probably
b. probably not

3. If you live alone, or are at home alone for the evening, do you spend a lot of time on the phone with nothing much to say?
a. frequently
b. sometimes
c. seldom or never

4. Do you have problems concentrating, reading, or doing creative things?
a. frequently
b. sometimes
c. seldom or never

5. When you are alone, is it hard to get anything accomplished?
a. frequently
b. sometimes
c. seldom or never

6. Do you enjoy—or feel comfortable—being alone?
a. frequently
b. sometimes
c. seldom or never

ANALYSIS OF YOUR ANSWERS

Section I.

The questions in this section reveal your level of anxiety. Anxiety, Dr. Feinstein says, is a feeling of impending danger to yourself or the people and things around you. "Anxiety is a perfectly normal reaction when real danger is present. It becomes pathological when it is either all out of proportion to the actual danger, or when no actual danger exists." Furthermore, he says, pathological anxiety is continuous. The individual who may need professional help is one whose thinking is dominated by a general sense of danger, "someone who isn't able to differentiate between safe and non-safe." Untreated, such a condition can become dehibilitating, making a basically healthy person worry himself sick (as in question 1), or keeping him from doing the things he'd enjoy (as in question 2). "Only Woody Allen can function effectively under a pathological anxiety," Dr. Feinstein says. An *a* answer to each of the questions in this section indicates a possibly high anxiety level: the more *a* answers you have, the more likely that you have an anxiety neurosis.

Section II.

Depression is a feeling we all experience at some time. If it doesn't go away, the depression is neurotic. "We can classify the symptoms for this condition by what psychiatrists call the 'depressive triad': negative conception of self; negative interpretation of life experience; negative view of the future," Dr. Feinstein explains. "The individual suffering acute depression feels he is somehow becoming trapped, that his life has become intolerable." The resulting feelings of boredom, restlessness, or entrapment make the depressed person want to escape by running away, by escaping into drugs or alcohol, by making radical changes (such as altering a life style or abandoning a mate), even by suicide. At the same time, that negative self-image and pessimistic outlook will convince the depressed person that new relationships won't work (question 1), that love and friendships are undeserved (question 4), that the worst will probably happen before the better (question 9). "Feeling depressed is natural at times," says Dr. Feinstein. "The loss of a spouse or of a position in society can cause a 'healthy' grief. Depression becomes neurotic when it continues—when, for example, the individual continues to grieve deeply over a significant loss that happened more than a year or so in the past, to use a somewhat arbitrary yardstick."

Section III.

Anger, says Dr. Feinstein, is a natural reaction to a stress situation. "In all animals it's part of the fight-or-flight reaction to a threat, though of course, since man has more options open to him than other animals do, he ought to exercise them. What may be natural to an animal may be pathological in man." He suggests that the healthiest reaction to an angry attack is to try to resolve it verbally—calmly, if possible. But, he adds, "the person who responds to anger by becoming angry and counterattacking is aggressively pathological. Just as pathological—passively so—is the individual who responds by becoming paralyzed with anxiety, who is unable to deal with the stress situation at all." Worse, the psychiatrist says, is to feel rage and retaliate "even when the frustrating agent is justified, nonarbitrary, or reasonable." It's unhealthy, in other words, to attack when your boss yells at you for burning down the office (assuming you did it). It's also unreasonable, and unhealthy, to become angry with your husband for getting stuck in a traffic jam he couldn't avoid. (Answer *b* is not satisfactory, either, since he may not have been able to reach a phone.) For each of the questions in this section, you are probably healthier if you chose the last answer.

Section IV.

If you answered yes to any or all of the questions in this section, you may have a phobia, which Dr. Feinstein defines as "the unreasonable anticipation of physical or psychological harm." It differs from anxiety in degree: With a phobia, what you fear is limited to a specific definable situation. The phobic person experiences the same anxiety symptoms whether he is placed in that specific situation or merely reminded of it. If you have a phobia about tunnels, says Dr. Feinstein, you may break out in a cold sweat in a real tunnel or when you see a picture of one. But, he adds, having a phobia doesn't necessarily mean you need treatment. If you feel at ease when you aren't in the specific situation, and if you can easily avoid being placed in it, chances are you'll be able to function pretty well. It's when your circumstances change and you are forced into the phobic situation that you may need professional help. For example, you may fear elevators and lead a normal life, but when you take a new job on the fortieth floor you may need help coping. For every yes answer in this section, chalk up one point for your phobias.

Section V.
If you have a phobia, you may exhibit what this section deals with: compulsion. Dr. Feinstein says a compulsion is "the attempt to allay excessive doubts or obsessions through actions." Thus the anxious person may worry about his house catching fire; the compulsive person will check half a dozen times to make sure the pilot light isn't out. Since the characteristic of a compulsion is its non-thinking nature, the physical response to whatever one is compulsive about may not be the right one to solve the problem. Compulsive people, Dr. Feinstein says, frequently exhibit ritualistic behavior, such as repeated handwashing or floor scrubbing, using the ritual almost as a magic charm which can't be understood but seems to ward off the danger. The more *a* answers in this section, the more compulsive you may be. Obviously, whether you need help depends on how much your compulsive behavior gets in the way of your life (as in question 5).

Section VI.
Of all the states of mind, loneliness is least neurotic, says Dr. Feinstein. He adds that lonely people have not really developed to the stage of a separate, mature individual. They are caught in the immature struggle for attachments and security, and are therefore more vulnerable to feelings of loss and separation. "There is a big difference between aloneness and loneliness," says Dr. Feinstein. "Aloneness is the capacity to enjoy solitude. It's a mature, comfortable feeling. Loneliness is really a kind of separation anxiety—a feeling of vulnerability and abandonment, even a dread that something terrible will happen." The mature individual, he says, enjoys periods of aloneness, particularly since these are the times when one is creatively productive. "Lonely people have trouble being creative or productive, because the necessary prerequisite for many such endeavors (such as writing or painting) is solitude. In fact, the woman who is a poor housekeeper may be neither lazy nor sloppy. She may just dread being alone in the house. Outside, in the business world, she may perform beautifully." He adds that lengthy phone conversations may be a way lonely people cope with their isolation. Number 6 is the only question for which *a* is a healthy response.

☛ THE SELF-RATING DEPRESSION SCALE

This depression scale was developed by Dr. William W.K. Zung, a psychiatrist specializing in depression and anxiety. Dr. Zung notes that while depression can be used to describe an affect or feeling of short duration, or a mood or emotion sustained over a longer period of time, it can also be a disorder with characteristic and complex symptoms.

The Self-rating Depression Scale is not intended to differentiate types of depression. It serves rather to measure the intensity of depression and rate it as a disorder.

Read the statements below and circle the answer which best describes your feelings.

1. I feel down-hearted, blue and sad
  a. none or a little of the time
  b. some of the time
  c. good part of the time
  d. most or all of the time

2. Morning is when I feel best
  a. none or a little of the time
  a. some of the time
  c. good part of the time
  d. most or all of the time

3. I have crying spells or feel like it
  a. none or a little of the time
  b. some of the time
  c. good part of the time
  d. most or all of the time

4. I have trouble sleeping through the night
  a. none or a little of the time
  b. some of the time
  c. good part of the time
  d. most or all of the time

5. I eat as much as I used to
  a. none or a little of the time
  b. some of the tme
  c. good part of the time
  d. most or all of the time

6. I enjoy looking at, talking to, and

being with, attractive women/men
a. none or a little of the time
b. some of the time
c. good part of the time
d. most or all of the time

7. I notice that I am losing weight
a. none or a little of the time
b. some of the time
c. good part of the time
d. most or all of the time

8. I have trouble with constipation
a. none or a little of the time
b. some of the time
c. good part of the time
d. most or all of the time

9. My heart beats faster than usual
a. none or a little of the time
b. some of the time
c. good part of the time
d. most or all of the time

10. I get tired for no reason
a. none or a little of the time
b. some of the time
c. good part of the time
d. most or all of the time

11. My mind is as clear as it used to be
a. none or a little of the time
b. some of the time
c. good part of the time
d. most or all of the time

12. I find it easy to do the things I used to
a. none or a little of the time
b. some of the time
c. good part of the time
d. most or all of the time

13. I am restless and can't keep still
a. none or a little of the time
b. some of the time

c. good part of the time
d. most or all of the time

14. I feel hopeful about the future
a. none or a little of the time
b. some of the time
c. good part of the time
d. most or all of the time

15. I am more irritable than usual
a. none or a little of the time
b. some of the time
c. good part of the time
d. most or all of the time

16. I find it easy to make decisions
a. none or a little of the time
b. some of the time
c. good part of the time
d. most or all of the time

17. I feel that I am useful and needed
a. none or a little of the time
b. some of the time
c. good part of the time
d. most or all of the time

18. My life is pretty full
a. none or a little of the time
b. some of the time
c. good part of the time
d. most or all of the time

19. I feel that others would be better off if I were dead
a. none or a little of the time
b. some of the time
c. good part of the time
d. most or all of the time

20. I still enjoy the things I used to do
a. none or a little of the time
b. some of the time
c. good part of the time
d. most or all of the time

HOW TO SCORE

Tally your total score based on the points for each question and answer.
Questions 1, 3, 4, 7, 8, 9, 10, 13, 15, 19: a–1, b–2, c–3, d–4
Questions 2, 5, 6, 11, 12, 14, 16, 17, 18, 20: a–4, b–3, c–2, d–1

WHAT YOUR SCORE MEANS

To determine your depression rating locate your score on this table.

Below 39: Within normal range, no depression disorder.

40–47: Presence of minimal to mild depression.

48–55: Presence of moderate to marked depression.

56 and over: Presence of severe to extreme depression.

Interpretations of the scores are based on data comparing seriously depressed versus non-depressed subjects in the 20–64-year-old range. If you received a high score, it does not necessarily mean you are suffering from depression as a disorder. It merely indicates the presence of symptoms which may be significant enough to have you seek professional assistance.

☞ THE SELF-RATING ANXIETY SCALE

This scale, developed by noted psychiatrist Dr. William W. K. Zung, contains twenty items that relate specific characteristics of anxiety as symptoms of certain anxiety disorders. After reading each statement below, choose the answer that best applies to you.

1. I feel more nervous and anxious than usual
  a. none or a little of the time
  b. some of the time
  c. good part of the time
  d. most or all of the time

2. I feel afraid for no reason at all
  a. none or a little of the time
  b. some of the time
  c. good part of the time
  d. most or all of the time

3. I get upset easily or feel panicky
  a. none or a little of the time
  b. some of the time
  c. good part of the time
  d. most or all of the time

4. I feel like I'm falling apart and going to pieces
  a. none or a little of the time
  b. some of the time
  c. good part of the time
  d. most or all of the time

5. I feel that everything is all right and nothing bad will happen
  a. none or a little of the time
  b. some of the time
  c. good part of the time
  d. most or all of the time

6. My arms and legs shake and tremble
  a. none or a little of the time
  b. some of the time
  c. good part of the time
  d. most or all of the time

7. I am bothered by headaches, neck and back pains
  a. none or a little of the time
  b. some of the time
  c. good part of the time
  d. most or all of the time

8. I feel weak and get tired easily
  a. none or a little of the time
  b. some of the time
  c. good part of the time
  d. most or all of the time

9. I feel calm and can sit still easily
  a. none or a little of the time

  b. some of the time
  c. good part of the time
  d. most or all of the time

10. I can feel my heart beating fast
  a. none or a little of the time
  b. some of the time
  c. good part of the time
  d. most or all of the time

11. I am bothered by dizzy spells
  a. none or a little of the time
  b. some of the time
  c. good part of the time
  d. most or all of the time

12. I have fainting spells or feel like it
  a. none or a little of the time
  b. some of the time
  c. good part of the time
  d. most or all of the time

13. I can breathe in and out easily
  a. none or a little of the time
  b. some of the time
  c. good part of the time
  d. most or all of the time

14. I get feelings of numbness and tingling in my fingers, toes
  a. none or a little of the time
  b. some of the time
  c. good part of the time
  d. most or all of the time

15. I am bothered by stomach aches or indigestion

  a. none or a little of the time
  b. some of the time
  c. good part of the time
  d. most or all of the time

16. I have to empty my bladder often
  a. none or a little of the time
  b. some of the time
  c. good part of the time
  d. most or all of the time

17. My hands are usually dry and warm
  a. none or a little of the time
  b. some of the time
  c. good part of the time
  d. most or all of the time

18. My face gets hot and blushes
  a. none or a little of the time
  b. some of the time
  c. good part of the time
  d. most or all of the time

19. I fall asleep easily and get a good night's rest
  a. none or a little of the time
  b. some of the time
  c. good part of the time
  d. most or all of the time

20. I have nightmares
  a. none or a little of the time
  b. some of the time
  c. good part of the time
  d. most or all of the time

HOW TO SCORE

Tally your total score based on the points for each answer.

1. a–1, b–2, c–3, d–4
2. a–1, b–2, c–3, d–4
3. a–1, b–2, c–3, d–4
4. a–1, b–2, c–3, d–4
5. a–4, b–3, c–2, d–1
6. a–1, b–2, c–3, d–4
7. a–1, b–2, c–3, d–4

8. a–1, b–2, c–3, d–4
9. a–4, b–3, c–2, d–1
10. a–1, b–2, c–3, d–4
11. a–1, b–2, c–3, d–4
12. a–1, b–2, c–3, d–4
13. a–4, b–3, c–2, d–1
14. a–1, b–2, c–3, d–4

15. a–1, b–2, c–3, d–4
16. a–1, b–2, c–3, d–4
17. a–4, b–3, c–2, d–1
18. a–1, b–2, c–3, d–4
19. a–4, b–3, c–2, d–1
20. a–1, b–2, c–3, d–4

WHAT YOUR SCORE MEANS

Each statement in the Anxiety Scale refers to the following specific anxiety symptoms:

1. anxiousness
2. fear
3. panic
4. mental disintegration
5. apprehension
6. tremors
7. body aches and pains
8. easy fatigability
9. restlessness
10. palpitation

11. dizziness
12. faintness
13. dyspnea (breathing difficulty)
14. paresthesias
    (numbness, loss of feeling)
15. nausea and vomiting
16. urinary frequency
17. sweating
18. face flushing
19. insomnia
20. nightmares

While anxiety can be simply feeling a little anxious or a tense moment in an anxious situation, if severe enough it can become an emotional disorder requiring professional treatment. Locate your total score below to determine your anxiety rating.

20–35: Within normal range, no anxiety present.

36–47: Presence of minimal to moderate anxiety.

48–59: Presence of marked to severe anxiety.

60 and over: Presence of most extreme anxiety.

☞ HOW WELL DO YOU COPE WITH STRESS?

Read the twenty conditions below and truthfully indicate whether they never occur, occur sometimes, or occur frequently.

1. Do you breathe rapidly and shallowly?
   a. never
   b. sometimes
   c. frequently

2. Are your hands and feet cold?
   a. never
   b. sometimes
   c. frequently

3. Do you have vague aches and pains?
   a. never
   b. sometimes
   c. frequently

4. Do you suffer from heartburn?
   a. never
   b. sometimes
   c. frequently

5. Do you feel your heart palpitating?
   a. never
   b. sometimes
   c. frequently

6. Does your face flush and/or feel hot?
   a. never
   b. sometimes
   c. frequently

7. Do your hands shake?
   a. never
   b. sometimes
   c. frequently

8. Are you always running to the bathroom?
   a. never
   b. sometimes
   c. frequently

9. Are you too busy to eat?
   a. never
   b. sometimes
   c. frequently

10. Do you have trouble falling or staying asleep?
   a. never
   b. sometimes
   c. frequently

11. Are you too tired to think?
   a. never
   b. sometimes
   c. frequently

12. Are you bored?
   a. never
   b. sometimes
   c. frequently

13. Do you feel indispensable?
   a. never

b. sometimes
c. frequently

14. Do you feel trapped?
    a. never
    b. sometimes
    c. frequently

15. Do you feel like you never have enough time to get things done?
    a. never
    b. sometimes
    c. frequently

16. Do you need a tranquilizer or a drink before facing a group or making a decision?
    a. never
    b. sometimes
    c. frequently

17. Do you feel depressed and don't know why?
    a. never
    b. sometimes
    c. frequently

18. Do you feel anxious and don't know why?
    a. never
    b. sometimes
    c. frequently

19. Do you fly off the handle easily?
    a. never
    b. sometimes
    c. frequently

20. Are you reluctant to stand up for your rights?
    a. never
    b. sometimes
    c. frequently

HOW TO SCORE AND WHAT YOUR SCORE MEANS

While all of us could answer "b. sometimes" to all these questions, if you responded with "c. frequently" to any one of them you may have difficulty controlling stress.

☛ HOW MUCH STRESS CAN YOU TAKE?

The Holmes Stress scale assigns point values to changes, good and bad, that often affect us. If you've had any of these changes during the past year log their point value.

Life Change	Points
Death of spouse	100
Divorce	73
Marital separation	65
Jail term	63
Death of close family member	63
Personal injury or illness	53
Marriage	50
Fired from Job	47
Marital reconciliation	45
Retirement	45
Change in health of family member	44
Pregnancy	40
Sex difficulties	39
Gain of new family member	39
Change in financial status	38
Death of close friend	37
Change to different kind of work	36
Change in number of arguments with spouse	35
Foreclosure of mortgage or loan	30
Change in work responsibilities	29
Son or daughter leaving home	29
Trouble with in-laws	29
Outstanding personal achievement	28
Wife beginning or stopping work	26
Beginning or ending school	26
Revision of personal habits	24
Trouble with boss	23
Change in residence	20
Change in schools	20
Vacation	13
Minor violations of law	11

HOW TO SCORE AND WHAT IT MEANS

Total your points. If you tally 300 or more for changes that occurred in the last year, you have reached a danger point.

A recent population study by Dr. Thomas H. Holmes, professor of psychiatry at the University of Washington, and the creator of this scale, showed that 80% of those people exceeding 300 points became seriously depressed and had heart attacks or other serious illnesses.

Appeared as "Social Readjustment Rating Scale" by Dr. Thomas Holmes in the *Journal of Behavior Therapy and Experimental Psychiatry*. Reprinted with permission of Pergamon Press, Ltd.